The Unofficial Ark Guide

Publishing company:
BILDNER Verlag GmbH
Bahnhofstraße 8
94032 Passau
Germany

http://www.bildner-verlag.de
info@bildner-verlag.de

Cover design: Aaron Kübler
Author: Andreas Zintzsch
Editor: Christian Bildner
Translator: Lisa Bildner
Proofreader: Patrick Mutual

Translated from the original German version

Image chapter 1: © Catmando - Fotolia.com
Image chapters 2 and 9: © Herschel Hoffmeyer - Fotolia.com
Image chapter 10: © Elenarts - Fotolia.com

© 2020 BILDNER Verlag GmbH Passau, Germany
All information in this book is published regardless of any patent protection. All trademarks are used without guaranteeing free usability. The utmost care was applied during compilation of texts and images. Nevertheless, errors cannot be completely eliminated. The authors and the publisher can in no way be held responsible or made legally liable for any such errors or their potential consequences. The publishing company and the editor are grateful for any suggestions for improvement and for pointing out any errors. Nearly all hardware and software notations and trademarks mentioned in this book can, without special marking, be subject to trade- or brand mark protection or are protected by patents.

This book is not an official or licensed product of Studio Wildcard, Kirkland.

All rights to this work including all or any of its parts are reserved. The General Terms of License apply to the BILDNER Verlag GmbH Passau, Germany.

Introduction

Ark Survival Evolved was released in 2015 on Steam as an "Early Access Game" for the computer and shortly afterwards on Xbox One. Since December 2016, ARK is also available on Play Station 4.

ARK offers the player various possibilities in single player as well as in multiplayer mode. You can opt for player versus environment (PvE) or player versus player (PvP), become a tribe member, and experience all kinds of adventures. Regardless of whether you want to create cool forts and bridges, try to catch and tame every dinosaur and creature in the ARK, build your own perfect dino breeding facility, or fight and defeat all the other tribes – ARK provides possibilities for almost every form of gaming: building, exploring, surviving, collecting, and fighting.

If that alone isn't enough, you'll surely find what you're looking for amongst the many modifications (mods) that are currently available. ARK's modding community is extremely active, so there are consequently various mods available on computer and Xbox One. Everything from simple game improvements and new maps to "Total Conversions" is available.

Purchasable DLCs have already been released as well (downloadable content): *ARK Scorched Earth*, *ARK Aberration*, and *ARK Extinction*. With the *ARK Genesis Season Pass* you obtain two additional DLCs. The first one, *Genesis Part 1*, has already been released and *Genesis Part 2* is said to be released in the beginning of 2021. These add-ons tremendously extend the game with new maps, a lot of new creatures, and some new game mechanics.

The beginning of the game isn't easy. The player dies because of dehydration, heat stroke, or is eaten by a Raptor. Food, water, shelter, and weapons are just the beginning of survival. With a well-protected base and different tamed creatures that are working for you, survival (and life) becomes easier.

This guide is intended to help new players get started in ARK and describes the basic game mechanics. Players who have already gained some experiences in ARK, can find information in this book that makes surviving, crafting, and fighting in ARK easier.

In ARK, you can tame and train creatures for a variety of different tasks and make them work for you: collecting resources, transporting loads, guarding, traveling, and fighting. This is why the overview of all the different creatures takes up so much space in this book. There, you can find the most important information and data for each animal and decide which animals you want to catch and tame.

When the term dinosaur or dino is used in this book, we are referring to every type of creature that appears in ARK. There are a number of animals from all kinds of different periods (dinosaurs, reptiles, fish, insects, mammals, and many more). However, dinos like the T-Rex or Brontosaurus will certainly stick out to you.

This book provides complete information regarding the basic game *ARK Survival Evolved* as well as the add-ons *ARK Scorched Earth*, *ARK Aberration*, *ARK Extinction*, and *ARK Genesis Part 1*.

The game is frequently updated with new features and content. For the future, the developer of the game has already announced that additional content and amendments will be released, which couldn't be addressed in this book.

This book was created using the computer version of ARK Survival Evolved and is based on version 307.1 from March 2020. Basically, the version released for Xbox and PS4 are identical compared to the computer version even though some updates and changes are published with a slight delay.

Since the console commands to summon dinos and other items are partly very long and inconvenient and there are also tons of them, we decided to summarize them on two pages which you can access via our website. You can copy and paste them into your ARK console easily with just one click:

bildnerverlag.de/ark_items

bildnerverlag.de/ark_creatures

Spelling

Commands, names of control panels, and items are highlighted in color and italics for better distinction, for example, the command *Inventory* or the item *Stone Axe*.

In this book, you will frequently encounter listings with the most important facts and instructions in a nutshell. If you're a hurried reader, the inquisitive raptor in the margin indicates those lists in order to make them easier for you to find.

Now, we'd like to wish you a lot of fun with the book and good luck in ARK.

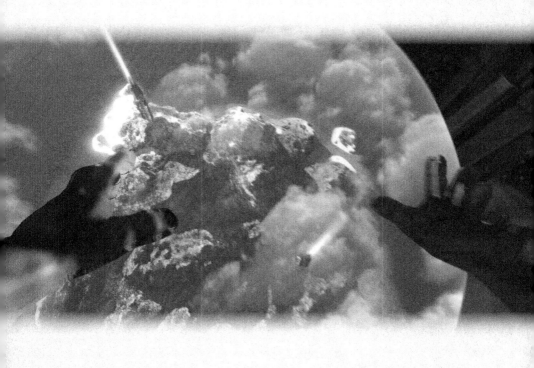

Table of Contents

1: ARK Basics 13

1.1 Getting Started 14
Host\Local 15
Join Multiplayer Game 20
Options 21
Tips for Graphic Settings 21

1.2 Game Basics 24
Enter the Game 24
First Minutes of the Game 25

2: Game Mechanics 33

2.1 Experience 34
2.2 Attributes 35
Overview 35
Status Effects 37

2.3 Engrams & Crafting 42
Learning Engrams 42
Resources 45
Crafting Stations 48
Recipes for Food, Coloring, and Kibble 50
Coloring 55
Level of Technology 56
Armors 58

3: BUILDING 61

3.1 Quick Construction Guide 62
3.2 Basics: structures 63
Materials 63
Foundations 64
Snapping and Adjustment 65
Pillars on Slopes and Bridges 68
Building Ramps 70
Building Pillars in Alignment with the Roof 71
3.3 Building Fence Foundations 74
Example: Octagonal Tower 76
3.4 Raft and Platform Saddles 77
Building on Platforms: The Basics 77
Lowering Foundations 78
3.5 Additional Building Tips 82
Triangle Foundations 83
Flexible Power Lines and Water Pipes 85

4: MAPS 87

4.1 Exploring the area 88
Supply Crates 88
Explorer Notes 89
Caves and Artifacts 99
4.2 The ARK - The Island 100
Resource Overview 104
4.3 The Center 105
Resource Overview of „The Center" 108
4.4 Ragnarok 109
Resource Overview 111
4.5 Valguero 112
Resource Overview 116

5: SCORCHED EARTH 117

    5.1   New Features in Scorched Earth 118

    5.2   Map Overview 120

            Resources 121

    5.3   How to Survive in Scorched Earth 122

6: ABERRATION 123

    6.1   New Features in Aberration 124

    6.2   Map Overview 128

    6.3   Tips for Aberration 130

7: EXTINCTION 131

    7.1   New Features in Extinction 132

    7.2   Map Overview 137

    7.3   Resources & Tips 139

8: GENESIS PART 1 141

    8.1   New Features in Genesis Part 1 142

    8.2   Biome 142

    8.3   Missions and Hexagons 144

    8.4   Map Overview 146

    8.5   Resources Overview 149

    8.6   Tips for Genesis Part 1 150

9: Catching and Taming 151

- 9.1 **Quick Guide: Taming** 152
- 9.2 **Basics: Taming** 153
  - Pros of Taming Creatures 153
  - Preparations for Taming 154
  - The Taming Process 154
- 9.3 **Taming by Increasing Torpidity** 155
  - Hunting Techniques 155
  - Narcotics 157
  - How to Feed Stunned Animals 158
  - Taming By Starvation 159
- 9.4 **Taming by Active Feeding** 159
- 9.5 **Kibble** 160
  - Kibble & Egg Production 160
  - Kibble Production 161
  - Kibble Recipes 161
  - Old Kibble System 163
- 9.6 **Unique Taming Methods** 164

10: Breeding and Rearing 165

- 10.1 **Breeding: Quick Guide** 166
- 10.2 **Selection and Mating** 167
  - What's the Point of Breeding? 167
  - Choosing the Parents 167
- 10.3 **Breeding and Pregnancy** 168
- 10.4 **Raising Animal Babies** 170
- 10.5 **Imprinting Animals** 172
- 10.6 **How to Breed Better Animals** 174
  - Enhancing Values 174
  - Mutations 175

11: Creatures in General 177

- 11.1 Values in Detail 178
- 11.2 Different Versions of Creatures 180
- 11.3 Terrestrial, Aerial, and Aquatic Creatures ... 182
  - Bosses 182
  - Mini Bosses 182

12: Terrestrial Creatures 183

13: Aerial Creatures 379

14: Aquatic Creatures 431

15: Bosses 481

- 15.1 General Info about Bosses 482
- 15.2 Broodmother Lysrix 486
- 15.3 Megapithecus 488
- 15.4 Dragon 490
- 15.5 Scorched Earth (Manticore) 492
- 15.6 The Center Boss 494
- 15.7 Ragnarok Bosses 496
- 15.8 Aberration 498
- 15.9 Extinction - the Titans 500
  - Ice Titan 500
  - Forest Titan 502
  - Desert Titan 504
  - King Titan 506

15.10 Valguero Bosses 508

15.11 Genesis - Part 1 510
    Moeder 510
    Corrupted Master Controller 512

16: Ascension 517

16.1 Preparations 518

16.2 Tek Cave 519
    Additional Useful Equipment: 521
    Tips for Crossing the Cave: 521

16.3 Overseer 522

17: Game Assistance 525

17.1 Console Commands 526

17.2 DLC / Add-on 528

17.3 How to Install Mods 529

17.4 Selecting Mods 531

Index 533

1: ARK Basics

1.1 Getting Started

When you start ARK Survival Evolved, the following screen appears:

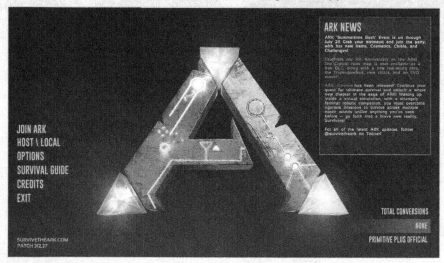

Click on a link to get to the following options:

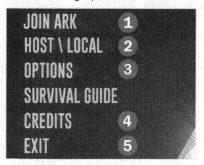

1. Join ARK: Start a multiplayer game or join a local-area network (LAN).
2. Host\Local: Start a single-player game.
3. Options: Sub-menu comprising all settings related to sounds, graphics, and controls.
4. Credits: Development team.
5. Exit: Leave the game.

HOST\LOCAL

If this is your first encounter with ARK Survival Evolved, we recommend starting in single-player mode until you've learned the basics.

Select *host\local* and the following window will appear on your screen. Here, you can adjust various settings and parameters for your local game.

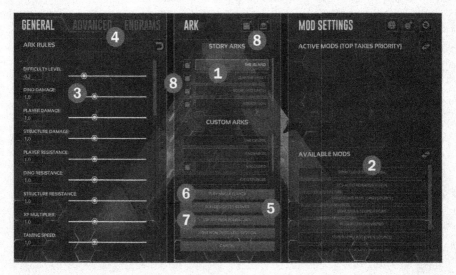

1. Choose the map you want to play.
2. If you have any mods (modifications) installed, you can select the ones you want to use, here.
3. Adjust individual parameters (e.g. difficulty level).
4. Specify diverse configurations.
5. Create a dedicated server (for network games without individual user interface).
6. Play in single-player mode or start a multiplayer online game.
7. Create a new and randomly generated map.
8. The file symbol indicates that a saved game is available. By clicking on it, you can delete the savegame. On the upper edge of the screen you can delete all savegames at once with only one click.

Select a map
At the very beginning, there's only one available map: *Ark - The Island*. This map is sufficient for hours of gaming fun, however, you can download other DLC maps for free: *The Center*, *Ragnarok*, and *Valguero*.

In case you've installed one of the add-ons, you also obtain the following maps: *Scorched Earth*, *Aberration*, *Extinction*, and *Genesis: Part 1*.

Additional maps can be downloaded in the form of mods. A couple examples of the most popular map mods would be *Valhalla* or *Shigo Island*. You'll learn how to download and install mods for the computer in another chapter.

You can also create a randomly generated map by clicking on ❼ *create procedural ARK*. On the next screen, you can individually adjust various settings, select names, and, lastly, generate a new map.

> **Warning:** randomly generated maps might change or even get deleted when updating the game.

The function to generate maps is still only usable on an experimental basis. The classical maps normally provide more gaming fun.

Mods
Mods (modifications) change the base game. You can, for example, add new dinosaurs, change the features of creatures and weapons, take advantage of better crafting facilities, and more. Read more about mods in chapter 12.

In order to actually be able to click on ❷ *mods*, you have to make sure that you've installed mods in the first place; otherwise you have no access to this function.

> Only activate the mods you want to use. Too many mods affect your system negatively and can slow down your gaming speed.

On the lower right side of the screen, the available mods are listed. Select those you'd like to activate and continue by clicking on the arrow next to the headline. On the upper right side, you can see the mods that are currently in use. You can also delete them in the same way.

Warning: when you remove mods, all associated benefits/items will be removed as well (e.g. newly added building structures).

Detailed Settings

In the following, we would like to give you a deeper understanding of the detailed settings that go along with numbers ❸ and ❹.

For adjustment, you can either use a slide control like the one below or enter the values directly into the box. By doing so, you can easily exceed the slide control's range.

Click on a box with a number and put in a value that goes beyond the slider's limitation.

Difficulty Level

The settings for the difficulty level determine the maximum level of the creatures in the game and the quality of the loot.

The standard value of 0.2 equals a max. creature level 30 and loot at 100%. In single player mode, the max. value of 1.0 keeps the wild dinos at a max. level of 150 and the quality of loot increases by 500%. These are also the settings of the official PvP and PvE servers.

For multiplayer servers, all data gets changed and saved in the form of a config file. The level of difficulty is determined a bit differently here.

Overview of difficulty level in local multiplayer mode:

Difficulty	Max. Creature Level	Loot Quality
0.20	30	100%
0.40	60	200%
0.60	90	300%
0.80	120	400%
1.00	150	500%

Prohibiting ARK Tribute Downloads
This is only of interest in a multiplayer server network. This function allows or prohibits transferring characters to another sever within the same server network.

Flyer Carry (PvE)
If this setting is turned on, flying creatures are allowed to transport other wild creatures in PvE mode. Then, you could do something like, throw a wild Carno into a stranger's base so that it eats all of their dinosaurs. That's why this function is disabled by default. It's definitely more fun when this feature is enabled. Otherwise, pterosaurs can't carry other wild creatures in PvE mode.

Hardcore Mode
If this function is enabled, you only have 1 life. If your character dies, you have to restart with a new one at level 1.

PvE Mode
When player versus environment is selected, you don't play against each other in multiplayer mode. It's not possible to kill, attack, or destroy dinos or structures from other players. In PvE mode, this is only possible when one tribe declares war on another and the declaration is accepted by the other tribe. If the PvE mode is disabled, you can attack, plunder, or destroy other players and their property at any time (this would be the PvP mode = player versus player).

Determines how many structures can be located within a certain area. If you want to build a lot in one spot, increase this value.

Day Cycle Speed
The higher the value, the faster the time passes.

Day/Night Time Speed
The higher the value, the shorter the day or night.

XP Multiplier
The higher the value, the more experience the player gains.

Taming Speed
The higher the value, the faster dinosaurs are tamed and the lower the amount of narcotic required.

Dino Character Food Drain
We highly recommend keeping the value at 1.0. On the one hand, the dino needs less food the lower you set the value, but on the other hand, the taming process takes longer since the dino needs to eat as frequently.

Player Character Food Drain
The lower the value, the longer you can go without food or water.

Harvest Amount
The higher the value, the more things you receive when farming.

Harvest Health
The higher the value, the more resources you gain from an item (e.g. wood/thatch from a tree).

Resources Respawn Period
The lower the value, the faster the re-growth period of resources.

Join Multiplayer Game

Go to the main menu and click on *Join ARK* to play in multiplayer mode.

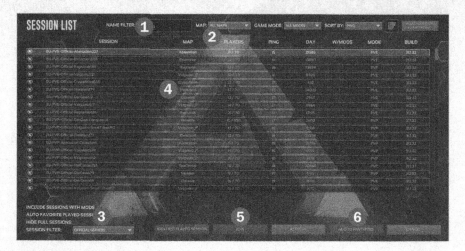

1. Server name filter: Enter a part of a name to find a specific server (unofficial servers often include descriptions in their names, for example, Tame x4, which indicates that the taming speed is set to 4x).

2. Click on this panel to select one of the available maps (e.g. *Ragnarok*). Under game mode, you can choose between PvE and PvP servers.

3. Session filter: Here, you can filter whether you search for an official or unofficial server, servers your friends are on, or the one you've already played on (*my survivors*). LAN servers (local networks) are also indicated here.

4. The main screen displays all servers and any related information ARK is able to find.

5. Click on a server on the main screen ❹ and select "join" to enter the game.

6. Select a server and click on this panel in order add it to your favorites (found under ❸). Servers you've played on recently are added to your favorites automatically.

Options

In this section, you can adjust a lot of ARK-related settings. Here, you can see the options from the computer version:

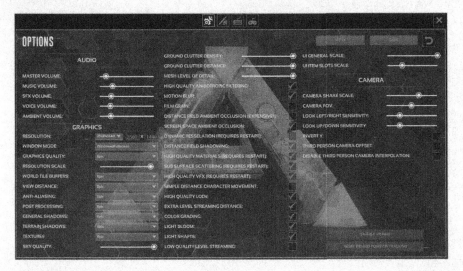

By clicking on the four symbols at the top of the screen, you can display the keyboard layout of the controls and, if required, change it according to your needs. On the left-hand side of the options, you can find all graphic and audio settings.

Tips for Graphic Settings

ARK requires a very high operating level. Especially on the computer, the game quickly pushes the computer and the graphics card to their performance limits.

In gameplay, place your character on a hill with a view of the ocean under sunny light conditions and with a forest in proximity. Now, try various settings and take a look around in the game. By doing so, you can find out which effects you can do without and which ones you want to keep.

Provided you reduce the values, the following settings come along with a remarkable increase in performance without a loss in gaming ambiance:

- Post processing
- Anti-aliasing

- *General shadows*
- *Terrain shadows*
- *Sky quality*

Window Mode: Choose full-screen for a better performance.
Ground Clutter Density

Disabled ground clutter density yields better performance and provides yet another advantage:

> By turning off ground clutter density, in-game resources and little items on the ground are better recognizable and can be found easier (e.g. small eggs).

Almost every adjustable setting in the left corner at the bottom (e.g. *motion blur*) can be disabled in order to improve performance. The following things can remain activated since they only have a small impact on the performance:

- *Sub surface scattering*
- *Simple distance character movement*
- *Color grading*
- *Light bloom*
- *Light shafts*
- *Low quality level streaming*

How to Change Starting Parameters

On the computer, you can change your starting parameters in Steam to achieve better in-game performance. It is, however, always dependent on your system whether these settings benefit an increase in performance or not. In addition, these alterations decrease the graphics quality significantly.

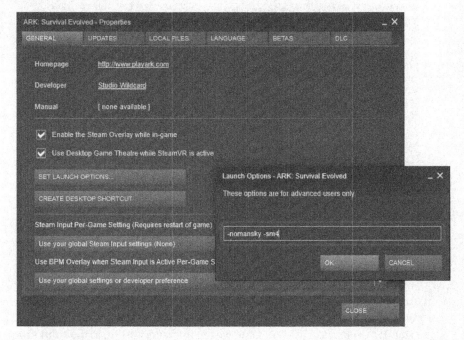

- Pull up Steam and go to your *library*. Right click on the game *ARK: Survival Evolved* and select the last point on the list *properties*.
- In the next window, under the *general* tab, click on *set launch options*.
- Type the following commands into the launch options and confirm with OK. You can also use every command individually:
    - *-UseallAvailableCores* (only for multi-core processors)
    - *-sm4* (utilizes DirectX 10 Shader instead of the latest version, DirectX 11)
    - *-nomansky* (sky effects are disabled)
    - *-lowmemory* (for systems with a main memory of 4 GB and smaller)

In order to erase these settings, delete the corresponding item in the launch options.

1.2 Game Basics

Enter the Game

When you first start a game you have to create a character:

1. Adjusting the appearance: First, choose between a male or female character. Use the slide control to change your appearance.

2. Preview: Here, you can see how your character will look.

3. Spawn location: Select a zone to determine your starting position. Depending on the map, the area you start in can be more or less dangerous. In regard to the standard map *The ARK - The Island* we recommend starting in the southern area (provided you're a beginner) since it's not as dangerous. The north, in contrast, is more densely populated by predatory animals.

4. Name your character and start the game by clicking on *create new survivor*.

5. With *download ARK survivor*, you can use a character you've saved in an obelisk on another server. By doing so, you can transfer a character from one server to another. This is only possible on a server network (e.g. official PvP servers).

First Minutes of the Game

Your character appears on the island naked and without any equipment. Survival is key. At any time, you can view and change the game control and keyboard layout in the options menu.

It's very likely that you will quite often die during the first few minutes of the game. Wild creatures that eat you, hunger, thirst, fall damage, and more will cause your death. Even though it's annoying to lose all the equipment you've collected every time your character dies, it's not that bad. By collecting and crafting new equipment, you will become stronger and gain experience.

Below, is a small list with a few tips that will help you survive during the first few minutes:

- Stay close to the beach at the beginning. Advantages: There's a lot of water that satisfies your thirst and not too many dangerous animals.
- Harvest wood and thatch with your bare hands and collect berries, fibers, and stones.
- Craft a stone pick and gather flints.
- First, depending on how you play, you'll want to increase your health (for longer survival), weight (to carry more objects), or movement speed (to run away faster and track animals better).
- After you've leveled up, you have to learn the following Engrams: stone pick, spear, and campfire. Then, craft cloth clothing, a hide sleeping bag, and a box.
- Hunt little dinos (e.g. Dodos) to gain raw prime meat and hide.
- Craft clothing. It better protects you from heat and cold and also provides armor protection.
- Build your own little base with a sleeping bag (onetime spawn point after death), a campfire (to cook meat), and a storage box (to store important items).
- Gain some more experience and you will soon be able to learn the first Engrams for a (thatch) building structure and a bed. Then, build them.
- Search for a suitable place where you can live near water and protected (e.g. on cliffs or against rock faces). Additionally, make sure that it's as flat an area as possible where you can build and in proximity to wood and stones.

- Build your first little thatch shed with walls, a roof as well as a door, and furnish it with a bed, cooking place, and storage boxes or shelves. Save some space for things like a mortar and pestle, or even a forge that can be built at a later time.

- Try to tame some dinos as soon as you can. Don't try to tame the high-leveled dinos at the beginning. Dino levels from 5-20 are enough to help you through the first hours. Advantage: They don't need as many narcoberries yet to get stunned and it takes less time to tame them. Always bring a sufficient amount of narcoberries, feed, bolas, and clubs for taming. Later on, narcotics, bows, and tranquilizer darts are, of course, more suitable. Here are some dinos you can tame relatively easily at the beginning and which are of great use as well:

  - Dilophosaur: Knock it unconscious with the club or your fists and tame it with meat. 2-4 of them provide good protection for your base or during excursions. Their eggs can be useful for kibble.

  - Parasaur: Catch it with a bola, knock it unconscious with a club or your fists, and use berries to tame it (preferably mejoberries). The Parasaur is your first riding creature and can carry goods for you. Besides that, it makes harvesting berries easier compared to using your bare hands.

  - Iguanodon: a slightly better alternative to the Parasaur, but requires more time to tame and the use of a saddle can't be unlocked until level 30.

  - Raptor: With a bola and a club, a low-leveled Raptor is knocked out very quickly. Tame it with meat. The Raptor is a fast riding creature, can kill small animals quickly, and gather meat and leather. It's better than a Dilo because it's stronger and you can also ride on it.

  - Trike (Triceratops): with a Parasaur, you can gather the required amount of narcoberries and mejoberries you need for taming a Trike more quickly. Since a Trike is very defensive, it's better to use tranquilizer darts from a safe distance or to skillfully approach it. A Trike may be quite slow, but provides a relatively good weight capacity and collects berries way faster than the Parasaur.

Now, you should have reached around level 20 and be well-prepared for further progress.

You'll get to know more about experience, attributes, and Engrams in chapter 2.

How to Become a Tribe Member

A tribe is the merger of several players on a multiplayer server. You can create a tribe at any time and invite other players to join you. In order to do so, go to the *tribe menu* in your inventory (or directly by pressing "L" on your keyboard) and type in the future name of your tribe.

A tribe comes with the following advantages:
- Players gain experience for actions of tribe members in the proximity.
- It's easier to fight and survive in a team.
- Task sharing makes a lot of things go faster.
- Buildings, resources, and tamed dinos can be used mutually (depending on the settings).

> You can only be a member of one tribe. That's why you shouldn't create a one-man tribe on a server right at the beginning. It is, however, possible to leave a tribe and enter a new one, but depending on the settings, you can potentially lose your buildings or tamed creatures.
>
> In addition, other tribes may not invite you into their tribe because they see that you're already a member of a tribe.

Tribe Manager

On the tribe manager screen, owners and admins can define the settings of their tribe.

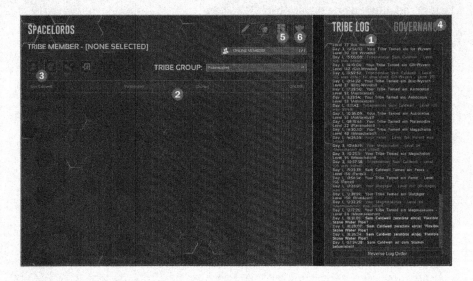

1 Tribe Log: Here, you can see an overview of your tribe's recent events. You can also do things like, check if any dinos have been killed during your absence.

2 Overview of all tribe members.

3 Change the rank of tribe members (for owners and admins only).

4 Adjust the tribe governance (only owners and admins can change it).

5 Create and manage further ranks and the corresponding authorization of members.

6 Alliance overview and creating new alliances (for owners and admins only).

Tribe Ranks

In general, a tribe has three different types of ranks:

- Owner: The founder of the tribe with full rights.
- Admin: Has the same rights as the owner (except for removing the owner).
- Member: Has limited rights. For members, up to 10 additional groups with different assignments of rights can be created.

As an owner or admin, you can create and change the ranks under the menu item *manage tribe group ranks*:

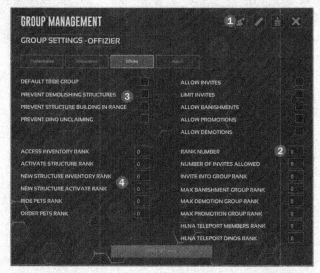

At first, create a *new group* ❶, name it, and set the values accordingly.

The setting for the *group ranking* ❷ is very important. The higher the group ranking (0 - 10), the more rights the member has. You can also set these rights individually ❹ to do things like, assign *structure ranking* or *riding animals ranking*.

Under point ❸, you can determine further rights.

If you have created more groups with different ranks, you still have to assign the corresponding rank to each member of yours in the main menu under tribe manager.

Now, you only have to determine the activate ranks for doors, boxes, cabinets, tamed animals etc. In order to do so, look at an object (e.g. a door) and hold the *use button*. In the radial menu, you can now either increase or decrease the *activate rank* (or access rank).

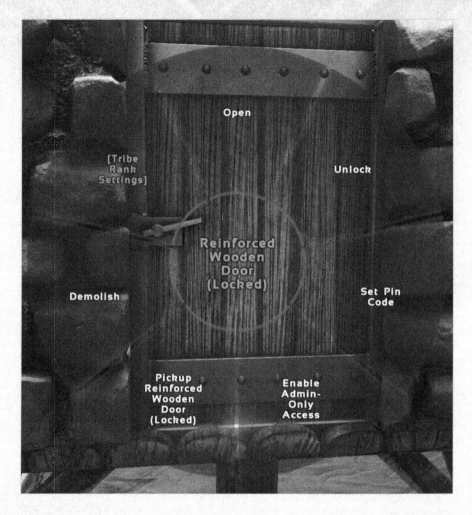

Here are examples for the different types of ranks:

A trial member has group rank 1.

A full member has group rank 2.

An officer has group rank 3.

A door has the tribe activate rank 2.

This means that the door can only be opened and closed by full tribe members or higher, admins, and owners.

Tribe Governance
The type of tribe governance specifies the ownership of and access to tamed animals and structures. In case a member leaves the tribe, it also determines whether dinos and buildings remain in the tribe's or member's possession. Owners and admins can change the governance.

Creature Ownership:

- *Tribe owned:* All dinos belong to the tribe. When you leave the tribe, your dinos remain in the tribe's possession.
- *Personally owned, tribe ridden:* Already existing dinos remain in your possession, but the tribe is also allowed to use them (e.g. releasing them as well).
- *Personally owned, personally ridden:* Already existing dinos remain in your possession and can only be used by the owner.

Tame Settings: (only changeable when personally owned)

- *Tribe taming:* Newly tamed dinos belong to the tribe.
- *Personal taming:* Newly tamed dinos belong to the player that has tamed it.

Structure Ownership:

- *Tribe owned, admin demolish:* Structures remain in the tribe's possession, only admins are allowed to destroy them.
- *Tribe owned:* Buildings belong to the tribe; all members can demolish them.
- *Personally owned, tribe Snap, admin demolish:* Buildings belong to the player; members can, however, replace objects. Admins can even destroy them.
- *Personally owned, personal snap:* Only the player owns the property and demolishing rights.

Locks & Pin Codes: (only available in personally owned structure ownership)

- *Tribe locks & pin codes:* Tribe members don't need a pin code for locks (provided that they are in use).
- *Personal locks & pin codes:* Even tribe members need to know the pin codes (in case they are used).

Dino Release Allowed:

- *It's possible for tribe members to release them.*
- *Only admins can release them.*

> Before joining a tribe, take a look at the type of governance the tribe has determined. Be aware, that your property may completely fall into the tribe's hands and you can never reclaim it if you decide to leave.

Tribal Alliance

In regard to tribal governance, owners and admins have the option to establish alliances. In order to do so, they have to invite another tribe's owner or admin who, in turn, must accept it.

An alliance comprises up to twelve tribes and each tribe can have only five members at the most.

An alliance offers the following advantages:

- Mutual use of electricity and troughs.
- You can't be attacked by creatures or weapons owned by the alliance.
- There's a private alliance chat and an individual colored marking for alliance members (players, structures, and buildings).
- Pillars don't prevent the construction of new alliance buildings.

Especially on PvP servers, alliances are for the benefit of a lot of tribes. You can safely move through an alliance tribe's territory and therefore, a lot of small tribes can become a powerful force as well.

2: Game Mechanics

2.1 Experience

You're going to gain experience during the game. Once you've gained enough experience, you level up and, consequently, increase your attributes and learn new Engrams.

You gain experience for every action you carry out in ARK:

- Over time, you automatically gain experience (when in-game, of course)
- Harvesting and gathering resources
- Crafting items
- Killing enemies
- Taming and breeding creatures
- Gathering explorer notes
- Actions of tribe members in proximity (you receive 50% of their experience)

Actually, you don't need to carry out specific actions to gain experience. Simply gather, hunt, and build like normal, and you'll level up accordingly.

The higher the level of the item you're crafting or the more expensive it is to craft, or the more dangerous the enemies, the more experience you gain.

> Try to join a tribe as quickly as possible and play with or around other tribe members. As a result, you gain 50% of the experience they gain.

Collecting explorer notes (usually found in ruins or caves) doubles your gain in experience for the next 10 minutes. Therefore, use these 10 minutes to gain as much experience as possible.

> An explorer note can only be collected once.

2.2 Attributes

Overview

Each character has 11 attributes and a few other additional values that determine its survival. Pull up the *inventory* to get a full overview of your character's most important values in the center of the screen.

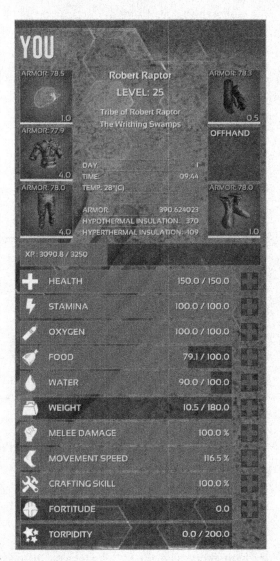

As soon as you've gained enough experience, you level up and, consequently, can increase one out of ten attributes. In order to do so, click on the plus icon next to the attribute. Each attribute has the following individual effect on the game:

Health:
affects your current life value. The higher it is, the longer you can keep up a fight.

Stamina:
the higher the value, the more actions you can perform without getting exhausted (e.g. running, fighting, farming).

Oxygen:
the higher the value, the longer you can stay under water without drowning.

Food:
the higher the value, the longer you can cope without food.

Water:
the higher the value, the longer you can do without drinking.

Weight:
the higher the value, the more you can carry without being overloaded.

Melee Damage:
the higher the value, the more damage you cause with melee weapons.

Movement Speed:
the higher the value, the faster you can run. With a value of 120-130 you can get away from almost any dino.

Crafting Speed:
the higher the value, the faster you can craft items.

Fortitude:
the higher the value, the longer you can cope with heat, cold, and poison until negative effects occur.

Torpor:
this value indicates how quickly you pass out from the effects of poison. When your torpor reaches a value of 50, you black out. This value can't be raised. Increase your fortitude to prevent you from passing out quickly. You can't increase the torpor value!

You can find further values on your inventory screen:

Armor:
the higher the armor value, the better you can cope with damage. This also applies to damage caused by torpor (e.g. induced by a Titanoboa).

Hypothermic Insulation:
the higher this value, the better you're protected from freezing to death or cold in general. Depending on your clothing/armor, this value enhances or declines. Fire increases the value (e.g. a torch in your hand or a campfire in the proximity). The food *Fria Curry* increases the value as well.

Hyperthermic Insulation:
the higher this value, the more you're protected from heat. This value increases or decreases according to clothing/armor. In addition, *Calien Soup* increases this value.

> The game's highest level, by default, is 100. After ascension, the maximum level increases (depending on the level's difficulty) by 5 (gamma), 10 (beta), or 15 (alpha) steps.

STATUS EFFECTS

When playing ARK Survival Evolved, you are constantly affected by a variety of environmental influences like heat or torpor. This is what the symbol in the left corner at the bottom of your screen indicates. If you're riding an animal, the corresponding item is displayed above the animal's values in the upper edge of the screen.

Symbol	Effect	Description
	Cold	You're cold and your stamina drops.
	Hypothermia	You're slowly freezing to death, your stamina drops, and you slowly take damage.
	Hot	You're hot and your stamina drops.

Symbol	Effect	Description
	Burning (internal)	The heat causes you to burn internally, your stamina drops faster, and you slowly lose health.
	Enflamed (external)	You're set on fire by dragon's breath, flame thrower, or heat wave. (only in Scorched Earth)
	Heat Stroke	You've been in the heat for too long. Sprinting is not possible, vision clouds, and you lose health. (only in Scorched Earth)
	Starving	You're in urgent need of food. You slowly lose health. You're not able to regenerate stamina.
	Dehydrated	You urgently need to drink something. You slowly lose health and you're not able to regenerate stamina.
	Encumbered	You're carrying too much. Your movement is slowed or you're completely unable to move.

Symbol	Effect	Description
	Exhausted	You have no remaining stamina. Wait a moment for your stamina to recover or you'll pass out.
	Food Poisoning	You ate poisoned food. You lose health.
	Venom (blind)	You were blinded (e.g. by a Dilophosaurus).
	Crafting/Repairing	You're crafting something at the moment. That's why your movement speed is decreased.
	Suffocating	You're out of oxygen. If you don't get oxygen quickly, you'll die. Get some air!
	Injured	You are extremely injured and your movement is massively hindered.

Symbol	Effect	Description
	Tranquilized	You've been tranquilized (e.g. by a Titanoboa) and your torpor level decreases.
	Knocked Out	You're knocked out and you can't move until the torpidity decreases.
	Webbed	You've been slowed (e.g. by a spider web).
	Leeched	A leech attached itself to your body and your health drains. Remove the leech as fast as possible. Walk into a fire in order to remove it.
	Gashed	You have a large wound (e.g. from an Allosaurus). You lose 5% health for five seconds and are slowed.
	Gaining Exp.	You gained experience.

Symbol	Effect	Description
	Experience Bonus	You've collected an explorer note and you receive a bonus for 10 minutes because of the experience you've gained.
	Iced Water	You drank iced water (from the fridge). Your resistance against heat increases and resistance against cold decreases.
	Shelter	The shelter icon appears on the right edge of the screen above your values. You're under a roof in a house. For this reason, you're better protected from weather.
	Healing	You regained health (e.g. by food or a healing elixir).
	Lesser Antidote	You've consumed a lesser antidote and you're healing from swamp fever.

2.3 Engrams + Crafting

With the corresponding items, you can craft the so-called Engrams which, in plain English, are recipes you can learn in-game. Once you've learned an Engram (e.g. stone hatchet), you can craft that item in the crafting menu. The following criteria need to be met in order to be able to craft items in the first place:

- The corresponding Engram has to be learned or available as a recipe (blueprint).
- Required resources need to be fully available.
- You have to work at the corresponding crafting station (e.g. your inventory or a forge).

Learning Engrams

Each Engram costs a certain number of Engram points (EP) to learn.

Engrams require a certain minimum level to learn. With each new level, you get access to additional Engrams.

You receive EPs whenever you level up. The higher the level, the more Engram points you get; high-level Engrams, however, are more expensive.

After leveling up, the Engram window appears on your screen automatically. You can, of course, pull up the Engram menu at any time. Open your *inventory* and switch to *Engrams* in the menu displayed on the upper edge of the screen.

In the following, you can find an overview of all Engrams.

The Engram Menu

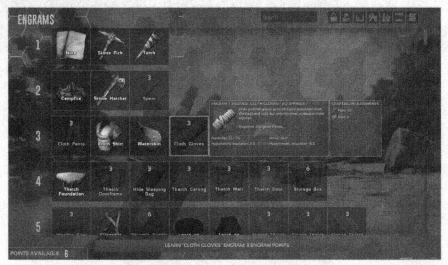

The colors of each Engram mean the following:

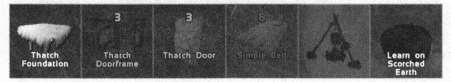

- **White**: Engram has already been learned.
- **Blue Text / Light Grey Symbol**: Engram has not been learned yet. Costs are displayed. Double-click to start learning.
- **Blue Text / Yellow Symbol**: another Engram needs to be learned first (by double-clicking, you can learn all required Engrams at once).
- **Dark Grey Font / Red Symbol**: you don't have enough Engram points to learn this Engram.
- **Blackened**: your level is too low to learn this Engram. The required Engram is displayed on the left edge. If it's part of another DLC, the name is indicated.

There are requirements that need to be met in regard to various Engrams. For example, you have to learn the slingshot Engram before being able to learn the bow Engram.

> Don't spend your Engram points all at once. Save some of your Engram points to be able to learn important new Engrams as soon as you've leveled up.

Finding Engrams/Blueprints

You can also find Engrams in the form of blueprint notes. With these notes, you can craft items without learning the respective Engram.

These kind of Engram recipes can be found in loot crates.

All you have to do is put the blueprints into the corresponding crafting tool (inventory, forge, fabricator) in combination with the sufficient amount of resources. Start the crafting process with a *right click* on the recipe.

A variety of loot crates can be found on the main land, in caves, and underwater. The higher the level of the loot crate, the better the blueprints it contains.

An orange circle around the loot crate (like in the picture above), means that it contains twice the amount as usual.

Resources

In order to be able to craft items, you need resources. You can find them anywhere on the map, receive them from creatures, or find them in caves.

Below, you can see an overview of all essential resources that can be found in ARK. Resources that need to be crafted from other resources and can't be found in another way, are not listed here (e.g. metal pipes or charcoal from burnt wood).

Symbol	Resource	Source	Best Harvesting Dinos & Tools
	Fiber	Plants: everywhere	Therizinosaur, Gigantopithecus, Dire Bear, sickle
	Thatch	Trees: everywhere	Megaloceros, Brontosaurus, Woolly Rhino, pick
	Wood	Trees: everywhere	Castoroides (beaver), Therizinosaur, Mammoth, hatchet
	Stone	Rocks: everywhere	Doedicurus, Dunkleosteus, Ankylosaurus, hatchet
	Flint	Rocks: everywhere	Ankylosaurus, pick
	Metal	Golden, iron-containing rocks: mountains, caves	Ankylosaurus, pick
	Cement	Manufactured, beaver dams, insects (by Beelzebufo)	Beelzebufo
	Achatina paste (substitute for cement)	Achatina snails (swamp denizen)	Taming of Achatina
	Obsidian	Smooth, black Obsidian stone: large mountains	Ankylosaurus, pick

Symbol	Resource	Source	Best Harvesting Dinos & Tools
	Organic Polymer (subtitute for polymer)	Kairuku	Pelagornis, Wooden Club
	Fur	Hairy creatures (e.g. Direwolf, Mammoth, Castoroides)	Direwolf, Sabertooth, Hatchet
	Human Hair (substitute for fur)	Player	Scissors
	Wool (substitute for Fur)	Ovis (sheep)	Scissors
	Leather	Many creatures	Giganotosaurus, Direwolf, Sabertooth, Rex, Therizinosaur, Hatchet
	Chitin & Keratin	Insects, creatures with Horn	Sabertooth, Direwolf, Beelzebufo, Diplocaulus
	Crystal	High mountains and caves	Ankylosaurus, Pick
	Silica Pearls	Ocean floor, sometimes at the bottom of rivers and lakes, beaver dam	Hand, Otter (during fish hunting)
	Black Pearls	Eurypterid, Ammonit, Tusoteuthis, Alpha Mosasaurus	Megalodon, Pick, Otter (during fish hunting)
	Oil	Oil stones: ocean floor and in icy regions at the shore	Dunkleosteus, Ankylosaurus, pick
	Sap	Redwood trees	Tree Sap Tap

Symbol	Resource	Source	Best Harvesting Dinos & Tools
	Angler Gel	Anglerfish	Direwolf, Megalodon, Hatchet
	Rare Flower	Swamp plants, red alpine flowers, beaver dam	Moschops, Therizinosaur, Brontosaurus, Ankylosaurus
	Rare Mushroom	Swamp trees, beaver dam, crystal	Moschops, Therizinosaur, Brontosaurus, Mammoth
	Raw Meat	Almost every creature	Giganotosaurus, Mosasaurus, Rex, Pick
	Raw Prime Meat	Large creatures (e.g. Paracer, Bronto, Rex)	Giganotosaurus, Mosasaurus, Rex, Pick
	Raw Fish	All fish	Baryonyx, Pelagornis, Spinosaur, Pick
	Raw Prime Fish Meat	Big fish	Baryonyx, Spinosaur, Pick
	Berries (all kinds)	Plants: everywhere	Brontosaurus, Chalicotherium, Therizinosaur, Stegosaurus
	Element	Bosses	No harvesting: kill and loot boses

CRAFTING STATIONS

When you've learned an Engram or you're in possession of the corresponding blueprint note, you are able to craft an item. In order to do so, open the respective crafting station (e.g. your inventory or your workbench), put all required resources (and possible blueprints) into the station, double-click on the Engram that is shown in the crafting station, and the crafting process starts. If you want to craft several items, click on the Engram and choose the desired quantity.

Passive Crafting

You can also craft items passively in quite a few crafting stations by putting the required resources into the station. After doing so, wait the required period of time. It's usually additional resources that are crafted like this. Here's a small selection:

Symbol	Item	Crafting Station	Action
	Cooked Meat	Campfire	Place wood and raw meat on the campfire and ignite it.
	Spoiled Meat	Irrelevant	Meat spoils by itself after some time.
	Charcoal	Diverse (all fire objects)	Burn wood in a campfire or other places with fire.
	Metal Ingot	Industrial Forge	Put 2 metal objects and wood in a forge and ignite it.
	Gasoline	Industrial Forge	Put 3 oil and 5 hide objects in the industrial forge (plus wood) and ignite it.

List of Crafting Stations

Symbol	Crafting Station	Level	Utilisation
None	Inventory	1	For all basic items.
	Workbench	20	For better and elaborate objects (usually metal).
	Fabricator	48	For modern objects; usually made of polymer or electronics. Runs on gasoline.
	Tek replicator	Boss defeated	Creates all Tek items. Runs on Element.
	Campfire	2	Passive. Log fire.
	Industrial Grill	50	Passive. Runs on gasoline.
	Mortar & Pestle	6	Produces diverse items. (e.g. narcotics, sparkpowder, cement, gunpowder)
	Chemistry Bench	82	Enhanced mortar. Runs on gasoline & electricity.
	Cooking Pot	8	For food, coloring, soap, kibble. Passive. Log fire.
	Industrial Cooker	89	Enhanced cooking pot. Passive. Runs on gasoline.

Symbol	Crafting Station	Level	Utilisation
	Refining Forge	20	Production of metal ingots and gasoline. Passive. Log fire.
	Industrial Forge	80	Enhanced forge. Runs on gasoline.
	Industrial Grinder	64	Destroys objects to reclaim ressources. Runs on gasoline.
	Beer Barrel	36	Makes beer using 40 straw and 50 berries. Passive station.

Recipes for Food, Coloring, and Kibble

With the right ingredients, you can craft a lot of dishes, coloring, kibble for taming, jerky, and many other items. You can get some recipes from defeated enemies and others you need to figure out by yourself. But here's a little list for you:

„Duration" indicates the duration of effect and „spoilage" how long the item can be kept in your inventory without spoiling. The durability of all perishable products extends accordingly when storing them in different containers.

Durability of perishable goods:

- Inventory (1x)
- Tamed creatures (4x)
- Smoking chamber (10x) (runs on gunpowder)
- Refrigerator (100x) (powered by electricity)
- Trough (4x) (only for all types of food)
- Bed (200x) (as long as it's unfertilized and not harvested)
- Compost pile (only for feces)

Calien Soup (cooking pot)

Recipe	Effect	Duration	Spoilage
■ 10 mejoberries ■ 20 amarberries ■ 20 tintoberries ■ 5 lemons ■ 2 stimulants ■ 1 water container	+50 heat protection -25% water consumption	15 min.	5 hours

Enduro Stew (cooking pot)

Recipe	Effect	Duration	Spoilage
■ 10 mejoberries ■ 9 cooked meat ■ 5 carrots ■ 5 potatoes ■ 2 stimulants ■ 1 water container	+35% melee damage +1.2% health	15 min.	5 hours

Focal Chili (cooking pot)

Recipe	Effect	Duration	Spoilage
■ 10 mejoberries ■ 9 cooked meat ■ 20 amarberries ■ 20 azulberries ■ 20 tintoberries ■ 5 lemons ■ 1 water container	+25% movement speed +100% crafting speed	15 min.	5 hours

Fria Curry (cooking pot)

Recipe	Effect	Duration	Spoilage
■ 10 mejoberries ■ 20 azulberries ■ 5 corn ■ 5 carrots ■ 2 narcotics ■ 1 water container	+50 hypothermic insulation -25% food consumption	15 min.	5 hours

Lazarus Chowder (cooking pot)

Recipe	Effect	Duration	Spoilage
10 mejoberries 9 cooked meat 5 corn 5 potatoes 2 narcotics 1 water container	-85% oxygen consumption underwater +1.2% stamina per sec. Very helpful for long expeditions underwater without oxygen tank.	10 min.	5 hours

Shadow Steak Saute (cooking pot)

Recipe	Effect	Duration	Spoilage
20 mejoberries 3 cooked prime meat 2 rare mushrooms 1 carrot 1 potato 8 narcotics 1 water container	+50% heat protection +50% hypothermic insulation -80% weapon recoil night vision	3 min.	5 hours

Battle Tartare (cooking pot)

Recipe	Effect	Duration	Spoilage
20 mejoberries 3 raw prime meat 2 rare flowers 1 lemon 1 corn 8 stimulants 1 water container	+60% melee damage +15% fortitude +50% movement speed stamina regen. +50% food/water consumption -90 health	3 min.	5 hours

Medical Brew (cooking pot)

Recipe	Effect	Duration	Spoilage
20 tintoberries 2 narcotics 1 water container	+40 health	5 sec.	2 hours

Energy Brew (cooking pot)

Recipe	Effect	Duration	Spoilage
20 azulberries 2 stimulants 1 water container	+40 stamina	5 sec.	1 hour

Nirvana Tonic (cooking pot)

Recipe	Effect	Duration	Spoilage
200 mejoberries 24 cooked prime meat 20 rare mushrooms 20 rare flowers 72 narcotics 72 stimulants 1 water container	resets attributes, but saves Engrams	immediately	5 hours

Sweet Vegetable Cake (cooking pot)

Recipe	Effect	Duration	Spoilage
25 fiber 7 sap 2 corn 2 carrots 2 potatoes 4 stimulants 1 water container	+500 health +15% health regeneration only for herbivores tames Ovis and Achatina	immediately	1.3 hours

Broth of Enlightenment (cooking pot)

Recipe	Effect	Duration	Spoilage
10 mejoberries 2 lemons 2 corn 2 carrots 2 potatoes 5 wo. Rhino horn 1 black pearl 1 water container	+50% experience tames Arthropluera	20 min.	5 hours

Cooked Meat Jerky (smoking chamber)

Recipe	Effect	Duration	Spoilage
■ 3 sparkpowder ■ 1 oil ■ 1 cooked meat	Extended spoilage Common ingredient for other recipes Crafting process for one piece: 36 min.	Immediately	2 days

Prime Meat Jerky (smoking chamber)

Recipe	Effect	Duration	Spoilage
■ 3 sparkpowder ■ 1 oil ■ 1 cooked prime meat	Extended spoilage Common ingredient for other recipes Crafting process for one piece: 36 min.	immediately	2 days

Soap (cooking pot)

Recipe	Effect	Duration	Spoilage
■ 3 polymer ■ 2 oil ■ 1 water container	removes color from colored or dyed objects	immediately	infinite

Kibble

Kibble is made from dino eggs, fiber, different vegetables, jerky, and a lot of other ingredients. It is made in a cooking pot with water. Usually, kibble is the best food for taming creatures.

Since each type of kibble has a different recipe, you'll find the right one for each respective creature shown in chapters 8, 9, and 10.
Kibble has a spoiling time of 3 days.

Coloring

By using coloring and a paintbrush (or a spray gun), you can color a lot of items:

- Drag and drop a color in order to apply it to an item in your inventory. By doing so, you can also color a paintbrush.
- Take the colored paintbrush and use it on a creature, an item of furniture, or building structures.
- In the following window, you can now paint or color the object.

Coloring is made in a cooking pot. In order to create the desired color, put a container filled with water and the following ingredients into the cooking pot and cook it until the process is done:

15 narcoberries
2 charcoal

4 amarb. | 1 azulb.
7 tintob. | 6 narcob.
1 sparkpowder

6 narcoberries
12 stimberries
1 gunpowder

15 azulberries
2 charcoal

12 azulberries
6 narcoberries
1 sparkpowder

12 azulberries
6 stimberries
1 gunpowder

12 tintoberries
6 narcoberries
1 sparkpowder

12 amarberries
6 narcoberries
1 sparkpowder

12 narcoberries
6 stimberries
1 sparkpowder

6 amarb.| 9 tintob.
3 azulb.| 2 charcoal

9 amarberries
9 tintoberries
2 charcoal

4 amarb. | 1 azulb.
7 tintob. | 6 stimb.
1 gunpowder

7 amarb. | 4 stimb.
7 tintob. | 1 sparkp.

12 amarberries
6 stimberries
1 gunpowder

7 amarb. | 7 tintob.
4 narcob.| 1 gunp.

6 amarberries
12 azulberries
1 sparkpowder

12 tintoberries
6 stimberries
1 gunpowder

15 stimberries
2 charcoal

6 amarb. | 7 azulb.
4 narcob. | 1 gunp.

9 azulberries
9 tintoberries
2 charcoal

15 amarberries
2 charcoal

9 amarberries
9 azulberries
2 charcoal

15 tintoberries
2 charcoal

9 azulberries
9 tintoberries
1 sparkpowder

7 azulb. | 7 tintob.
4 narcob.| 1 gunp.

Level of Technology

In ARK, there's no consistent classification of the different levels of technology since you can learn new Engrams in every level. There are, however, some significant leaps forward in your development, for example, the moment you're able to craft metal tools.

Therefore, we want to breakdown the newest and most important crafting stations and which resources you'll primarily need at which stage of development. You'll still need the crafting stations and resources of previous levels, of course, but at this point, those are way more easily available and in larger quantities at that. Below, you can see just a small selection of crafting stations, resources, and weapons, even though there are more things available in the respective level.

Stone Age
Approx. level 1 - 20
Activities: building a basic shelter, surviving, taming easily tamable dinos.

Crafting Stations	Important Resources	Tools & Weapons
Inventory	Fiber	Stone Pick
Campfire	Thatch	Stone Hatchet
Mortar & Pestle	Wood	Spear
Cooking Pot	Stone	Club
	Flint	Bow

Iron Age
Approx. level 20 - 50
Activities: expanding and embattling your base, exploring the area, taming, exploring the first caves.

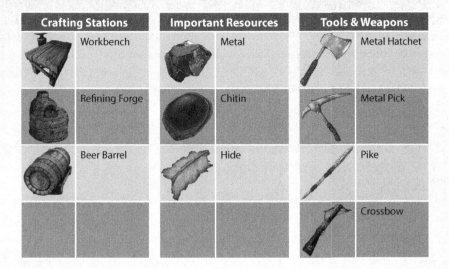

Modern Age

Approx. level 50 - 85

Activities: spreading bases all over the island, breeding, exploring the ocean, looting caves.

Crafting Stations	Important Resources	Tools & Weapons
Fabricator	Obsidian	Assault Rifle
Industrial Grill	Cementing Paste	Pump-action Shotgun
Industrial Forge	Oil	Rocket Launcher
Industrial Cooker	Silica Pearls	
Chemistry Laboratory	Crystal	

Tek Age

Approx. level 85 - 100

Activities: defeating bosses, gathering Elements, building bases underwater; Tek cave and ascension.

Crafting Stations		Important Resources		Tools & Weapons	
	Tek Replicator		Element		Tek Rifle
			Black Pearls		

ARMORS

In order to protect yourself from dangers of the island, you should wear appropriate armor:

Cloth Armor

Lvl	Set	Resources	Description
3	5 items - in total crafted in your inventory	145 fiber 10 hide	The first armor in the game. Better than nothing and provides moderate protection against heat & cold.

Hide Armor

Lvl	Set	Resources	Description
15	5 items - in total crafted in your inventory	33 fiber 82 hide	Better armor than cloth. Protection against cold. Negative values for hyperthermic insulation.

Chitin Armor

Lvl	Set	Resources	Description
37	5 items - in total crafted on the workbench	18 fiber 40 hide 82 chitin	Good armor protection but expensive regarding resources. Slight hypothermic insulation and negative heat protection values.

Flak Armor

Lvl	Set	Resources	Description
56	5 items - in total crafted on the workbench	18 fiber 40 hide 53 metal i.	Best-value armor. Slight hypothermic insulation, negative heat protection values.

Riot Armor

Lvl	Set	Resources	Description
98	5 items - in total made in the fabricator	3 fiber 7 hide 35 crystal 50 polymer 25 silica p.	Very good protection, slightly better than flak armor. Best protection against torpor. Quite expensive. Moderate cold and negative heat protection.

Ghillie Armor

Lvl	Set	Resources	Description
33	5 items - in total crafted in your inventory	18 fiber 40 hide 26 org. polymer	Provides camouflage: +50% visibility range. Good heat protection and slight hypothermic insulation.

Fur Armor

Lvl	Set	Resources	Description
23	5 items - in total crafted on the workbench	18 fiber 40 hide 53 metal i. 320 Pelz	Armor for cold areas. Very good hyperthermic insulation, very negative heat protection.

Heavy Miner's Helmet

Lvl	Set	Resources	Description
65	1 item - head in fabricator 30 electronics 20 metal ingots	8 fiber 15 hide 30 crystal 14 polymer	The helmet for exporing caves. Built-in headlight. Very good protection.

SCUBA Armor

Lvl	Set	Resources	Description
81	4 items - no hand protection made in the fabricator	13 fiber 87 hide 12 chitin 16 metal i. 6 cementing paste 7 silica pearls 43 polymer 10 crystal	Head: provides enhanced underwater vision. Body: oxygen mask (infinite oxygen supply). Legs: very high hypothermic-insulation. Feet: fast swimming.

Tek Armor

Lvl	Set	Resources	Description
--	5 items - in total made in Tek replicator has to be learned from boss enemies	600 polymer 2250 metal i. 600 crystal 100 Element 275 black p.	Head: night vision & helmet scanner. Body: jetpack (flying). Legs: fast walking ability. Hands: devastating punches. Boots: no fall damage.

Gas Mask

Lvl	Set	Resources	Description
85	1 item - head made in fabricator	220 polymer 85 crystal 10 absorb. substrate	Helps in the case of poison and gas attacks. Degrades while wearing it.

Night Vision Goggles

Lvl	Set	Resources	Description
84	1 item - head in fabricator 250 crystal 30 angler gel	240 polymer 180 metal i. 250 electronics 210 cementing paste	Provides night vision. Expensive. Only interesting in PvP mode. 15 absorbent substrate

3.1 Quick Construction Guide

- Craft the structures you want to create at the crafting station (inventory, workbench).
- Look for a preferably flat area where you can start crafting.
- Place structures in your hotbar and choose the ones you need.
- First, place the foundation.
- Pillars with roof structures on top can be used instead of foundations. For plain fences, you can use pillars or fence foundations with walls.
- Then, place the wall structures on the edges.
- After doing so, place the roof structures.
- Single parts snap into already existing structures. When placing the structure, move sideways slightly back and forth in order to change the snap point.
- With *snap point cycles* (default: Q or Z), you can switch between snap points during the crafting process.
- With the *use key* (default: E), you can flip the direction of a wall when placing it.
- Aim at a structure you've already built and press the *use key* (default on the computer: E) for a bit longer to activate to the radial action menu, which allows you cancel, demolish, or repair structures.
- When demolishing structures, you only get half of the used materials back.
- In case you've placed something incorrectly, you can take it back for 30 seconds immediately after placing the object.

3.2 Basics: Structures

Materials

Structures can be crafted with 7 different kinds of material:

Symbol	Material	Crafting Station	Description
	Thatch	Inventory	Resources: fiber, thatch, and wood. Cheapest structure, weak resistance. Good for beginners or testing purposes in order to find the right building site.
	Wood	Inventory	Resources: fiber, thatch, and wood. Sufficient protection against small dinos. For buildings in secure areas, interiors, roofs, or decoration.
	Clay	Inventory	Resources: fiber, thatch, wood, and clay. Can only be used within the Scorched Earth add-on and some other maps. Best heat protection. Stability similar to wood.
	Stone	Inventory	Resources: thatch, wood, and stone. Sufficient protection in PvE. Only a few dinos can destroy stone. For solid buildings.
	Metal	Workbench	Resources: metal ingot, cement. Can't be destroyed easily (only 2 dinos or a lot of explosives can do it). Most important type of protection in PvP; best when double or triple reinforced.
	Element	Tek Replicator	Resources: metal ingot, polymer, crystal, Element. Just like metal, difficult to destroy. Unlocked by defeating boss enemies. Offers some new possibilities in terms of building, for example, underwater domes.
	Greenhouse	Workbench	Resources: metal ingot, crystal, cement. Is used for greenhouses: enhances efficiency of beds. Also suitable for decoration.

Foundations

In order to build walls, ramparts, doors, and roofs, you must first build a foundation. Without a foundation, buildings collapse or can't even be built. The only building structures that don't require foundations, are dinosaur gates.

> Since dinosaur gates stand firm without foundation, you can use them to quickly erect ramparts and fenced-in areas without having to use foundations.

In addition, a foundation prevents resources or creatures from spawning in the proximity. Other players have to keep a certain distance from the foundation in order for them to start building.

Foundations comprise the following:

- *Foundation*: prevents other player's resources or creatures from spawning in the proximity. Allows you to create additional structures. Range for overhanging building structures (e.g. a balcony made out of roofs): 2 building blocks.
- *Pillars*: even a simple pillar prevents other players from building in the proximity; dinos and resources do spawn nevertheless. That's why people like putting pillars in an area in order to claim it for themselves. Pillars with a roof on top, however, are considered the same as a normal foundation and likewise prevent spawning.
- *Fence foundation*: prevents other player's resources or creatures from building and spawning in the proximity. The range, compared to that of a foundation, is slightly shorter. It only servers as foundation for building walls. It's not possible to build a lateral extension onto it.

SNAPPING AND ADJUSTMENT

The snap function makes it possible to create connected buildings. Foundations connect by snapping into place. This also applies to walls, ceilings, etc.

If the item is highlighted in green, this means that building is possible in that spot. The color red, however, indicates that you can't build there for many reasons.

Here, you can build on the right-hand side of the stone foundation. The foundations line up precisely with each other and are connected.

On the left-hand side, however, you can't place a foundation since it would extend too far into the ground or mountain. As a consequence, the foundation is blocked and highlighted in red.

You could get away with building a roof (e.g. a stone roof) instead of a foundation. This is also the case in the rear. You could, in fact, place a foundation in the front, but the slope is too steep and the foundation would end up in too low of a position and both foundations wouldn't be connected to each other.

Here, you can also resort to a roof in order to create a flat and connected surface:

Keep in mind, that you can only build two building blocks outwards without a foundation. Here's an example:

- Two roofs away from a foundation.
- One roof and one wall on the roof plate.

If you want to build further away than two blocks, you have to arrange a construction connected to the foundation again, for example, with a pillar that reaches the ground and connects the roof.

In our example, we could expand in all four directions with one foundation and three roofs:

Unfortunately, as you can see in the picture above, roofs don't line up completely evenly with foundations, so there's still a slight elevation.

> If you're not sure whether you can build large structures in a specific spot, do a test run first by using cheap resources like thatch instead of wasting expensive ones like stone and metal. If everything works out fine, you can build over the thatch structures with better ones and you even get back 50% of the thatch resources you've invested.

The construction functions are a bit sluggish sometimes and it often happens that they don't snap to connecting points of the structure. If this is the case, you can try the following:

- Change your position, move a bit to the side.
- Crouch or lie down.
- Approach the object from another side (if possible).
- Get closer or further away.
- Use the buttons, Q and Z, in order to switch between snap points.

Building with Pillars

Pillars offer the possibility to build foundations even in difficult locations. Below, you can read some tips for the use of pillars.

Snapping Pillars into Place

Pillars can also be connected by snapping. This only works, however, when building on a flat surface. On a slope, pillars only snap into place bottom-up. This doesn't work downhill.

> Build pillars from the bottom up, if possible, as it enables you to snap them into other pillars.

Pillars snap to the following snap points and make it possible to create connected buildings:

- In the middle and on both sides of foundation blocks.
- In the center of roof plates.
- At full distance or half way between adjacent pillars.
- An entire block away from fence foundations with a wall on top. This makes the building of catwalks or ramps next to fences possible.

In the following, we would like to show you some examples for the use of pillars.

Pillars on Slopes and Bridges

It's easy to create a group of straight pillars of equal height since they easily snap into each other. In case they don't snap into place, increase the height of the pillars in order to compensate the inclining plane.

As soon as you've connected the pillars with roofs at a desired height, the construction counts as contiguous building with connected foundations. By using this construction, you can build a „bridge" without any further pillars:

You can use this construction, for example, as a bridge across a river or as a ramp on a cliff. In a river, the foundation Elements would be on the riverbed and barely visible. You would only see the upper part of the bridge.

Building Ramps

With the previously explained technique, you can build a ramp at the hillside. First, build the foundation made of pillars and roofs. Make sure all pillars are connected so that it counts as one construction with a foundation:

Now, you can build a ramp from the top to the bottom.

Without the foundation, you could build a ramp at a range of max. 2 blocks.

Be careful though. The foundation has to stay in place. If a pillar or a roof gets destroyed, the ramp completely collapses in the same spot because there's no longer a consistent and connected foundation.

This type of construction offers many possibilities:

- Bridges
- Ramps
- Air bases (with a connection to the ground)
- Jetties for lakes and the ocean
- Making a lake completely flat
- Bases in the ocean (above the water and underwater)

Building Pillars in Alignment with the Roof

When building something, it often happens that you decide you want to expand the roof and many times need to brace it from beneath with pillars.

In the example below, you wouldn't be able to expand the roof further to the right because the foundation at the bottom is missing. Another pillar is required to support the entire construction.

Subsequently, pillars can only be snapped to the roof when building top down. However, as you can see on the picture below, an unsightly piece of the pillar sticks out of the roof.

You can avoid this with a little trick. Don't build the pillar as in the picture shown above, but rather move it to the top so that it's placed right in the center:

Don't worry, the pillar will be removed at the end. Unfortunately, you're wasting resources when you build it like this. Therefore, we recommend crafting this pillar with wood since it's cheaper.

Now you have to continue building the pillar downwards; but be careful. You have two snap points when building downwards. The standard snap point is further up and the pillar would, consequently, stick out of the roof again. The second snap point is further down and is in alignment with the roof. Building the second pillar (as shown in picture below: right) often involves a little tinkering and a few attempts before it works:

Now, complete the pillar by building it to down to the ground. Finally, you can destroy the pillar that sticks out of the roof on the upper side:

3.3 Building Fence Foundations

Fence foundations don't serve just for building a fence. You can also use them to construct your base in many creative ways.

Positioning and Alignment

On top of placed fence foundations you can construct walls to any height. It is important, however, to build the fence foundations in the same direction to avoid the walls facing the wrong sides.

You can, indeed, change the alignment of a wall (outside/inside) by pressing the *use key* (default: *E*), but walls and foundations would ultimately not be in perfect alignment.

Fence foundations are marked with a color, which indicates where the external side is to be placed. One half of it is marked in dark green, the other in light green. Unfortunately, these colors can only be distinguished under very dark or very shady light conditions. You can't tell the difference when the sun is glaring.

When the dark side points towards you, the external side of the wall will be at the left-hand side later:

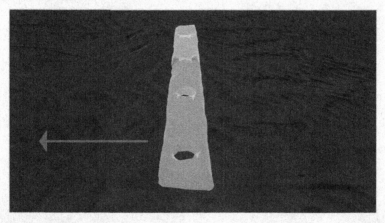

By pressing the *use button* (*E*), you can change the alignment of the fence foundation during the building process.

When the dark side is pointing away from you, this means that the exterior of the wall is on the right-hand side:

Fence Foundation: The All-purpose Tool

Just like pillars and other foundations, fence foundations have multiple snap points to precisely connect additional fence foundations.

Fence Foundations can be snapped into place in eight different directions:

Fence foundations can also be placed on top of other foundations and roofs, which enables you to construct additional shapes on a foundation.

Example: Octagonal Tower

First, start by building a flat platform made of foundations or roofs (on top of pillars):

Now, you can place fence foundations on the platform in the desired shape.

We want to build a simple octagonal tower. Arrange the fence foundations accordingly. Begin with the external side of a foundation and place the fence foundation there. This way, everything gets connected.

After placing the fence foundations, you can construct the walls. Since everything is connected, you have a firm foundation and can use things like roofs, ramps, etc.

Our little tower is now finished. You can, of course, build it two or three times larger using the same technique. You just have to make sure that the foundation is large enough.

In the interior of the tower, you can create an entire living and working area by building floors made of roofs.

3.4 Raft and Platform Saddles

Building on Platforms: The Basics

You can also make a building on rafts and platform saddles. You cannot, however, use just any amount of building structures. Depending on the creature, there's a restricted number of maximal objects on a platform. This also includes items of furniture, like beds, cupboards, wall torches, and workbenches. For this reason, we recommend saving as much space as possible when building.

This restriction can only be changed in the server settings. The values indicated above, are the ones from the official servers.

Depending on the platform, you can also just build a foundation made of 3x3 or 2x2 foundations and expand it with two roof blocks on each side. The height is restricted as well.

The following platforms are available:

By Land
- **Paracer** platform saddle: max. 32 structures
- **Bronto** platform saddle: max. 63 structures
- **Titanosaur** platform saddle: max. 250 structures

By Sea
- **Plesiosaur** platform saddle: max. 50 structures
- **Mosasaur** platform saddle: max. 70 structures
- **Raft**: max. 88 structures
- **Motorboat**: max. 80 structures
- **Megachelon**: (in Genesis part 1)

In the Air
- **Quetzal** platform saddle: max. 40 structures

Every kind of weight on a platform is added to the total loading capacity of the respective animal: content of chests, the tare weight of transported dinos and their inventory, etc.

For transport on a platform (e.g. on a Quetzal), we recommend using dinos with weight reduction for resources (e.g. Doedicurus for stone) since you can then transport more.

Lowering Foundations

When you build foundations on a raft, they significantly protrude beyond the raft's edges. With the following construction manual, you can lower the raft's foundations. The advantages are:

- Low superstructure.

- The raft is wrapped in foundations and therefore can't be attacked (except for Leedsichthys, which ignores all structures during its attacks and, consequently, destroys any raft).

This superstructure can be used as a basis for all types of rafts you want to build.

First, build a pillar at the center of the raft's front. Use the sail as an aid. You can stand next to the rudder with the selected pillar in order to place it in the middle automatically.

Now, build a foundation next to it. It should snap into the pillar.

Hide the sail, demolish the first pillar, and build a new one in the center of the foundation. Then, build a new foundation next to it. It should snap into the pillar and, in doing so, turn out slightly lower than the other foundation:

Destroy the pillar and the foundation you can see on the right-hand side of the picture. Then, repeat the whole process. Place a pillar in the middle of the already existing foundation and a lower foundation next to it.

By doing so, you can alternately continue to lower the foundation until it's in alignment with the raft's floor. Then, demolish the pillar and build nine foundations on top of it. See to it, that the foundation around the rudder is low enough so that you can still select the boat later.

You can expand the raft in every direction by using roofs. In the picture below, you can see a row of roof blocks attached to the foundations at the front:

Ultimately, the raft disappears almost completely because of the foundations and you can continue building on top of it according to your desires.

Ideas for Boats

On the basis of the platform's building technique described above, you can now build a bunch of different types of boats:

- Mission boat with a little base (bed, workbench, cupboards, additional crafting stations; everything walled in to make it secure).
- Attack craft with ballistas, cannons, or catapults on board.
- Transport boat for dinos.
- Taming boat.

Above, you can see an example of a taming boat: lure the dino (e.g. a Carno) via the ramp into your boat. It's then trapped in the cage and you can stun and tame it from a safe distance. When the taming process is over, you can conveniently take it out through the dino gate.

3.5 Additional Building Tips

With the *homestead update* in the beginning of the year 2019, the ARK main game has been extended with some new features from the mod *structures+*. This is why *triangle foundations* now offer more construction possibilities and flexible power lines and water pipes make it easier to set up new power supplies.

Additionally, you can undo structures for 30 seconds right after placing them. As a consequence, incorrectly placed Elements aren't lost immediately.

Triangle Foundations

With *triangle foundations*, you can also build „circular" structures without resorting to fence foundations. For hexagonal („circular") structures, you have the following two possibilities:

Alternate Building
- Start with an inner circle made of six triangles.
- Then, expand it externally with square foundations.
- Now, alternately put a triangle next to a square and then a square next to a triangle. The intermediate spaces are to be filled with other Elements.

Advantage: the coverage evenly expands at its exterior. Even in the case of very large layouts, the even structure on the edges is retained.

Disadvantage: it's difficult to combine the alternating structure with larger building structures since it's a bit confusing.

Linear Building
- Start with an inner circle made of six triangles.
- Then, expand it externally with square foundations.
- Expand the square foundations until you've reached the desired coverage.
- After doing so, intermediate spaces are to be filled with triangles.

Advantage: this coverage is built faster and can be easier combined with other building structures.

Disadvantage: the larger the coverage, the more uneven the edges get (e.g. five exterior walls and one exterior wall in alteration - ratio 5:1). This way of construction requires more triangle foundations the larger it gets and is, therefore, more expensive.

On the following page, you can see both constructions in comparison. In order to make it more distinguishable, we've alternated using wood and stone as material.

Alternate building:

Linear building:

With this size (3 exterior foundations; ensuing from the middle), the coverage of both structures is still identical. As soon as the surface is expanded externally, the coverage of the linear building looks more asymmetrical.

To make it more clear, you can see the coverage of the linear building type here:

FLEXIBLE POWER LINES AND WATER PIPES

Reinforced water hoses, formable metal pipes, and flexible power lines give you the possibility to lay the pipes and wirings suited to your requirements.

In former versions of the game, for example, you had to lay the pipes in one piece and from one end to the other since flexible adjustment wasn't possible. Additionally, the player only had branch lines at an 90° angle available.

Now, you can use flexible parts to connect several cables or pipes that run towards each other diagonally:

In the case of the example shown on the previous page, connecting with inflexible lines is impossible. Here, the reinforced water hose comes into use which accurately connects both pipes:

In case the pipes get moved or damaged, you don't have to demolish and re-build the flexible parts. Just go to the radial menu and select *reconnect* in order to reestablish the connection.

4: Maps

4.1 Exploring the area

Apart from the beautiful landscape, there are a lot of other things you can explore:
- Supply crates
- Explorer notes
- Caves on shore
- Underwater caves

Blue supply crate in a cave.

Supply Crates

In supply crates, you can find a great number of useful items and blueprints of Engrams. A lot of items have a better quality compared to items you've crafted on your own.

You can find different supply crates on shore, underwater, or in caves. The loot crates on shore can be detected from a distance since a colored beam marks its location. The color of the beam indicates the level of the crate:

	Island	Sco. E.	Aberr.
	3	3	10
	15	15	25
	25	30	35
	35	45	50
	45	55	65
	60	70	80

Violet supply crate on land.

Deep sea loot crates (only on "The Island") require you to be level 80.

> Crates contain better saddles, which offer your creatures better protection. You can also find weapons or construction plans for more powerful weapons. That's why you should always check every supply crate in the area if possible.

Explorer Notes

Ruins are spread all over the island, in which you can often find explorer notes left behind from other survivors. These notes increase your experience for the next 10 minutes. In addition, you obtain an achievement for finding a certain number of explorer notes.

Notes can be found in crates located in old ruins, caves, and specific locations.

When you collect several notes, you gain time in regard to your experience bonus.

> Make use of the gained experience bonus: don't collect crates immediately. Instead, wait until you expect to receive a lot of experience.

Explorer notes are only available on "*The Island*", "*Scorched Earth*", "*Aberration*", and "*Extinction*". They tell the story of the ARK. *Glitches* in *Genesis Part 1* have similar functions.

The notes you find tell the story of other survivors. By reading them, you learn a lot of new things about ARK. One of the survivors has even issued a dossier about every creature which you can find as well:

On "The Island", notes from four survivors can be found. Their stories are interconnected and reveal a lot of information about ARK.

Helena Walker

Helena comes from our time, she's a biologist, and probably Australian. She's also the author of all dinosaur dossiers and explores the general life in the ARK. She figured out how to open the Tek Cave. Most of the time, she accompanies Mei-Yin until she gets caught by Nerva. She reaches the Overseer's platform last and ascends.

Sir Edmund Rockwell

Rockwell is a chemist and a London citizen from the 19th century. He passionately explores the ARK and creates all the known recipes for kibble, soups, and potions. He considers Helena as a colleague but also as a competitor. Ultimately, he joins Nerva in order to find out more about the ARK. He accesses the Overseer's platform with Nerva and tries to operate devices there (Ascension) which is, probably, successful.

Gaius Marcellus Nerva

Nerva is a centurion from the Roman period between the 1st and 3rd century after Christ. He becomes the leader of a very aggressive tribe, "the Legion". They occupy a lot of areas and he tries to solve the secret of the ARK because he thinks this leads to incredible power. This causes him to come into conflict with Mei-Yin. Thanks to captive Helena, he opens the Tek Cave and loses all his men during a battle with the Overseer. There's a final battle with Mei-Yin, but you can't find out (yet) what happened to them.

Mei-Yin Li
Mei-Yin is a Chinese warrior from the three kingdom's period (about 250 after Christ). She has tamed a lot of creatures in the ARK and serves as a mercenary. That's why she has the name "Beast Queen". On behalf of Helena, she conquers the giant ape boss to get the second key for the Tek Cave. However, all of her creatures are killed by Nerva's legion and she's barely able to escape. Out of revenge, she follows Nerva into the Tek Cave and her fate remains, for now, uncertain.

Scorched Earth Explorer Notes
Helena Walker and Sir Edmund Rockwell reached "Scorched Earth ARK" through their ascension on "The Island". There, you can find their new notes and dossiers. Rockwell discovered (among other things) the new resource "Element" there.

John Dahkeya

John Dahkeya is a Native American and wanted robber from the late 19th century wild west. In the ARK, he becomes the protector (sheriff/captain) of Nosti (settlement of Raia) and falls in love with her. During an earthquake, he and Raia escape but he gets killed by Wyverns.

 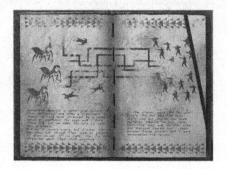 

Raia

Raia is an Egyptian priest. In "Scorched Earth" ARK, she becomes the leader of the Nosti settlement until it gets destroyed by an earthquake. After the death of her beloved Dahkeya (caused by Wyverns) she manages to create tamed Wyverns by hatching their eggs. With the tamed Wyverns, she protects the population of the ARK and they give her the name "Wali a Aswad". She takes Helena Walker and Edmund Rockwell to the portal of the Overseer's platform to help them leave the ARK.

Aberration Explorer Notes

In Aberration, we find explorer notes from *Helena Walker* and *Sir Edmund Rockwell* who arrived here after their adventure at Scorched Earth. In addition, you can find notes from *Mei-Yin Li* who, after her battle with Nerva (which she won by the way), came here directly after leaving "The Island".

Group of Students

Rusty Stufford (Kentucky), Emilia Müller, Boris, Trent, and Imamu are five students from the present age. They are fighting their way through the cave systems of Aberration and are able to get the three artifacts. However, their group's chance to escape decreases and their situation gets more and more hopeless. Only Imamu makes it into the TEK chamber and that's where he meets Rockwell. It seems like he has survived and backtracked, but nobody knows what has become of him.

Diana Altares

Diana is a pilot from the United Republics of Earth Army (URE) from the future. She and her group are stranded on the ARK and search a portal that leads back to earth.

In the course of time, they meet Mei-Yin who decides to join them and becomes their "animal keeper". They also meet Helena Walker and, finally, Sir Edmund Rockwell. They work together to find the portal to earth and open it. They search for the three artifacts and are able to find them as well.

Rockwell, however, is more interested in his research activities and experiments concerning "Edmundium" (what he calls Element). He injects himself with fluid Element which transforms him into a monster. During this process, he kills Diana Altares. Helena and Mei-Yin activate the portal in order to reach the planet beneath them (earth?). This is also the place you end up at after you've defeated Rockwell. Have fun in the 3rd DLC:

Extinction Explorer Notes
In Extinction, you can find explorer notes from *Helena Walker*, *Mei-Yin Li*, and the FAF soldier *Santiago*.

Santiago
Santiago was a soldier of the "Federation Armed Forces" and a member of Diana Altares' group. Together with Helena and Mei-Yin, he made it and they end up on

earth which is infested with Element. Santiago is a technical specialist and builds Meks in the course of events.

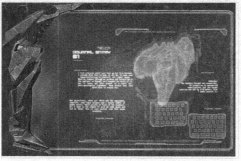

He's only able to build a few Meks and dies during a battle with a Titan before he was able to finish his last project, the "Mega Mek". His grave is at Sanctuary.

The One Who Waits
You may also come across explorer notes from "The One Who Waits". *The One Who Waits* is an ascended human being; a Homo Deus, as people call him. In fact, he's probably the most recent and last version of his kind. He also enlightens the player about the story of the earth, which Helena Walker was able to find out as well.

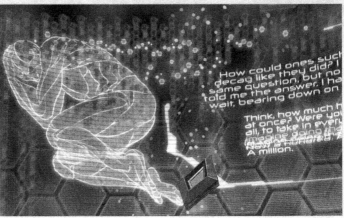

The earth was divided into two camps: United Republics of Earth and Earth Federation. Both were at war against each other and made use of Element. Where Element originates is uncertain but it probably came from space (maybe a meteorite?). The human race advanced the growth of the liquid Element which had became very important to them. In the process, slowly but surely, it penetrated every being on earth and mutated as well as corrupted them. Ultimately, the human race worked together in order to safeguard the existence of the human race, but it was already too late. The mutated creatures took possession of the last human strongholds. In small areas of the earth, the humans built refuges containing everything the earth had to offer – the ARKs. Their aim was to send them into space using AI.

The last secure city, Sanctuary (in which the player finds himself), was overrun and unable to witness the successful launch of the ARKs. Meanwhile, the ARKs arrived in space safely and are still awaiting the moment in which they can return to earth – when the corrupted Element has been extensively destroyed.

After Helena Walker had discovered that, she made it to the Grave of the Lost and, consequently, Helena began to transform into a Homo Deus.

Diana Altares
Mei-Yin was completely alone at this point but something incredible happened: *Diana Altares* came back. As she assumed, she had been cloned with one of Santiago's cloning chambers and her former consciousness was transferred to her new body.

Together, they tried to cleanse the earth from Element by destroying manifestations – the so-called Titans. They succeeded in injuring the King Titan, but they weren't able to achieve the final victory. They pulled back and now someone else has to finish the job.

Now it's up to the player to destroy the Titans so that the ARKs can begin their return to Earth and bring it back to life.

Genesis Part 1 Explorer Notes (Glitches)
In *Genesis Part 1*, you can't find any explorer notes. Instead, every time you find and repair a glitch, HLN-A tells you the corresponding story. Additionally, for each repaired glitch, you receive hexagons as a reward. The majority of the story will make the most sense when watching the video after the final battle. Spoiler alert:

HLN-A Glitches
Helena Walker, who ascended to a Homo Deus, has created an artificial creature bearing the name HLN-A with the aim to support the player during their challenges to come. HLN-A has many character traits from Helena Walker as well as her voice.

After the ARKs came back to the earth in Extinction, the most successful survivors were sent to a new planet in a spaceship (or possibly even several) in order to settle it and to make a new start. The survivors are in cryofridges on board the spaceship and don't even know that they're traveling. The player first learns of this in the end credits. In order to prepare the survivors for their difficult task and to continue training them, a virtual simulation is created where the survivors have to pass several tests in five biomes.

Every biome has a Master AI (Artificial Intelligence) that is supervising it and there's a central Master Controller program that keeps the whole system running. During the simulation, the player finds several life-threatening glitches (e.g. a harmless gas in the swamp turns into a gas that causes your death). HLN-A forces the player to fix the glitches and pass the test so that the player is allowed to finally leave the simulation.

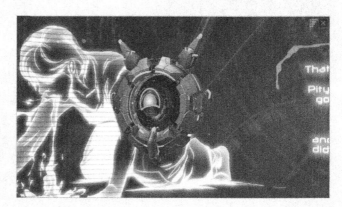

Something has infiltrated the system and is changing it. Four of five Master AIs seem to be destroyed. The fifth AI has gone insane and attacks the survivors (underwater boss – the Moeder).

As soon as you've forged ahead to the Master Controller, the infiltrator can be revealed. Edmund Rockwell has, somehow, survived the battle in Aberration and taken over the AI of the system.

Once you've defeated the corrupted Master AI bearing Rockwell's face, you can leave the cryofridge and, therefore, the simulation. You find yourself on board the spaceship that is just about to arrive at the planet; its final destination. HLN-A, however, is horrified when she discovers that some survivors in the cryofridges have already been infested with Element. The entire evil story threatens to repeat itself. The player quickly puts on a TEK suit and in the moment he wants to cross the bridge, one of Rockwell's tentacles pulls him back into the room. The end.

It remains to be seen if the player, Rockwell, and the other survivors will fight another battle in Genesis Part 2 on a new planet.

Caves and Artifacts

- Rare materials like crystal or obsidian
- Supply crates
- A lot of enemies (warning: they often spawn at a later time)
- Artifacts

You require several different artifacts to get access to an ARK obelisk from a boss. Usually, you can find artifacts in caves on land. Underwater caves house a substantial haul of resources and supply crates.

Artifact crate in a cave.

Many specific creatures can only be found in caves, for example, Arthropluera, Dung beetle, Onyc (giant bat), Megalosaurus, Araneo (giant spider), and Yeti.

> In some caves, creatures have an extremely high spawning level. In the Tek Cave, this can range from level 250 up to level 500. You can't tame these creatures. For these kind of caves, we recommend taking good equipment with you and bringing high level tamed dinos to support you!

4.2 The ARK – The Island

Here, you can find an overview of many interesting places on the standard map. You can use the teleport command only in single-player mode or when you own the admin rights of a server.

In order to teleport, open the console (*TAB*) and then type *enablecheats* and confirm with *enter*. Then, you can type in the teleport command.

Locations

Obelisks

Location	Lat.	Lon.	Teleport
Red Obelisk	79.8	17.4	admincheat setplayerpos -260600 239000 -10700
Green Obelisk	59.0	72.3	admincheat setplayerpos 178500 71700 -9600
Blue Obelisk	25.5	25.6	admincheat setplayerpos -195100 -196100 34300

Caves on Land

Cave	Lat.	Lon.	Teleport	Artfct.
Central	41.6	47.0	admincheat setplayerpos -23900 -67300 000	Clever
North-west	19.2	19.0	admincheat setplayerpos -247500 -246200 -11100	Skylord
Lower South	80.2	53.5	admincheat setplayerpos 28600 242300 -13200	Hunter
North-east	14.8	85.3	admincheat setplayerpos 283100 -281400 -13400	Devourer
Upper South	68.2	56.1	admincheat setplayerpos 49500 146100 -13400	Pack
South-east	70.6	86.1	admincheat setplayerpos 289100 165000 -14100	Massive
Swamp Cave	62.7	37.3	admincheat setplayerpos -101400 101700 -4300	Immune
Snow Cave	29.1	31.8	admincheat setplayerpos -144500 -165000 200	Strong
Caverns of Lost Hope	45.9	88.9	admincheat setplayerpos 00 00 00	Cunning
Caverns of Lost Faith	53.7	10.4	admincheat setplayerpos 00 00 00	Brute

Underwater Caves

Nr.	Lat.	Lon.	Teleport
01	16.0	10.1	admincheat setplayerpos -317000 -272000 -37000
02	10.0	21.5	admincheat setplayerpos -227000 -319000 -41000
03	10.4	39.5	admincheat setplayerpos -82000 -316000 -41500
04	07.9	90.1	admincheat setplayerpos 322000 -336500 -45000
05	36.3	91.5	admincheat setplayerpos 330000 -110000 -45500
06	50.5	11.2	admincheat setplayerpos -310000 4000 -42000
07	52.7	91.9	admincheat setplayerpos 334500 225000 -45500

Nr.	Lat.	Lon.	Teleport
08	83.0	09.9	admincheat setplayerpos -320000 267000 -41500
09	90.8	13.0	admincheat setplayerpos -290000 327000 -45500
10	89.8	36.8	admincheat setplayerpos -106500 320000 -44000
11	90.3	71.3	admincheat setplayerpos 171000 324500 -44000
12	87.1	90.2	admincheat setplayerpos 321000 297500 -44500

Artifacts

Artifact	Lat.	Lon.	Teleport
Clever	39.6	45.9	admincheat setplayerpos -32600 -83500 -6600
Skylord	19.6	18.4	admincheat setplayerpos -252700 -243100 -11500
Hunter	83.1	56.8	admincheat setplayerpos 54300 264600 -23700
Massive	67.1	86.0	admincheat setplayerpos 288000 136700 -24500
Devourer	16.1	84.5	admincheat setplayerpos 275600 -271100 -25100
Pack	71.9	60.9	admincheat setplayerpos 87100 174900 -26200
Strong	29.9	26.5	admincheat setplayerpos -188100 -160900 -6500
Brute	60.9	22.0	admincheat setplayerpos -224000 867000 -29000
Cunning	46.4	83.4	admincheat setplayerpos 267200 -28800 -43200
Immune	62.2	39.6	admincheat setplayerpos -83200 97300 -8800

Mountain Peaks

Artifact	Lat.	Lon.	Teleport
Volcano	43.4	37.6	admincheat setplayerpos -99000 -52600 46000
Frozen Fang	22.0	53.5	admincheat setplayerpos 28000 -224000 41500
The Radiant	25.7	24.8	admincheat setplayerpos -201800 -194100 39500
Far's Peak	33.6	79.3	admincheat setplayerpos 234000 -130900 25500
Frozen Tooth	35.7	59.1	admincheat setplayerpos 73100 -114500 25100
Grand Peak	56.6	48.0	admincheat setplayerpos -16000 53000 15400

Artifact	Lat.	Lon.	Teleport
Cragg's Island	87.0	24.7	admincheat setplayerpos -202200 295600 -5800
Weathertop	74.1	33.9	admincheat setplayerpos -128800 192700 -5800
Dead Island	16.2	83.2	admincheat setplayerpos 265900 -270600 -8000
South Haven	84.7	85.4	admincheat setplayerpos 283300 277900 -10400

Resource Overview

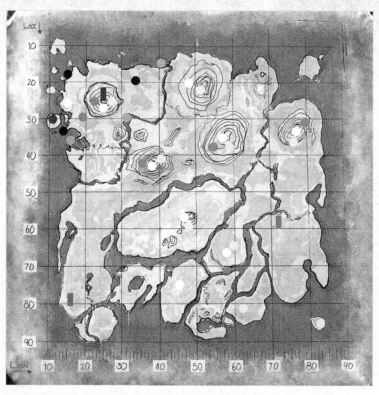

	Large Metal deposits
	Large Crystal deposits
	Large Obsidian deposits
	Silica Pearls on the surface
	Oil rocks on land or easily accessible
	Kairuku colonies (Organ. Polymer)

Oil can be found in the ocean all around the island and silica pearls at the bottom of the sea.

4.3 The Center

"The Center" is a DLC map. You can download it on Steam for free. On Xbox and PS4, this map will only be unlocked after you've defeated the boss of "The Island" and ascended accordingly.

You can also do this quickly, however, with a cheat command on the map "The Island":

> Open your console and type in the following cheat:
>
> **cheat playercommand Ascend1**
>
> Ascend2 and Ascend3 unlock the next ascension. In case the cheat doesn't work, key in **EnableCheats** in the console beforehand.

Obelisks

Location	Lat.	Lon.	Teleport
Red obelisk	8.2	57.4	cheat setplayerpos 36000 -209600 2000
Green obelisk	35.6	15.3	cheat setplayerpos -373200 42600 -14000
Blue obelisk	50.3	81.0	cheat setplayerpos 249600 193600 -8700

Underworld

In "The Center" is a huge underworld which is accessible from different locations. Here are some of them:

Location	Lat.	Lon.	Location
Access 1	53.6	53.9	Jungle South
Access 2	44.2	58.0	Jungle Mid
Access 3	66.1	51.7	Underwater, Jungle South

Underwater Domes

There are two large underwater domes in which you can breathe and build.

Location	Lat.	Lon.	Location
Dome 1	23.0	88.0	NE of Tropical Island North
Dome 2	67.0	64.2	West of Skull Island

Caves

Caves often have multiple entrances. To keep an overview, we've only listed one cave each:

Cave	Lat.	Lon.	Artfct.
The Center Cave	36.0	34.5	Devious
Jungle Cave	54.2	62.7	Immune
North Ice Cave	18.7	29.7	Clever & Devourer
South Ice Cave	60.0	22.5	Skylord
West Lava Cave	15.8	50.5	Hunter & Pack
East Lava Cave	11.2	67.4	Massive & Strong

Artifacts

Cave	Lat.	Lon.	Teleport
Devious	41.1	33.7	
Immune	49.2	65.5	cheat setplayerpos 100000 181300 -29900
Clever	19.2	24.2	cheat setplayerpos -296400 -106000 -8300
Devourer	24.0	26.1	cheat setplayerpos -277600 -59600 2600
Skylord	54.0	20.9	cheat setplayerpos -328200 228000 -1900
Hunter	16.7	54.3	cheat setplayerpos -7500 -130000 -13100
Pack	60.7	53.8	cheat setplayerpos -7800 -152500 -16900
Massive	10.2	52.9	cheat setplayerpos -20600 -192100 -24700
Strong	15.2	57.4	cheat setplayerpos 22500 -144600 -25900
Cunning	35.2	18.1	cheat setplayerpos -355700 45900 -47000
Brute	71.6	87.3	cheat setplayerpos 309000 395700 -104400

Resource Overview of „The Center"

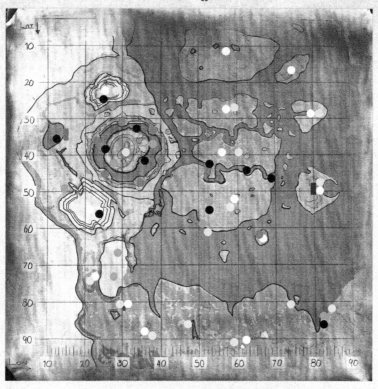

	Large Metal deposits
	Large Crystal deposits
	Large Obsidian deposits
	Silica Pearls on the surface
	Oil rocks on land or easily accessible
	Kairuku colonies (Organ. Polymer)

Oil can be found in the ocean all around the island and silica pearls at the bottom of the sea.

4.4 Ragnarok

Ragnarok is an official DLC map, just like "The Center". You can download it for free. It's one of the most popular ARK maps.

The map is about 2 ½ times larger than "The Island" and offers many creatures from the Scorched Earth add-on as well. There are also unique creatures you can only find here:

Ice Wyvern, Griffin, Lava Elementals, and Ice worms.

Megalania and Ovis (sheep) appear much more often than on any other maps.

This map offers a very Nordic flair with some interesting landscape features like huge waterfalls, ruins, frosty mountains, and a high plateau, for example.

Obelisks

Location	Lat.	Lon.	Teleport
Red Obelisk	35.0	85.7	cheat setplayerpos 467000 -195000 -14700
Green Obelisk	57.0	38.1	cheat setplayerpos -155000 91000 11700
Blue Obelisk	18.1	17.3	cheat setplayerpos -428000 -418000 -13600

Interesting Locations

Location	Lat.	Lon.	Teleport
Fort in the Swamp	21.2	40.8	cheat setplayerpos -121000 -377000 17000
Abandoned Lighthouse	22.7	85.6	cheat setplayerpos 466200 -357400 2900
Desert	65.3	65.3	cheat setplayerpos 200000 200000 -10400
Hidden House	24.5	83.9	cheat setplayerpos 444466 -333802 -13780
Bridge	40.1	38.4	cheat setplayerpos -152000 -130000 31600
Lava Cave	18.7	27.9	cheat setplayerpos -290000 -410000 -3400
Ice Cave	30.9	37.8	cheat setplayerpos -160000 -250000 31500
Boss Arena	51.3	37.8	cheat setplayerpos -159470 17181 -128688

Artifacts

Artifact	Lat.	Lon.	Teleport
Devious	39.0	45.3	cheat setplayerpos -61500 -144000 350
Immune	23.7	44.6	cheat setplayerpos -71000 -345000 3400
Clever	27.4	69.1	cheat setplayerpos 250000 -296000 11400
Devourer	47.4	2.3	cheat setplayerpos -624500 -34000 -59500
Skylord	27.5	28.9	cheat setplayerpos -276500 -294300 6700
Hunter	21.5	27.2	cheat setplayerpos -298934 -373125 -10664
Pack	33.6	43.4	cheat setplayerpos -86500 -215000 -14200
Massive	21.7	77.4	cheat setplayerpos 359200 -370600 3500
Strong	24.8	24.7	cheat setplayerpos -331500 -330300 1260
Brute	35.2	78.3	cheat setplayerpos 370200 -193600 19080
Cunning	20.3	46.0	cheat setplayerpos -52600 -390000 10300

Resource Overview

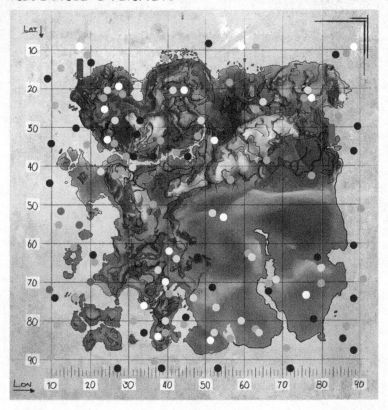

	Large metal deposits
	Large crystal deposits
	Large obsidian deposits
	Silica pearls
	Black pearls
	Oil rocks

Ragnarok is very large, therefore we can only give you a rough idea of the deposits' location.

4.5 Valguero

Valguero, just like the previous maps, was a Mod map that was taken over as an official DLC for free by the support of Studio Wildcard. Valguero is, again, significantly smaller than Ragnarok, but has some unique features in store:

- New sky effects (rainbows, auroras, shooting stars).
- A large underground ocean (The Abyss).
- An exclusive creature called Deinonychus.
- Scattered along the lake are corpses of Carbonemys and Ichthyosaurus, which you can also farm.

The map was created very beautifully and offers common biomes like woods, lakescape, jungle, redwood, tundra, and snowy mountains. The map is located in an area that ranges from moderate climate to snow zones. There are no deserts.

There's a trench with Wyverns in the north-east of the snow mountains (The Great Trench) where you can find Ice Golems and, in its deeper lava regions, Fire Wyverns as well.

Obelisks

Location	Lat.	Lon.
Red Oobelisk	76.1	17.1
Green Obelisk	48.8	76.1
Blue Obelisk	9.3	17.2

Artifacts

Location	Lat.	Lon.
Artifact of the Brute	47.7	88.0
Artifact of the Crag	35.0	52.2
Artifact of the Cunning	14.5	26.3
Artifact of the Destroyer	67.0	89.1
Artifact of the Devourer	48.7	90.3

Location	Lat.	Lon.
Artifact of the Gatekeeper	48.0	58.9
Artifact of the Immune	74.3	35.8
Artifact of the Pack	70.1	39.2
Artifact of the Skylord	13.4	72.7
Artifact of the Strong	72.2	36.5

Cave Access Points

Location	Lat.	Lon.
Artifact of the Cunning	15.5	27.3
The Great Trench	9.3	71
The Great Trench	8.9	78.8
The Abyss	32.0	8.3
The Abyss	31.8	9.3
Tundra Cave	32.8	9.4
Tundra Cave	33.6	9.1
Tundra Cave	33.4	9.6
Tundra Cave	33.3	10.3
Artifact of the Crag	34.3	51.4
The Emerald Forest	37.9	57.4
Mining Cave	30.8	94
The Emerald Forest	32.2	92.4
Teruki Falls Cave	34.9	89.7
Cave	37.0	90.9
Cave	38.9	89.3

Location	Lat.	Lon.
Cave	39.9	89.9
The Abyss	45.4	34
The Lost Temple	46.9	87.5
Cave	47.4	75.7
Tunnel	48.5	75.6
Tunnel	48.2	76
Cave	51.5	86.3
Cave	53.6	87.8
Tunnel	53.2	12.6
Tunnel	55.1	13.8
The Abyss	63.9	73.3
The Lair	73.1	40.6
Tunnel	74.2	59.3
Tunnel	75.3	60.1
Tunnel	96.1	20.6

113

Interesting Locations

Location	Lat.	Lon.
Snow Ruins	14.4	60.2
Skeleton Gorge	25.8	42
Mountain Fortress	33	21.3
Ruins of a bridge	33.3	42.2
Ruins	33.5	46.2
Ruins	32.3	52.8
Teruki Waterfall	34.5	89.3
Ruins of a bridge	36.4	82.8
Ruins of a bridge	36.8	81.5
Jungle Palace	37.9	90.4
Weathertop Ruin	40.5	67.2
Stonehenge	40.3	25.9
Lost Temple	43.4	84.5
Ruins	44.9	82.1
Ruins	45.6	68.7

Location	Lat.	Lon.
Ruins of a bridge	49.6	10
Ruins	54.6	52.8
The Stronghold	60.4	9.8
Ruins of a bridge	80.5	18.3
The Redwoods Stronghold	77.6	49.6
The Maul	79.8	67
Access to the Forgotten City	86.1	90.5
Access to the Forgotten City	91	87.9
Ruins of a bridge	80.5	18.3
Ruins of a bridge	84.6	17.1
Ruins	85.5	18.3
Ruins of a dam	87.8	11.1
Ruins	88.2	36.3
Ruins of a temple (Megapithecus)	91.5	29.8
Ruins of a bridge (broken)	95.7	39.6

Deinonychus

The Deinonychus is extremely suitable for taming. You can learn more about it in its listing which can be found in the chapter "Terrestrial Creatures". However, you can't tame it in the normal manner; you have to steal one of its fertilized eggs and hatch it. The nests of the Deinonychus can primarily be found in the south-east of the map:

Deinonychus Nests (excerpt)

Location	Lat.	Lon.	Location	Lat.	Lon.
Deinonychus nest	50.5	93.9	Deinonychus nest	78.7	72.6
Deinonychus nest	70.4	94.1	Deinonychus nest	82.3	95
Deinonychus nest	69.7	63.1	Deinonychus nest	91.9	91.5
Deinonychus nest	72.7	60.6	Deinonychus nest	96.1	81.3

Wyvern Nests (excerpt)

Location	Lat.	Lon.	Location	Lat.	Lon.
Wyvern nest	7.4	76.8	Wyvern nest	13.3	71.6
Wyvern nest	8.8	75.8	Wyvern nest	14	71.1
Wyvern nest	11.1	71.6	Wyvern nest	15.3	73
Wyvern nest	12.3	77.8	Wyvern nest	16.4	71.7

You will quickly find more nests in the proximity of the ones mentioned above.

Resource Overview

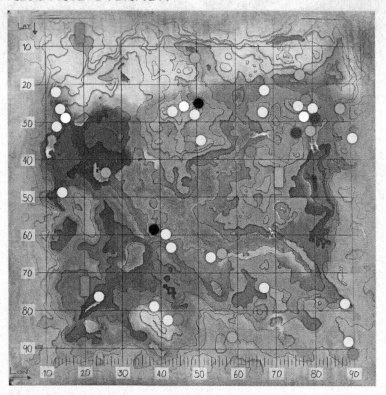

	Large Metal deposits
	Large Crystal deposits
	Large Obsidian deposits
	Silica Pearls
	Black Pearls
	Oil rocks
	Blue Gems
	Oil

5: Scorched Earth

5.1 New Features in Scorched Earth

The *Scorched Earth* add-on can be acquired separately and offers a lot of new features to your game in ARK:

New Map:

The map is extraordinary. It's a desert map and open water is rare, even though sufficient water is available.

New Creatures:

- Deathworm
- Jerboa
- Jug Bug
- Lymantria
- Manticore
- Mantis
- Morellatops
- Rock Elemental
- Thorny Dragon
- Vulture
- Wyvern
- Dodo Wyvern

New Final Enemies/Boss Battle:

The Manticore is a challenging, new boss. Not to mention the fact that Death Worms in the desert and Wyverns (dragons) are already a challenge you have to deal with in the normal game.

More Difficult Fight for Survival:

Due to the tremendous heat, you constantly have to fight against the lack of water and food and suffer from heat exposure.

There are a lot of sandstorms and electrical storms that make it even harder to make progress.

Over time, contents of your water tanks disappear and food spoils faster.

Stone and metal structures increase the heat. To create a space for living and crafting, make a building made of clay. Clay provides good heat insulation which makes for a better indoor climate.

New Resources and Objects (small excerpt)

Symbol	Resource	Description
	Sand	Required for crafting several new objects. Main ingredient for clay. Mined from stones with a metal pick.
	Raw Salt	Used to preserve food. Can be found in the mountains. Mined with a metal pick.
	Sulfur	For some highly dangerous weapons. Can be found in the mountains close by metal. Use a metal pick.
	Clay	Important for adobe structures. Made of sand and cactus sap.
	Cactus Sap	You can eat it and it's required for clay. Can be extracted from cacti. Use a whip or an axe.
	Boomerang	Returns back to you and increases torpor.
	Whip	Useful for gathering resources or to goad your tamed dino.
	Chainsaw	There's no better tool than a chainsaw to gather wood and chitin.
	Adobe Structures	As sturdy as wood, isolates and protects excellently from the tremendous heat.

5.2 Map Overview

In Scorched Earth, you can only find three caves; each with one artifact:

Caves

Cave	Lat.	Lon.	Artifact
Ruins of Nosti	78.5	75.6	Destroyer
Grave of the Tyrants	28.5	29.3	Crag
The Old Tunnels	58.6	47.7	Gatekeeper

Artifacts

Artifact	Lat.	Lon.	Teleport
Destroyer	79.8	81.3	Admincheat setplayerpos 250300 237800 -31500
Crag	35.2	28.1	Admincheat setplayerpos -175500 -118900 7200
Gatekeeper	58.2	43.4	Admincheat setplayerpos -52700 66000 -27300

Resources

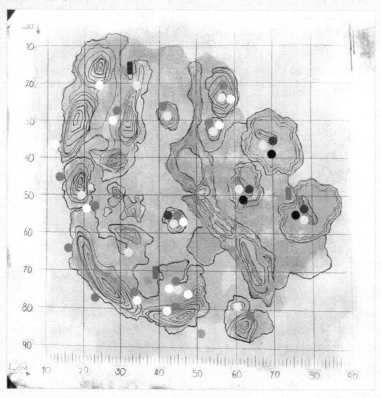

	Large Metal deposits
	Large Crystal deposits
	Large Obsidian deposits
	Silica Pearls on the surface
	Several Oil Wells
	Large Salt deposits

In Scorched Earth, you can find oil in form of springs on which you have to place oil pumps.

Next to the big trench in the western desert where Wyverns live, you can find large obsidian and metal deposits.

5.3 How to Survive in Scorched Earth

Here are some tips to help you survive more easily in Scorched Earth:

- Build an adobe shelter to create a living and crafting space. For better protection, you can build a stone or a metal structure around it.
- Jug Bugs provide water and oil and occur frequently.
- The calls of the Jerboas warn you of impending storms. Seek shelter quickly when you hear them.
- Cacti emit water during the harvesting process. Despite its name, cactus sap is considered as food and is readily available and in large amounts.
- Tame Morellatops. They're suitable as water reservoirs, pack animals, and for farming resources.
- Build in the proximity of water or water sources.
- Build wells on water springs.
- Build various water reservoirs under the open sky in case there's no source of water in proximity to your base; the reservoirs fill up during rare rainfalls automatically and are usually sufficient to provide your base with water.
- At the beginning, avoid the sand desert – Deathworms are waiting for you there.
- Avoid huge yellow stones; they're rock Elementals in disguise – don't get too close.
- Use preserving salt (made of salt and sulfur) in your inventory, in the inventories of your dinos, and in smoke houses. This makes food last two times longer and is important for valuable food and food that spoils very fast (e.g. filets or Wyvern milk).
- On Scorched Earth, power generators will be damaged as soon as they are running. You have to repair them approx. every 24 hours (real time). Wind turbines are more suitable. In the sand desert, there's 100% wind.

6: Aberration

6.1 New Features in Aberration

The *Aberration* add-on can be bought separately and offers new sceneries for ARK.

New Map:

This time, you play in a damaged ARK. The upperworld is contaminated by radiation and is scorching hot during the day, making it impossible to survive. You play in the underworld of the ARK. In the dark depths, the Nameless attack you without warning and in never-ending waves, save you're carrying one of the various new kinds of light sources. Since there are no flying creatures you can tame, you have to climb a lot. There is, however, plenty of new equipment available.

Fertile biome (green): this starting point is reminiscent of the normal ARK. There's lots of water and a fertile area with a bit of sunlight. You're not threatened by the Nameless. There's almost no metal and only a few advanced resources. It's a good region for your first base.

Bio-Luminescent biome (blue, see chapter cover art): there's no daylight. Instead, you'll mostly come across luminescent plants and mushrooms. The Nameless attack you if you're not carrying a charge light (e.g. from a Bulbdog or a lantern). Lots of metal (even in the blue luminescent stones) and better resources can be found here.

Element biome (red/purple): this biome has completely absorbed the Element and is toxic. Rock Drakes, Reapers, and many other dangerous creatures live here. The Nameless are even more numerous. Bring a sufficient amount of charge light and climbing equipment. You can find a lot of rare resources here.

Upperworld: the scorched upperworld is a toxic and contaminated place. You should only visit it by night while wearing a protective suit. During the day, the floor is burning, which makes surviving difficult. Reapers, Nameless, and Seekers inhabit this surreal area. Supply crates and access to the three ARK obelisks, can only be found on the surface.

> **Warning**: don't try to download creatures from another ARK in multiplayer mode. They will immediately die in Aberration – even fertilized eggs!

New Creatures:

- Basilisk (also alpha version)
- Bulbdog (has charge light)
- Featherlight (has charge light)
- Glowbug (charges batteries)
- Glowtail (has charge light)
- Karkinos (also alpha version)
- Lamprey (has charge light)
- Nameless (avoids charge light; also alpha)
- Ravager (can climb on zip lines)
- Reaper (several versions)
- Rock Drake (can climb and glide)
- Roll Rat (fast movement)
- Seeker (gets bonus from charge light)
- Shinehorn (has charge light)

A lot of known creatures appear in a specific "aberrant" version here: they have fluorescent colors and are therefore easier to see in the twilight of caves. Besides that, they're identical to their counterparts. There are no flying creatures.

New Final Enemies/Boss Battle:

Edmund Rockwell is already known due to many explorer notes. Here, he mutates because of his various experiments with "Edmundium" (Element) and is part of a challenging final showdown in ARK. You can read more about that in the chapter "Boss Enemies".

New Resources and Objects (small excerpt)

Mushrooms

Mushrooms grow everywhere in the Aberration ARK. The smaller ones can be collected by hand. Which mushrooms you get is chance. By using a sickle or the corresponding dinos for harvesting (e.g. Trikes), you get more mushrooms when harvesting them. You can cut down the bigger mushrooms like trees. You can use the wood of the mushrooms just like normal wood.

A lot of the smaller mushrooms secrete poison. That's why you should always pay attention to the type of mushrooms you're passing through. The toadstools in the Fertile biome cause hallucinations, for example.

Symbol	Resource	Description
	Auric mushroom	Removes radiation sickness and consumes water.
	Aggeravic mushroom	Heals a small percentage. Protects against toxins from the Fertile biome.
	Ascerbic mushroom	Increases the torpor level by 25 within 2 seconds. Good alternative to narcoberries. Provides immunity to toxins from the Element biome.
	Aquatic mushroom	Provides some water and decreases food level. Provides immunity to toxins from the Luminescent biome (blue).
	Fungal wood	Harvested and used like normal wood. Necessary for some recipes.

Additional Resources

Symbol	Resource	Description
	Green Gem	Can be found in the Fertile biome, during earthquakes, and next to the holes of Roll Rats.
	Blue Gem	Can be found in the Luminescent biome, during earthquakes, and next to the hole of Roll Rats.
	Red Gem	Can be found in the Element biome, rarely during earthquakes, and next to the holes of Roll Rats.
	Element Ore	Can be found on the surface.
	Congealed Gas Ball	You have to build a gas collector on top of a gas wire that emits violet smoke. Warning: the collector breaks rather quickly (within about 1 ½ days).

Tools & Essentials (small selection)

Object	Resource	Description
	Climbing Pick	You can even climb overhangs with a climbing pick. You should always have one with you.
	Zip Line Anchor	Shoot two of them by using a crossbow in order to create a zip line. Now, you can rappel quickly.
	Zip Line Motor	Attache a zip line to your pants so that the motor can pull you up.
	Gliding Suit	When attached to your chest armor, it enables sailing and gliding from an elevated point.

6.2 Map Overview

Obelisks

Obelisk	Lat.	Lon.	Teleport
Purple	22.5	78	cheat SetPlayerPos 223631 -219658 57270
Red	80.8	20.4	cheat SetPlayerPos -237063 246035 53430
Blue	19	16.2	cheat SetPlayerPos -270302 -248089 66730

Caves

Since Aberration is a cave system, transitions are smooth.

Cave	Lat.	Lon.	Teleport	Hint
Cave (Depths)	48.3	27.2	cheat setplayerpos -182400 -13600 43100	Without tames
Cave (Shadows)	55.2	65.9	cheat setplayerpos 127200 41600 15000	Diving suit and climbing tools
Cave (Stalker)	81	46	cheat setplayerpos -32000 248000 7600	Climbing tools and RockDrake

Artifacts

Artifact	Lat.	Lon.	Teleport
Depths	51.2	23.8	cheat setplayerpos -210000 11100 36000
Shadows	50.5	72.6	cheat setplayerpos 181170 4397 -7593
Stalker	91.7	51.3	cheat setplayerpos 11063 333564 31971

Interesting Places

Location	Lat.	Lon.	Teleport
Boss Terminal	42.7	36.8	cheat setplayerpos -105377 -58144 -102977
Rockwell's Arena	87.4	12.3	cheat setplayerpos -301600 299200 -215800
The Ancient Device	43.1	25.3	cheat setplayerpos -197600 -55200 49500
The Overlook	51.3	33.1	cheat setplayerpos -135200 10400 41200
The Grave of the Lost	57.4	51	cheat setplayerpos 8000 59200 -59400
The Fallen Nexus	14.9	41.7	cheat setplayerpos -66400 -280800 67700
Rock Drake Cave	66.3	61.8	cheat SetPlayerPos 94496 130414 -93749

Charge Nodes (battery charging station and Element production)

Location	Lat.	Lon.	Teleport
The Lost Roads	61.6	39.8	cheat setplayerpos -81600 92800 -3200
Hope's End	60.2	43.7	cheat setplayerpos -50400 81300 -15800
Mushroom Forest	36.8	37.9	cheat setplayerpos -96800 -105600 55400
Mushroom Forest	38	40.4	cheat setplayerpos -76800 -96000 38100
Mushroom Forest	36	45.3	cheat setplayerpos -37600 -112000 37100
Mushroom Forest	35.2	47.2	cheat setplayerpos -22400 -118400 37800
Mushroom Forest	27.8	47.6	cheat setplayerpos -19200 -177600 37100
Mushroom Forest	48.1	31.6	cheat setplayerpos -147082 -15596 58000
River Valley	36.3	49.7	cheat setplayerpos -2399 -109600 37700
River Valley	42.5	50.4	cheat setplayerpos 3400 -60000 37500
River Valley	30.3	61.5	cheat setplayerpos 92000 -157600 40700
River Valley	24.1	60.2	cheat setplayerpos 81600 -207200 49100
River Valley	25.2	53.9	cheat setplayerpos 31200 -198400 40100
River Valley	38.8	46.1	cheat setplayerpos -30996 -89595 48785
Luminous Marshlands	36.7	57.1	cheat setplayerpos 56800 -106400 33200
Luminous Marshlands	44.6	60.2	cheat setplayerpos 81600 -43200 15800
Luminous Marshlands	48.8	66.8	cheat setplayerpos 134736 -9505 18868
The Overlook	57.7	56.9	cheat setplayerpos 55200 61600 17100
The Overlook	56.7	43.3	cheat setplayerpos -53600 53600 7900
The Surface - northwest	18.5	15.5	cheat setplayerpos -276066 -251683 66731
The Surface - northwest	17.2	17.5	cheat setplayerpos -260193 -262639 57863
The Surface - northwest	13.6	17.1	cheat setplayerpos -262818 -291569 66072

6.3 Tips for Aberration

Here are a few tips to help you survive better in Aberration:

- You require a lot of water. Improve resistance (at least by 10) and take enough filled water tanks with you.
- Tame a creature with a charge light (e.g. a Bulbdog) and take it with you when you enter the darker regions. Its light will protect you from the Nameless. When the animal is sitting on your shoulder, you can turn its light on and off by using the emote "light" (e.g. similar to waving).
- Oil is very rare and not available in large amounts. By using charged batteries, you can also run electric devices. In order to do so, simply place them into the device's inventory. One battery, for example, can power a refrigerator for 2 ½ hours. You can recharge them on charge nodes or with the aid of Glowbugs.
- There are a lot of useful tools. Use them for climbing (climbing pick, natural zip lines, ladders, elevators, Rock Drakes). Without them, you won't reach many important places since flying dinos aren't available.
- Collect large amounts of mushrooms by using sickles or dinos. They will protect you from poisoning. Better eat a full stack at once (=100 pieces).

7: Extinction

7.1 New Features in Extinction

The *Extinction* add-on wraps up the story about the ARKs and is the last DLC you can buy from the first ARK season pass.

New Map:

You are on earth, which is infested with Element. The city of Sanctuary is your spawn point. This city was the humanity's last stronghold against the creatures that had been corrupted by Element.

Sanctuary City: it stretches over the entire center of the map and is a relatively safe place. There are several levels with balconies on top of the highest towers. Here, you can find trees, water, metal, and all important resources you need in the beginning. In addition, the city is secure against meteors, which impact the surrounding area constantly. Automatic drones and enforcers attack aggressive and corrupted creatures immediately upon detection.

Snow Dome: a large Snow biome houses the blue obelisk in the northeast and is protected by a dome.

Desert Dome: there's also a protective dome around the red obelisk in the southeast of the map. A desert area surrounds the obelisk.

Forbidden Zone: the zone in the north of the map leads to the boss "King Titan". You should stay away from this dangerous area.

The Crater: in the southwest, you can find a crater with hot springs that provide sulfur and condensed gas.

The Wasteland: this is the region between Sanctuary and the other areas and is a dangerous zone. A lot of corrupted creatures live here. You can, however, find advantageous *Orbital Supply Drops* and several new creatures here. In The Wasteland, meteors hit the earth frequently. Use a strong and fast riding mount if you're in this region.

Caves: three caves including their artifacts can be explored.

New Creatures:

Corrupted Creatures: a lot of animals were mutated and corrupted by Element. You can easily recognize them by their purple coloring. It doesn't matter which creature it is, they immediately attack every creature that hasn't mutated yet and hunt it till it's dead. Corrupted animals can't be tamed.

Drones: Scouts and Enforcers belong to Sanctuary's automatic defense system. They attack every corrupted and aggressive creature (including you, as soon as you become aggressive). Destroy them to obtain a construction plan in order to be able to build your own drones.

Tamable Creatures (excerpt):

Velonasaur: the machine gun among the dinos - he shoots spines.

Managarmr: a dragon similar to Rock Drake. He can leap very highly, is extremely fast, and can freeze enemies.

Snow Owl: the Snow Owl is a mixture between Daeodon and Argentavis. It's able to fly, heal, fight, and can carry a lot.

Gasbags: funny transport creatures with large lung capacity.

Gacha: peaceful omnivore (literally) that can create resources.

Forest Wyvern: red Wyverns that appear in the northern area.

New Final Enemy/Boss Battle:

Four giant Titans have to be defeated in order to save the wold. Three of them can even be tamed. Read more about it in chapter 13.

We consider the Alpha King Titan one of the strongest enemies in ARK. The one who tries to fight him unprepared, dies.

Meks

Meks are battle robots you can build and man. They have a Tek sword and a plasma pistol. You can also equip them with additional weapons and shields. The cannon module transforms a Mek into a dangerous tool that can be used to siege the enemy's base.

You can learn the corresponding Engram, but you can only achieve level 51 Mek with it. In OSDs (see next page), you can find construction plans for Meks far exceeding level 400.

For the battle with the King Titan, you can even build the giant Mega Mek. It's an effective weapon against the strong Alpha King Titan.

A Mega Mek faces the Alpha King Titan

Orbital Supply Drops

On the surface, you can't find any supply crates like the ones you know from The Island or Scorched Earth. There are, however, "*Orbital Supply Drops*" (short: OSDs) which occasionally fall from the sky but you can't loot them instantly.

When you enable an OSD, a force-field protects it. Then, several waves of numerous corrupted animals make an attack, but you have to keep them away from the OSD. If you accomplish destroying every wave and the OSD survives, you can initiate ejecting the items and discover a lot of useful things.

The colors indicate the difficulty of the assaulting waves as well as the loot quality. Yellow and red OSDs are the most difficult to defend but also offer the best loot. Several Gigas or a good Rex can master this task.

By doing this, you can find construction plans for really good Meks or Tek weapons.

You can easily recognize OSDs from a far distance by the black trail of smoke they emit. They can only be found in Wasteland.

Element Nodes are defended in a similar way. After successful defense, they can yield Element.

Resource and Objects (small excerpt)

Symbol	Resource	Description
	Fragmented Green Gem	Can be found in the blue crystal clusters. Replacement for the green gem.
	Blue Crystalized Sap	Can be found by harvesting from fungal trees. Alternative to the blue gem.

Symbol	Resource	Description
	Red Crystalized Sap	Can be found by harvesting from blood-ridden trees. Replacement for the red gem.
	Element Dust	Can be found in tools and devices in Sanctuary. A Doedicurus is very suitable for harvesting the Element dust.
	Unstable Element	Made of Element dust in city terminals and transforms into normal Element.
	Condensed Gas	Can be harvested from the yellow stones in the Sulfur Fields. Has to be processed in a refining forge. Replacement for congealed gas.
	Silicate	Harvested with a hatchet from silicate stones. Also provides obsidian. Alternative to silica pearls.

Tools & Essentials (small excerpt)

Objekt	Resource	Description
	Delivery Crate	Mark a position on the map. Place a delivery crate, fill it, and select a location in the menu. The goods are then delivered to the indicated location.
	Cryopod	You can store a dino in it. It's a type of ARK Pokéball. The pod can be used for 30 days.
	Cryofridge	Cryopods last forever in it. It's a giant dino deposit with low space consumption.
	City Terminal	Can be found anywhere on the map but mostly in the city. It's used to craft several Engrams (e.g. Element).

7.2 Map Overview

Obelisks

Obelisk	Lat.	Lon.	Teleport
Blue NW	21.8	78.2	cheat SetPlayerPos 262258 -225743 11000
Blue destroyed NE	25.4	22.5	cheat SetPlayerPos -189743 -199343 -123000
Red SE	77.6	76.9	cheat SetPlayerPos 215858 221458 -45500
Green Sanctuary	50.6	29.7	cheat SetPlayerPos -161671 5952 -21900

Caves

The position indicates the cave's access point, the respective artifacts, and boss terminals.

Cave	Lat.	Lon.	Teleport
Cave (Void)	20.3	62.2	cheat SetPlayerPos 97604 -236945 -11472
Cave (Growth)	11.8	39.3	cheat SetPlayerPos -86793 -305496 -132371
Cave (Chaos)	87.4	70.4	cheat SetPlayerPos 162457 299532 -39681

Artifacts

Artifact	Lat.	Lon.	Teleport
Void	13.5	84.0	cheat SetPlayerPos 272301 -291753 -38641
Growth	13.5	49.2	cheat SetPlayerPos -5816 -292372 -142660
Chaos	93.9	88.0	cheat SetPlayerPos 304100 351137 -61008

Boss Terminals

Location	Lat.	Lon.	Teleport
Snow Titan Terminal	6.7	85.8	cheat SetPlayerPos 286527 -346122 -40791
Forst Titan Terminal	15.9	50.5	cheat SetPlayerPos 3858 -272843 -146084
Desert Titan Terminal	97.1	90.1	cheat SetPlayerPos 321596 377337 -60039
King Titan Terminal	3.4	49.2	cheat SetPlayerPos -6273 -371982 36795

Interesting Locations in Sanctuary

Location	Lat.	Lon.	Teleport
Sanctuary City Terminal 1	58.1	36.3	cheat SetPlayerPos -109500 64821 -35923
Sanctuary City Terminal 2	47.9	42.3	cheat SetPlayerPos -61138 -16057 -9281
Sanctuary City Terminal 3	44.4	55.1	cheat SetPlayerPos 41125 -44385 -23837
Sanctuary City Terminal 4	51.1	63.6	cheat SetPlayerPos 109311 9452 -24198
Sanctuary City Terminal 5	53.2	26.3	cheat SetPlayerPos -189306 25790 -21754
Sanctuary City Second Level			cheat SetPlayerPos -65393 26892 -22327
Sanctuary City Third Level			cheat SetPlayerPos -49257 -15597 -9440
Sanctuary City Fourth Level			cheat SetPlayerPos -104240 -24735 -3923
Sanctuary City (Sanctuary Parkway Arch South)			cheat SetPlayerPos -51264 91750 -34536
Sanctuary City (Sanctuary Parkway Arch North)			cheat SetPlayerPos -49941 -89659 -20484
Sanctuary City Well	59.0	39.1	cheat SetPlayerPos -86694 72644 -35809
Sanctuary City (Sanctuary Park)	50.4	44.0	cheat SetPlayerPos -47938 3048 -23932
Sanctuary City (Downtown Hub)			cheat SetPlayerPos 48430 -30832 -20564
Sanctuary City (Memorial Park) eastern tip	49.7	60.3	cheat SetPlayerPos 82505 -1811 -24794
Sanctuary City Central Tower Balcony			cheat SetPlayerPos -50207 1446 99735
Sanctuary City Central Tower (tip)			cheat SetPlayerPos -50337 4725 127596
Sanctuary City Good Place			cheat setplayerpos 134736 -9505 18868
Sanctuary City Nice Balcony 1			cheat setplayerpos 55200 61600 17100
Sanctuary City Nice Balcony 2			cheat setplayerpos -53600 53600 7900
Sanctuary City Balcony at the Central Tower			cheat setplayerpos -276066 -251683 66731

7.3 Resources & Tips

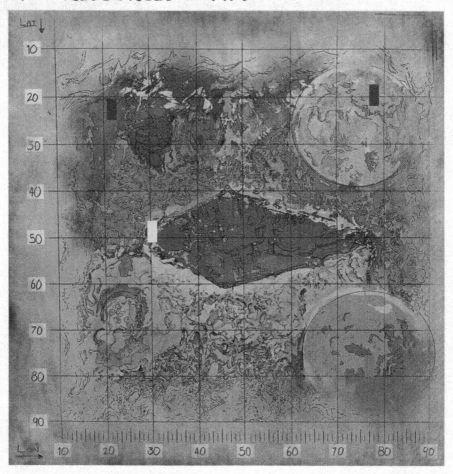

Resources:

- Oil can particularly be found in the north, south, and southwest of Wasteland.
- Obsidian as well; occasionally in Sanctuary.
- Metal and crystal can be found everywhere in sufficient amounts.
- In the trees, you can often find red and blue sap.
- Silicate chunks can be found and harvested in the Forbidden Zone in the north.
- Element dust can be found in Sanctuary in lamps, tables, benches, etc. Harvest it with a Doedicurus.

Tips:

- When you're wearing a Tek helmet, you're able to read the futuristic writing of humans.
- Try to get all OSDs; even the low-level ones. Inside, you can find a lot of cryo-pods, which you can use for transporting and storing dinos. Additionally, you get better construction plans for weapons, armor, and Meks.
- We recommend using a character that already has been played in other ARKs. With their level, Engrams, and Tek knowledge, it's way easier to make progress in Extinction.
- Are you playing ARK for the first time? If so, start with *The Island*. Extinction is the last chapter and quite difficult for beginners.
- Due to the fact that you get a lot of Element here (in comparison to the other ARKs), you should use and build Tek devices.

8: Genesis Part 1

8.1 New Features in Genesis Part 1

Genesis Part 1 can only be acquired in combination with the Genesis Season Pass. It includes Part 2, which should be released at the end of 2020/at the beginning of 2021.

Genesis Part 1 isn't a typical add-on for ARK. Several additional new Elements have been added to the game:

- **Shop & Currency System:** you can buy resources and loot crates from HLN-A. The corresponding currency for it are Hexagons.
- **Missions:** hexagons are mainly earned by completing missions, which can be found in all five biomes.
- **Biome Teleport:** you have to teleport from one biome to another.

8.2 Biome

Genesis Part 1 offers the player five new biomes. However, you can't just enter the biomes like you would in the open world game ARK. You have to get teleported from HLN-A. During the teleport process, a dome of energy builds up for a certain amount of time, just like with other ARK teleporters. Tamed creatures under the dome are teleported as well.

You can't find every resource in each biome. Some resources are just easier to buy from HLN-A with Hexagons.

Bog
- Annoying swarms of insects
- Creature: Bloodstalker
- Iron can be found easily here

Arctic
- Avalaches
- Creature: Ferox
- Blizzards

Ocean
- Dangerous whirlpools
- Creature: Megachelon
- Areas with air underwater

Volcanic
- Debris avalanches
- Volcanic Eruptions
- Creature: Magmasaur
- Lava lakes

Lunar
- Sun exposure harms you
- Air geysers
- Zero gravity
- Creature: Astrocetus

8.3 Missions and Hexagons

Every biome has eleven missions in three different levels of difficulty plus the mission of removing all the glitches in each respective biome, which means that there are 34 missions per biome in total. The Bog has two additional missions; therefore, 40 missions in total.

Finding Missions

Missions can be recognized by a terminal that has a mission symbol over it. In your inventory, you can display the missions in the bar at the upper edge of the screen. In this menu, you can see all of the important information about the missions. With the command "track mission", the selected mission and its distance is indicated on the screen in the form of a blue shield symbol.

The following mission types are available (recognizable by the terminal symbol):

Race: run/fly/ride through the gates and reach the finish within a certain amount of time.

Hunt: follow tracks and bring down one or several animals.

Gauntlet: you have to face several waves of enemies. Weapons are provided. Survive every wave and defeat the enemies.

Checkpoint: stop at each point. You have to defend yourself from assailants at the checkpoints and while running.

Escort: escort a creature to its target and protect it.

Boss: accept a battle against a boss enemy.

Fishing: fish at the lake and catch a fixed number of fish in a certain period of time.

Mini Games: do things like, play basketball with a Dodo and achieve a certain number of points.

Some missions can only played with several players (e.g. basketball matches with two teams). If playing Gamma difficulty (=easy), you can accomplish many missions on your own, but with Alpha difficulty (=very difficult), you'll need the help of several tames or/and fellow players. The racing mission (with Alpha difficulty) can only be accomplished at the last second, provided that your sprint is performed 100% flawlessly.

> The missions' objectives are slightly different for computer, PS4, and Xbox. This is why you have significantly less time for the race on the computer compared to the console.

The mission terminals also serve as normal consoles, just like the obelisks terminals on other maps. Here, you can transfer yourself, your creatures, and resources to and from other servers (provided that you're playing on a multiplayer server that makes it possible).

Earning Hexagons

Hexagons are used as a currency in ARK Genesis Part 1. There are three ways to earn Hexagons:

- **Completing Missions**: the more difficult the mission, the more Hexagons you get. Warning: when you repeat the mission, the number of the earned Hexagons decreases during the respective mission.
- **Repair Glitches**: for every glitch you've detected and repaired, you gain Hexagons and a part of the story.
- **Say Hello to HLN-A**: every now and then you can *say hello* to HLN-A in the radial menu. If you do so, HLN-A gives you 300 Hexagons in return.

> The Dodoball mission at the bog is quickly and easily completed. After starting the game and with a few repaired glitches, accomplishing this mission will make you a few quick Hexagons.

Hexagon Shop

You can spend Hexagons on items from HLN-A's shop in the radial menu:

- **Resources**: a lot of deposits are scarce or can't be found at all in the biomes. Very soon, you can buy Element from the shop to do things like, feed the Ferox (Arctic biome) in order to tame it.
- **Cryopods** : space-saving transport of your creatures.
- **Supply Crates**: yellow and red supply crates always contain a Tek replicator (as soon as you've unlocked it). Otherwise, they contain other random items.

8.4 Map Overview

Bog Glitches

Location	Lat.	Lon.
Glitch 1	57.7	61.8
Glitch 2	57.2	69.2
Glitch 3	57.6	84.8
Glitch 4	59.8	61.1
Glitch 5	60.2	59.5
Glitch 6	61.5	74.8
Glitch 7	63.8	76.5
Glitch 8	64.2	74.7
Glitch 9	66.2	67.5
Glitch 10	66.4	75.3

Location	Lat.	Lon.
Glitch 11	67.2	78.2
Glitch 12	66.5	85.0
Glitch 13	67.8	72.9
Glitch 14	68.1	59.8
Glitch 15	69.9	77.0
Glitch 16	70.2	76.6
Glitch 17	70.9	75.1
Glitch 18	71.6	75.4
Glitch 19	71.1	76.8
Glitch 20	72.5	76.6

Location	Lat.	Lon.
Glitch 21	73.5	76.9
Glitch 22	74.5	76.5
Glitch 23	75.3	75.8
Glitch 24	73.1	84.9
Glitch 25	73.7	83.7
Glitch 26	79.4	72.6
Glitch 27	84.2	74.8
Glitch 28	83.5	60.6
Glitch 29	72.6	70.0
Glitch 30	71.9	69.4

Arctic Glitches

Location	Lat.	Lon.
Glitch 1	85.4	30.7
Glitch 2	84.9	36.9
Glitch 3	82.4	21.4
Glitch 4	78.5	16.4
Glitch 5	80.4	26.6
Glitch 6	79.8	34.8
Glitch 7	72.3	43.4
Glitch 8	70.5	33.3
Glitch 9	70.0	31.0
Glitch 10	70.7	28.6

Location	Lat.	Lon.
Glitch 11	73.0	30.9
Glitch 12	74.7	30.4
Glitch 13	76.5	28.1
Glitch 14	71.2	19.6
Glitch 15	62.7	30.7
Glitch 16	61.4	32.9
Glitch 17	61.2	37.4
Glitch 18	64.0	37.4
Glitch 19	66.1	21.2
Glitch 20	68.0	21.9

Location	Lat.	Lon.
Glitch 21	86.1	15.2
Glitch 22	73.7	25.2
Glitch 23	67.3	32.6
Glitch 24	67.2	25.8
Glitch 25	70.7	26.2
Glitch 26	75.4	46.1
Glitch 27	75.6	53.1
Glitch 28	76.9	21.6
Glitch 29	82.6	41.9
Glitch 30	82.0	18.7

Ocean Glitches

Location	Lat.	Lon.	Location	Lat.	Lon.	Location	Lat.	Lon.
Glitch 1	15.9	47.5	Glitch 11	25.9	58.0	Glitch 21	33.3	51.4
Glitch 2	18.9	47.4	Glitch 12	26.7	51.1	Glitch 22	32.2	48.5
Glitch 3	18.9	51.8	Glitch 13	28.8	60.6	Glitch 23	32.2	46.2
Glitch 4	18.4	56.4	Glitch 14	28.8	47.8	Glitch 24	34.3	45.3
Glitch 5	20.2	50.1	Glitch 15	29.2	48.1	Glitch 25	34.5	51.0
Glitch 6	21.0	51.0	Glitch 16	30.7	56.2	Glitch 26	35.1	54.0
Glitch 7	21.8	50.3	Glitch 17	31.4	56.7	Glitch 27	35.9	45.7
Glitch 8	20.7	55	Glitch 18	31.8	57.3	Glitch 28	36.4	49.3
Glitch 9	23.1	51.3	Glitch 19	32.7	59.0	Glitch 29	39.1	47.1
Glitch 10	23.8	48.8	Glitch 20	33.1	51.9	Glitch 30	40.2	56.3

Volcanic Glitches

Location	Lat.	Lon.	Location	Lat.	Lon.	Location	Lat.	Lon.
Glitch 1	17.2	87.9	Glitch 11	47.4	66.7	Glitch 21	33	66.9
Glitch 2	37.3	37.3	Glitch 12	35.6	77.4	Glitch 22	35	86.4
Glitch 3	28.5	80.5	Glitch 13	27.9	66.7	Glitch 23	35	72.8
Glitch 4	17	71.2	Glitch 14	25.2	77.2	Glitch 24	19.8	72.8
Glitch 5	48.3	73.5	Glitch 15	12.4	76.2	Glitch 25	21.1	85.3
Glitch 6	41.5	75.9	Glitch 16	43.2	80.6	Glitch 26	40.7	73.6
Glitch 7	36.7	72.3	Glitch 17	43.6	76.1	Glitch 27	42.2	67.8
Glitch 8	28.2	73.9	Glitch 18	21.8	69.2	Glitch 28	30.9	80.0
Glitch 9	44.5	85.5	Glitch 19	28.1	80.2	Glitch 29	13.6	87.1
Glitch 10	26.8	77.1	Glitch 20	42.7	73.6	Glitch 30	22.2	69.7

Glitches in the Luna Zone (Moon)

Location	Lat.	Lon.	Location	Lat.	Lon.	Location	Lat.	Lon.
Glitch 1	12.4	38.8	Glitch 11	30.2	35.4	Glitch 21	40.8	38.2
Glitch 2	18.4	37.4	Glitch 12	32.3	37.7	Glitch 22	43.4	35.2
Glitch 3	21.4	14.5	Glitch 13	32.8	32.9	Glitch 23	46.4	21.5
Glitch 4	21.6	26	Glitch 14	31.9	14.8	Glitch 24	47.1	14.1
Glitch 5	22.3	31.3	Glitch 15	33.9	19.3	Glitch 25	47.4	23.7
Glitch 6	24.3	13.7	Glitch 16	34.2	26.8	Glitch 26	48.8	18
Glitch 7	23.6	25.7	Glitch 17	34.3	32.1	Glitch 27	50.9	13.9
Glitch 8	26.5	19.3	Glitch 18	37.3	24.5	Glitch 28	49.7	29.2
Glitch 9	27	27.6	Glitch 19	38.5	24.6	Glitch 29	50.5	27.8
Glitch 10	26.4	32.7	Glitch 20	40.9	12.7	Glitch 30	50.8	31.1

Blocked Areas (Building)

The areas where missions take place are blocked for building. You'll recognize it as soon as you want to place an object there. The blocked area is then highlighted with translucent, purple walls. In the example below, you can clearly see the blocked zones from the Ocean biome.

8.5 Resources Overview

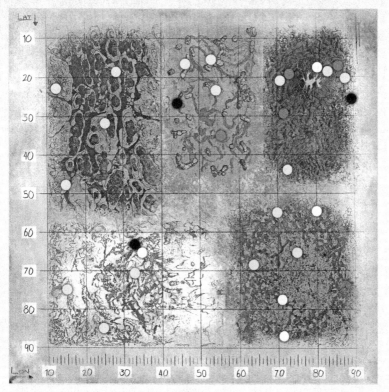

Large Metal deposits
Large Crystal deposits
Large Obsidian deposits
Gems
Oil

> In the shop, you can use Hexagons to buy desperately needed resources in any place and at any time.

8.6 Tips for Genesis Part 1

Annoying Swarm of Insects: try to hit the swarm with a torch. Instead of aiming for the air, aim straight ahead, like you would if a dino was attacking you. Later on, flamethrowers are very helpful. Water that reaches at least your waist makes the insects lose interest in the player.

Easy Start: the Ocean biome is very suitable for beginning the game. The level *hard* earns its title as soon as you're playing underwater. The Islands, however, are free from aggressive animals (except the annoying Pegomastax) and offer wood and fiber in abundance.

Taming Bloodstalker: try to tame a Bloodstalker in the swamp early on. He can climb, and walk on water and is, therefore, extremely useful for the Ocean biome as well.

Missions: we recommend completing the first missions in the swamp. Repair all the glitches you find on your way. By doing so, you quickly earn a bunch of Hexagons.

Taming Ferox: with the Hexagons you've earned, you can buy fur and use it to craft fur armor for the Arctic biome. When in the Arctic biome, look for caves in the large mountain. There, you can usually find the cute Ferox. Buy some Element from the shop and feed the Ferox with it. Escape from the Monsterferox and feed it again as soon as he has retransformed. Do this and you'll tame your first Ferox in less than no time. You can transform the cute little thing into its monster form at any time by feeding it Element. Its a very useful helper in all biomes, as it can climb, leap very high, and is very strong. You can get Element from the shop at any time for its transformation. In addition, it's a cute little animal on your shoulder.

Magmasaur: In the Volcanic biome, a Magmasaur is very helpful since it makes its rider immune to heat exposure. This also applies to the volcanic eruptions that occur from time to time.

9: Catching and Taming

9.1 Quick Guide: Taming

Taming by Increasing Torpidity
- Optional: if possible, lure the animal into a prepared trap (e.g. a bola, a bear trap, or a pen).
- Increase the creature's torpor with the corresponding weapons (e.g. narcotic arrows) or animals (e.g. scorpions).
- Place suitable food (see dino dossiers) and narcotics into the creature's inventory.
- Check its torpor level and force-feed it with narcoberries or narcotics in order to re-increase torpor.

Taming by Active Feeding
- Since a lot of these animals tend to flee or become aggressive, wear ghillie armor and sneak up on them (*crouch*).
- Place the appropriate food (see dino dossiers) into the last inventory slot, creep up on the animal, and press *use*.
- Repeat this process until the animal has finally been tamed.

Taming Troodons
- Troodons have to kill several tamed creatures of yours in order to be tamed.
- Set one of your tames to passive.

Taming Titanosaur
- Optional: lure the Titanosaur into a narrow place so that it gets stuck there.
- Increase its torpor by shooting it with a cannon or a stone catapult (for best results, aim for its head).
- As soon as it's stunned, saddle it and you're done.

Taming Rock Elementals/Golems (Scorched Earth)
- Optional: lure the Elemental into a narrow place until it gets stuck there.
- Increase its torpor by shooting it with a cannon or a stone catapult until it gets stunned (for best results: aim for its head).

- As soon as it's stunned, place the appropriate food in its inventory. Depending on the food, narcotics as well.
- Now proceed as you normally would when taming by increasing torpor.

9.2 Basics: Taming

Pros of Taming Creatures

Besides the fact that it's a lot of fun to create your own zoo comprising various dinos, tamed creatures provide the following advantages and possible applications:

- Riding animals for fast and safe movement.
- Transport animals with a huge carrying capacity.
- You can access hard-to-reach areas (e.g. by riding flying dinosaurs or deep sea creatures).
- Gathering resources: tamed creatures are an indispensable help in this regard.
- Tames support you during fights and guard your base.
- Many bosses can hardly be defeated without the help of tamed creatures.
- By using platform saddles, you can even create mobile bases on the back of some dinos (e.g. on a Brontosaurus, Paracer, Quetzal, or Mosasaurus).
- They assist you with stunning, taming, or breeding.
- You can gain experience (you share the experience you've gained with every one of your tames in the vicinity).

Preparations for Taming

When you head out to tame creatures, be appropriately prepared. Depending on the type of dino you want to catch, you should bring the following items:

- Good armor to prevent damage; a lot of victims will try to defend themselves.
- Enough food and water for yourself. Hunting makes you hungry and it would be a pity to have to interrupt the taming process because you're starving.
- Suitable weapons to increase the dino's torpor (see next heading).
- Enough of the appropriate food for the type of animal you want to tame. The best choice is always kibble, of course. You have to craft it first, though.
- A sufficient amount of narcotics (narcoberries, anesthetics, poison).
- Escort or transport dinos for your protection.
- Traps and trapping aids (e.g. bolas or bear traps).
- You might even build a fenced in area into which you can lure or herd the animal you're trying to tame. To remain mobile, you can also do this on a raft.

The Taming Process

During the taming process, you should pay attention to the following things:

- Keep an eye on the stunned animal's torpor level and, if required, feed them with narcotics or narcoberries.
- When taming via active feeding, make sure that you don't get too close to the animals since it can make them aggressive or scare them off.
- The better the quality of the food you use for taming, the better the taming efficiency and the faster it's done. It also has a positive effect on the tame's level.

Here's an example for taming a level 50 Rex with default settings:

Type of Feed	Required Quantity	Required Narcotics	Duration min:sec	Level Gained
Kibble (Exceptional Kibble)	14	0	44:48	+24
Raw Filet	37	1	74:00	+21
Raw Meat	110	239	220:00	+10

9.3 Taming by Increasing Torpidity

Hunting Techniques

Dino Traps

Always try to stun strong and defensive animals from a safe distance. In this case, we recommend using a trap you can lure the animals into. Here are some examples:

Taming trap on a raft:

The Allosaurus you can see in the picture above can be stunned from a safe distance. The dangerous part is luring him on the boat. It helps to increase your movement speed to 120 or 130.

The same trap with a roof is suitable for catching a flying creature, an Argentavis, for example:

A similar trap can be used on shore. You can build these traps to any size and for every creature. Here, we quickly built a frame made of stone gates after the Rex walked into the trap. The specific gate you see below is actually unnecessary for the Rex:

> If you don't want to build these kinds of traps, use bolas or bear traps to keep the animals locked in.

You can also build traps like this for flying dinos (e.g. on top of a Quetzal). Fly in front of them and make them fly into the trap. Since no flying creature can fly backwards, you've caught them – just like that.

Further Hunting Techniques
- You can try to lure or herd the animals into natural obstacles like narrow passages or dead ends in order to safely stun them.
- Another technique is to go hunting with a partner. In this case, riding animals with two or more saddles are advantageous (e.g. Tapejara or Procoptodon). One player directs and hunts the creature (or flees) while the other one shoots narcotic arrows at the animal.
- A more dangerous technique is to let one of the players fly an Argentavis while the shooter is being carried in its claws. If you do so, don't forget to bring parachutes.

NARCOTICS

You can try to stun creatures with the following weapons. We've only listed useful weapons and creatures:

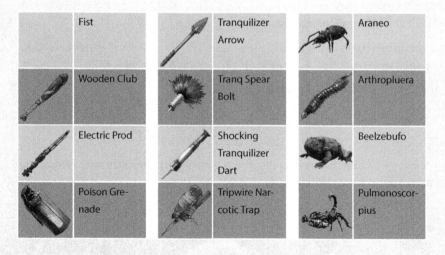

	Fist		Tranquilizer Arrow		Araneo
	Wooden Club		Tranq Spear Bolt		Arthropluera
	Electric Prod		Shocking Tranquilizer Dart		Beelzebufo
	Poison Grenade		Tripwire Narcotic Trap		Pulmonoscorpius

You can use these long-range weapons with the appropriate arrows:

	Boomerang (only for small animals)		Slingshot (only for small animals)		Bow (shoots very fast)
	Compound Bow (not so good)		Crossbow (best cost effectiveness)		Longneck Rifle (great with shocking darts)

In combination with narcotic darts, the crossbow is the weapon with the best cost effectiveness and is also easy to handle. A long-neck rifle with shocking darts is the most effective weapon; it reloads slowly, though.

When the animal is finally unconscious, all you need to do is feed it in order to tame it.

How to Feed Stunned Animals

When the animal is stunned, all you need to do is place the appropriate food and the necessary narcotics or narcoberries into the animal's inventory.

The animal will eat on its own as soon as it gets hungry, and every time it eats something it has a positive effect on the taming process. You can see the animal's current torpidity level in its inventory. Don't let it reach zero or the animal will wake up and it was all for naught.

Click on the narcotics in the animal's inventory and then click on *use* to force-feed the animal with narcotics. As a result, its torpidity will re-increase:

Narcoberries: increase the torpidity level by 7.4 points.

Narcotics: increase the torpidity level by 40 points.

Organic poison: increases the torpidity level by 80 points.

Attention: you have to force-feed some animals with narcotics very frequently (almost every minute), like the Therizinosaur, for example.

Taming By Starvation

This method is normally used for taming carnivores. Instead of putting food into the dino's inventory after its torpor has increased, you only put narcotics into it and feed it only as much as is required to prevent it from waking up.

After doing so, you let the animal's food level (hunger) decrease to a very low value. You can use the time to gather raw filets. Since this kind of food spoils very quickly (in about eight minutes), you need a good, fast meat collector (e.g. Carno, Rex, etc.) that can collect as many raw filets as possible within 6 minutes.

You can place the collected raw filets into the carnivore's inventory all at once. Since the tame-to-be is going to be very hungry, he'll eat it up before it can even spoil. By doing this, you can tame a creature by just feeding it with raw filets, which is faster than using normal raw meat. However, taming with kibble (if available) is always preferable. You can also use this method for herbivores. Mejoberries, however, spoil way slower than filets.

> Another advantage of this taming method is that you remain in possession of your resources until the end of the process. If the animal dies early, you haven't wasted your resources.

9.4 Taming By Active Feeding

When actively feeding an animal, proceed as described in the following:

Secure the animal's surrounding area. Kill other dangerous creatures that could be a disturbing factor during the taming process.

Place the appropriate food into the last slot of your hotbar.

Creep up on the animal silently. Preferably, use ghillie armor to be well disguised, and try not to touch the creature; many of them tend to flee or get aggressive when you do that.

When the prompt appears on the screen, press the *use* (E) button; that's how you feed the animal. You have to wait for a while until the animal gets hungry again.

Repeat the process until the creature is tamed.

9.5 Kibble

Kibble + Egg Production

Kibble is often the best choice to tame creatures quickly and effectively. Large and high-leveled creatures require many more hours to tame and receive significantly less bonus levels if you don't use *kibble*.

When you've finally stunned a Quetzal (level 150), you want to get the best out of it, which, in this example, is only possible with *exceptional kibble* made of multiple Bronto or Rex eggs.

Usually, *kibble* consists of one egg of a specific size, fiber, mejoberries and/or one of the four types of vegetables, and water.

The type of kibble each dino prefers is listed beneath it in this book's creature overview. If the creature lays eggs, the size of the egg is indicated as well.

Unfertilized eggs are sufficient for the production of kibble. To get them, all you need is one male and one female of the same species who are standing close to each other. Their levels don't play a role here. The heart symbol indicates that your dinos are close enough to each other for mating. Consequently, the female lays eggs at random intervals. Mating doesn't have to be enabled since the female is able to lay unfertilized eggs.

Three important things you should know about egg production:

- One single male is enough for multiple females.
- The more females you have, the more eggs are being laid (often only by one female, however, more frequently).
- An Oviraptor that is set to wandering around, accelerates the egg-laying process by more than three times. You will recognize this acceleration by an egg symbol next to your dinos.

> In case you need dinos for egg production only, low-leveled dinos are perfectly fine. They're easier and faster to tame.

For good egg production of one species, we recommend building a little stable with four to six females, one to two males, and one Oviraptor. The Oviraptor can, of course, enhance the efficiency of multiple different species.

> Load up an Oviraptor to capacity with stones and it will be unable to move, but can still be set to wandering around. That makes it stay in one place and specifically accelerates your egg production.

Kibble Production

A creature's eggs are categorized by their size. For instance, an *extra small egg* from a *Dodo* or *Parasaurus* can be used to craft *basic kibble* with which you can tame a variety of creatures (e.g. Phiomia or Parasaurus). Kibble is made in a cooking pot or industrial cooker. Put all the ingredients into the device and enable it (of course, you also need wood or gasoline depending on the device). With the cooking pot, one serving of kibble is done in 30 seconds.

Kibble Recipes

Basic Kibble:

1x extra small egg, 5x fiber, 5x mejoberries, 10x amarberries, 10x tintoberries, 1x cooked meat

Simple Kibble:

1x small egg, 5x fiber, 5x mejoberries, 2x carrots, 1x cooked fish meat

Regular Kibble:

1x medium egg, 5x fiber, 2x longrass, 2x savoroot, 1x cooked meat jerky

Superior Kibble:

1x large egg, 5x fiber, 2x citronal, 2x rare mushroom 1x prime meat jerky, 1x sap

Exceptional Kibble:

1x extra large egg, 5x fiber, 10x mejoberries, 1 rare flower, 1x Focal Chili

Extraordinary Kibble:

1x special egg, 5x fiber, 10x mejoberries, 1x Giant Bee honey, 1x Lazarus Chowder

Egg Sizes

The following list shows the creature's eggs categorized by size:

Extra Small Egg: Dilo, Dodo, Featherlight, Kairuku, Lystrosaurus, Parasaur, Vulture

Small Egg: Archaeopteryx, Compy, Dimorphodon, Gallimimus, Glowtail, Hesperornis, Morellatops, Microraptor, Oviraptor, Pachycephalosaurus, Pegomastax, Pteranodon, Raptor, Triceratops

Medium Egg: Ankylosaurus, Baryonyx, Carbonemys, Carnotaurus, Dimetrodon, Diplodocus, Ichthyornis, Iguanodon, Kaprosuchus, Kentrosaurus, Pachyrhino, Pelagornis, Pulmonoscorpius, Sarcosuchus, Stegosaurus, Terror Bird, Thorny Dragon, Troodon, Velonasaurus

Large Egg: Allosaurus, Argentavis, Mantis, Megalania, Megalosaurus, Moschops, Snow Owl, Spinosaurus, Tapejara, Titanoboa

Extra Large Egg: Basilisk, Brontosaurus, Giganotosaurus, Megachelon, Quetzal, T-Rex, Therizino

Special Egg: Deinonychus, Golden Hesperornis egg, Magmasaur, Rock Drake, Wyvern, Yutyrannus

Unused Eggs: Anglerfish, Araneo, Beelzebufo, Bloodstalker, Diplocaulus, Allo, Lymantria, Tusoteuthis (these eggs aren't used for creating kibble)

> One dino pair of each size is enough to get all the necessary eggs for every type of kibble.

Kibble and Creatures

The list below states which creatures are tamed with which type of kibble:

Basic Kibble: Dodo, Dilophosaur, Kairuku, Mesopithecus, Parasaurus, Phiomia

Simple Kibble: Archaeopteryx, Diplocaulus, Gallimimus, Giant Bee, Ichthyosaurus, Iguanodon, Megaloceros, Morellatops, Pachy, Raptor, Triceratops

Regular Kibble: Anglerfish, Ankylosaurus, Baryonyx, Beelzebufo, Carbonemys, Carnotaurus, Dimetrodon, Diplodocus, Doedicurus, Gigantopithecus, Ichthyornis, Kaprosuchus, Kentrosaurus, Lymantria, Pelagornis, Pteranodon, Pulmonoscorpius, Purlovia, Sabertooth, Sarco, Stegosaurus, Terror Bird, Thorny Dragon, Velonasaurus

Superior Kibble: Allosaurus, Argentavis, Castoroides, Daeodon, Direbear, Direwolf, Dunkleosteus, Gasbag, Mammoth, Megalodon, Megalosaurus, Megatherium, Paracer, Plesiosaur, Snow Owl, Tapejara, Woolly Rhino

Exceptional Kibble: Basilosaurus, Brontosaurus, Giganotosaurus, Karkinos, Managarmr, Mosasaurus, Quetzal, Spinosaurus, T-Rex, Therizinosaur

Extraordinary Kibble: Griffin, Megalania, Rock Elemental, Thylacoleo, Yutyrannus

> You can also feed kibble from a higher category to any creature. For instance, an Allosaurus will accept exceptional kibble and extraordinary kibble as well as superior kibble and it yields the same result.

OLD KIBBLE SYSTEM

If you've played ARK in the past, you may be familiar with the old kibble system. With the DLC, Extinction, a new system was introduced for test purposes and the adjusted version was applied to the main game after a general update.

Now, the old kibble recipes can't be created anymore. Should you be playing on a server that's been running for a long time and you're in possession of old kibble, you can use it just like the new stuff. The kibble is in the same category as the corresponding eggs. Here's an example: old *argentavis kibble* corresponds to *superior kibble*.

9.6 Unique Taming Methods

Some creatures have specific requirements. In the following, you will find a more detailed description next to the respective creatures:

Troodon: let it kill some of your tamed dinos. This increases its taming value.

Titanosaur: due to its size, we recommend stunning it with only cannons or catapults.

Rock Elemental & Astrocetus (Genesis Part 1): due to its size and armor, we recommend stunning it with only cannons or catapults.

Tusoteuthis: needs to hold a creature in its tentacles in order to be able to feed him.

Wyvern, Rock Drake (Aberration), Deinonychus (Valguero), Magmasaur (Genesis Part 1): can't be tamed. You have to steal a fertilized egg and breed it at the suitable temperature (air conditioners).

Titanoboa: put some fertilized eggs it can eat in front of it. The Boa can't be aggressive when you do this, otherwise it will ignore the eggs.

Phoenix: hit the Phoenix with flame weapons to tame it (flamethrower, flame arrows, the breath of a Fire Wyvern). This has to take place during a heat wave and takes a very long time.

Otter and Hesperonis: feed them with dead fish by hand (not with fish filets).

Reaper (Aberration): you have to get hit by the Reaper Queen's tail to get impregnated and bear the cubs on yourself.

Basilisk (Aberration): just like in the case of the Titanoboa, you have to put some fertilized eggs in front of the Basilisk's snout.

Bloodstalker (Genesis Part 1): you have to be carrying blood packs in your inventory and get caught and sucked by the Bloodstalker.

Megachelon (Genesis Part 1): lead a swarm of Microbes to the Megachelon and let it eat them without interruption in order to tame it.

10: Breeding and Rearing

10.1 Breeding: Quick Guide

Mating
- Find and tame one male and one female animal of the same species.
- Build a little fenced-in area where you can lock up both animals.
- Set both dinos to wandering.
- The female dino will lay an egg after a while or get pregnant. Collect the egg.
- After 18 to 48 hours, the animals mate again.

Pregnancy (e.g. mammals)
- Make sure that there are large amounts of food available for the female until she gives birth.

Hatching (eggs)
- Build a small area surrounded by five to ten air conditioners (more for huge creatures like Wyverns).
- Place the egg on the floor of the hatchery (turn on the air conditioning and keep it running continually).
- When the breeding time is over, a baby dino hatches from the egg.
- After hatching, claim the baby for yourself.

Raising
- Feed the baby immediately (place food into its inventory).
- Babies eat faster and need larger amounts of food; always keep an eye on them.
- After about 10% of their growth period has passed, the little dinos start eating from troughs (you will need a lot of food then).

Imprinting (increases the animal's stat-values during the maturation process)
- Little dinos demand one of the following three things frequently: a specific type of kibble, going for a walk, cuddling.

10.2 Selection and Mating

What's the Point of Breeding?

- Every creature has different values. Taming makes it possible to pass on the best values to the offspring.

- The offspring has a higher starting level than their parents (the level their parents had in their wild states is what counts).

- Offspring can be imprinted in order to increase their level even more.

- By breeding multiple times, you can further increase the values and raise your own "hyper-dino".

Choosing the Parents

Try to find parents (one male and one female) with the highest possible values. In this case, only the values the dinos had when they were wild are of interest. Progression from leveling up, taming bonus, or imprinting are irrelevant in regard to breeding. Therefore, when you're stunning and taming a high-leveled creature, write down its values as a wild animal so that you can make a good choice later regarding the creatures you're about to breed. We recommend mating two high-level dinos, for example, one with high health values and the other with high damage values. For the following example, we chose two Carnos which both had a level of 150 as wild dinos (meanwhile, they've reached level 228 and 229, which, as stated, is irrelevant in regard to breeding):

Then, build a shed and lock up the two dinos. Don't forget to add a roof if you want to prevent flying dinos from escaping. If you own an *Oviraptor,* put it in there too. Disable the dinos' *follow commands* function and set them to *wandering around.* Look at them and keep the *use key* pressed down until the *radial menu* appears.

Your dinos will now start mating. Due to the constant spread of pheromones, the Oviraptor additionally accelerates the process (the Oviraptor has to be set to *wandering around* as well).

As soon as the female has laid an egg, collect it before it spoils.

You can then easily store the fertilized egg in a refrigerator or in a normal cupboard for quite a long time. The dinos will start mating again in the next 18 to 48 hours.

10.3 Breeding and Pregnancy

During a pregnancy, you don't have to pay attention too much. Simply provide the pregnant animal with enough food, as she needs considerably more until she gives birth.

Make sure that the appropriate temperature is maintained for the incubation of the egg:

- With campfires (very inconvenient and difficult to maintain the right temperature).

- With a Dimetrodon in the proximity (functions as an air conditioner during the incubation process).
- With air conditioners (10 is sufficient for most eggs, but the more, the better).

Below, you can see a provisional hatchery for a Rex egg:

A secure room with air conditioning and refrigerators filled to the brim with feed is better suited for rearing:

Place the egg in the center of some air conditioners. Now, you just have to wait until your dino baby hatches. Check the state of your egg frequently in order to make sure that you're there when it hatches, as the baby will starve if you don't feed it immediately.

In the picture above, almost half of the breeding time has passed and the egg is still in good health thanks to the sufficient amount of air conditioning. The decrease in health is the result of the time at which it was collected (it wasn't found for quite some time).

10.4 Raising Animal Babies

By the way, you can put eggs back in a cupboard in case you want to incubate them later. By doing so, you can collect eggs that are 99% incubated and let them hatch at an opportune moment.

If a baby hatches or is born, it counts as a wild dinosaur.

> Warning: automatic turrets and dinos set to aggressive immediately attack babies just like a wild animal. Before the baby is born, set everything in the proximity to passive or neutral.

Now, every player has the possibility to claim the baby for himself. That's why we recommend being close by in order to be able to immediately claim it for yourself (*use button* while looking at the baby).

After you've taken it into possession, immediately bring up its inventory and place the appropriate food into it. Babies can't eat from troughs and have to be fed manually by placing food into their inventory. You will have to repeat this quite often at the beginning and take care of the baby for a while. Since it doesn't have a great loading capacity yet, you can only place two to five food items into its inventory.

As soon as they have grown by 10%, they are able to eat from troughs.

> Growing dinos eat a lot. Make sure in advance that there's enough food stored for the rearing process.

Little Carno in infancy.

Baby Carno with his mother from which he obviously got his color, and the proud breeder.

Young Carno - approx. 85% mature.

10.5 Imprinting Animals

Only the breeder/owner of the baby can do the imprinting. In order to do so, they must perform one of three actions within a certain period of time.

Imprinting has the following advantages (with 100% imprinting):

+ 20% is added to all values.

+ 30% damage and resistance, if the imprinting person is riding the dino.

It's not so bad if you miss or overlook an action. You won't reach the full 100%, but you still gain bonus points. At 50% imprinting, you only get 50% of the bonus points.

This Carno baby needs attention again in three hours and seven minutes.

A dino baby randomly demands the following three actions:

- Going for walks.
  Set the young dino to follow and take a few steps until it follows you. After a short distance, the task is done.
- Cuddling.
  Press the *use* button while facing the young dino.
- Feeding a specific type of kibble.
  No matter what species, maturing dinos always want a randomly chosen kibble from the following list:
  - Specific kibble (every type except for extraordinary)
  - Specific berries (mejo-, amar-, azul-, or tintoberries)
  - Meat or fish (cooked or smoked)

  Exceptions:
  - Wyverns: only Wyvern milk
  - Rock Drake: only poison from the Nameless
  - Magmasaur: only ambergris
  - Ferox: only Element

10.6 How to Breed Better Animals

Enhancing Values

When mating, there's about a 70% chance that the better values of a parent will be passed on to the child. Unfortunately, there's also a 30% chance that it will get the "worse" values of a parent.

A very successful breeding process, spanning three generations, could look like the following:

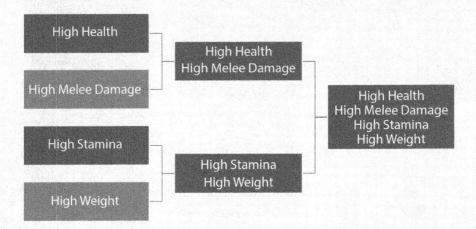

The animal's level always reflects the number of its improvements (also the ones that were lost, in the case of wild animals (e.g. movement speed)). This is why the parents of the first generation could have an untamed level of 145 and 150, but their matured child could have a level of 210, as it gets about 60-65 better values than its parents. In the example above, the third generation would be able to reach an even higher level.

Assuming a wild animal's level of 150, leveling up to 350 during a long breeding process is absolutely possible. Theoretically, you could even reach levels beyond 400.

Mutations

In regard to breeding, mutations only occur randomly. It's possible for one child to get up to three mutations. Every mutation that can occur has a probability of 2.5%. This means that offspring have about a 7% chance of getting at least one mutation.

Mutations always have an effect on the animal's fur color and on one of its values. The affected value will be increased by 2 points.

In the best case, the mutation increases a positive value even further.

Within the breeding line of several animals, no more than a total of 20 mutations can occur.

Color mutations can also create colors that can't be found among the ARK's wild animals.

> Imagine the following Rex:
> - Intentional breeding over several generations (especially: health, stamina, damage).
> - Mutations that affect the important values.
> - Imprint 75% to 100%.
> - Increased values due to leveling up.
> - An advanced saddle with high armor protection.
>
> A troop comprised of these kind of Rexes (with the appropriate support), could even square off with the alpha bosses.

11.1 Values in Detail

In the following chapters, we'd like to show you all the creatures that exist in ARK Survival Evolved. The values indicated correspond to a level 1 creature.

APPEARANCE: tells you where the creatures can usually be found. This especially applies to *The Island* or the main map on which the creature is found. This can deviate on DLC or MOD maps.

DAMAGES: specifies materials the creature is able to damage. Wood includes adobe and greenhouse as well.

BEHAVIOR: we've roughly differentiated the behavior into four levels, which is also indicated by the symbol next to the creature's name. Please note that every creature has a specific type of behavior, which is often specified in the text.

- Cowardly: the creature never attacks the player. It's fearful and flees as soon at it gets attacked (example: Dodo, Parasaurus).

- Passive: the creature doesn't attempt to attack the player and is peaceful. If it gets attacked or disturbed in some other way (e.g. looting a Castoroides' dam), it will attack the player (Trike, Bronto, Castoroides).

- Aggressive: the creature attacks the player. However, it doesn't specifically look for the player and stays peaceful at a distance. It loses interest quickly too (Chalicotherium, Dire Bear).

- Highly aggressive: they're the hunters among the creatures. They start hunting you even at a far distance, they're dangerous, and can't easily be stopped from hunting you (Raptor, Megalodon, T-Rex, Yutyrannus, Allosaurus).

ATTACK 1, ATTACK 2, ATTACK 3: describes the attack the creature is able to perform and it also corresponds to the respective control shortcuts. Instead of attacks, it can also indicate other actions, for example, *use* or *collect*.

CHEAT: enter the cheat into your console to summon a creature. In single-player mode, entering this cheat is sufficient. On a server you own the admin rights to, you have to add *admincheat* or *cheat* before the text. If you want to summon a creature that's already been tamed, type *summontamed* instead of *summon*. If you want to determine the level of the creature yourself, you need a longer command that's so complex it surpasses the scope of this book. For this purpose, we've created a list online under the following link: **/bildnerverlag.de/ark_creatures**

Saddles

 No saddle, riding impossible.

 No saddle, riding possible without saddle.

 Normal saddle (sometimes for two or more players (e.g. Tapejara or Diplodocus).

 Specific saddle.

 Platform saddle.

 Tek saddle; often equipped with additional features (e.g. laser guns).

Additionally, you can find information about the animal's taming procedure, its special features and possible applications thereof, the food it prefers during the taming process, and its egg size (if available).

In some cases, we left out unimportant and ineffective values regarding information about the drops creatures are able to release, information about its farming efficiency, and taming feed.

11.2 Different Versions of Creatures

You probably will come across different versions of specific creatures on every kind of map. They often only differ in stats (better or worse), coloration, or were intended to be bosses. These creatures aren't part of the following chapters since it would go beyond the constraints of this book.

In the following, you can see a small overview of the different versions. As an example, we've chosen the Triceratops and, in two other cases, the Tyrannosaurus Rex:

Normal Creature

Alpha Version

A little boss enemy: red, taller, stronger, more aggressive, and untamable (e.g. Raptor, Carno, Rex).

Image on the right: Alpha Rex

Aberrant Creature

Creatures in Aberration: different coloration and slightly worse values. Can be tamed.

Corrupted Creature

Occur in Extinction, always aggressive, and attack everything in the proximity. Untamable.

Enraged Creature

The Alpha Boss version is a corrupted creature. Only occurs in Orbital Supply Drops. Untamable.

TEK Creature

Robot version of a creature. Can be tamed.

X Creature

Only occurs in Genesis Part 1. Stronger and has better values than a normal creature.

Event Creature

Special appearance in accordance with different occasions (e.g. bunny ears at Easter or skeletons for Halloween).

Skins

Items that only change the appearance of your tamed creature.

Image on the right: Bionic Rex

11.3 Terrestrial, Aerial, and Aquatic Creatures

The following chapters divide the creatures into terrestrial, aerial, and aquatic animals. This classification only reflects the creature's favorite habitat and where it is more likely to be found. There are creatures capable of living and acting in two or even all three habitats.

One good example is the Pelagornis, which is a bird, and therefore an aerial creature, but also a very good swimmer. You can also find him waddling on shore sometimes.

The giant tortoise Megachelon from Genesis Part 1, which you can usually find underwater, can also swim on the water's surface or even go on shore.

Bosses

Bosses are challenging opponents and normally part of a map's final battle. The boss battles have their own mechanics and are fought in a specific arena. In order to be able to get to them, you need to fulfill certain requirements, and often you need to gather certain items first. These kinds of enemies can only be defeated by well-equipped and experienced players.

For this reason, you can find all the bosses listed and described in an extra chapter.

Mini Bosses

On many maps, you can find creatures that function as a sort of mini boss. These are usually significantly stronger versions of normal animals. They can appear randomly on maps (e.g. *Alpha creatures*), in fixed places like small arenas (e.g. like a *Lavagolem* boss in its cave on *Ragnarok*), or on special occasions (e.g. an *Enraged Trike* fighting for an *Orbital Supply Drop* in *Extinction*).

Since these creatures are just stronger, more difficult versions of their original embodiment, we have neither listed nor described them. Definitely don't underestimate these enemies, and make sure to be as well equipped as possible. Unfortunately, it's impossible to tame them.

ACHATINA

Basic Stats:

Health	75	Food	450	Speed (Land)	50
Stamina	100	Weight	150	Speed (Water)	300
Oxygen	∞	Melee Damage	0	Torpidity	50

Habitat: Swamp and Redwoods, Caves
Damages: -
Behavior: Passive

Type: Invertebrate
Diet: Herbivore
Names: -

Attack 1: -
Attack 2: -
Attack 3: -

Specifics:
- Can be picked up and carried by the player.
- Retreats into its shell and suffers almost no melee damage during an attack. Therefore you should aim for the soft parts of its body.
- Warning: the region where Achatina spawns is also a common place for dangerous creatures.
- Only feeds on Sweet Vegetable Cake.
- Produces Achatina Paste that can be used like Cementing Paste.

Utility:
- Storing Organic Polymer (3x spoil timer multiplier).
- Produces 1x Achatina Paste per minute (enable wandering around).
- Produces 1x Organic Polymer in an interval of 45 min. (enable wandering around)

Drops	Harvests	Breeding
Raw Meat	Provides Organic Polymer and Achatina Paste	Not breedable
Chitin		

THE ISLAND **SC. EARTH**
~~ABERRATION~~ **EXTINCTION**
~~GENESIS I~~ **RAGNAROK**
THE CENTER **VALGUERO**

CHEAT: summon Achatina_Character_BP_C

CARRYABLE BY: Kaprosuchus, Megalosaurus, Tapejara, Pteranodon, Argentavis, Quetzal, Griffin, Wyvern, Tusoteuthis, Karkinos, Procoptodon

EGG SIZE: –

USEFUL TRAPS: Bola, Bear Trap, Plant Species Y Trap

TAMING METHOD:
Knockout

SUITABLE FOOD FOR TAMING:
- Sweet Vegetable Cake

Allosaurus

Basic Stats:

Health	630	Food	3000	Speed (Land)	650
Stamina	250	Weight	380	Speed (Water)	300
Oxygen	150	Melee Damage	35	Torpidity	1000

Habitat: Mountains and Warm Jungles
Type: Dinosaur
Damages: Thatch, Wood
Diet: Carnivore
Behavior: Highly Aggressive
Names: Allo

Attack 1: Bite/Harvests
Attack 2: Gore (only leaders): decreases the speed of the enemy
Attack 3: Roar (only leaders): intimidation

Specifics:
- Usually spawns as a pack of three (or more).
- There's always a pack leader (glows) that reinforces the pack.

Utility:
- Riding animal: a fast and secure mount with acceptable loading capacity that can also defend itself well.
- Hunting: very suitable for hunting Meat.
- PvP battle: very dangerous opponent in a large pack.
- In packs of 3-5, including the bonus of female and male animals, they can even be used to hunt Alphas.

Drops	Harvests		Breeding	
Raw Meat	Raw Prime Fish	■■■	Type	Egg
Raw Prime Fish	Raw Meat	■■■	Egg Temp.	26°-32°
Hide	Chitin/Keratin	■■	Incubation	1h:39m
Keratin	Pelt	■■	Maturation	46h:18m
Allosaurus Brain				

~~THE ISLAND~~ ~~SE. EARTH~~
~~ABERRATION~~ EXTINCTION
~~GENESIS I~~ RAGNAROK
THE CENTER VALGUERO

Level	67
Engram Cost	35
Hide	320
Fiber	170
Metal Ingots	30

CHEAT: summon Allo_Character_BP_C
CARRYABLE BY: Tusoteuthis, Wyvern, Quetzal
EGG SIZE: Large

USEFUL TRAPS: Chain Bola, Large Bear Trap, Plant Species Y Trap

TAMING METHOD:
Knockout

SUITABLE FOOD FOR TAMING:
- Superior Kibble
- Raw Mutton
- Cooked Lamb Chop
- Raw Prime Fish
- Cooked Prime Meat
- Raw Prime Fish Meat
- Raw Meat
- Cooked Prime Fish Meat
- Cooked Meat
- Raw Fish Meat
- Cooked Fish Meat

ANKYLOSAURUS

Basic Stats:

Health	700	Food	3000	Speed (Land)	120
Stamina	175	Weight	250	Speed (Water)	300
Oxygen	150	Melee Damage	50	Torpidity	420

Habitat: Hills, Mountains
Damages: Thatch, Wood
Behavior: Passive

Type: Dinosaur
Diet: Herbivore
Names: Ankylo/Anky

Attack 1: Tail Attack (farms all kinds of Metal, Stone, and Wood)
Attack 2: Tail Attack (collects plants: Berries)
Attack 3: –

Specifics:
- Slow movement on shore but faster than expected in the water.
- We recommend fighting it with ranged weapons (e.g. Bow).

Utility:
- One of the best resource collectors for Metal, Flint, and Crystal.
- Can also be used underwater for things like collecting Oil. Make sure to increase the Ankylosaurus' oxygen level.
- Can withstand a lot. Therefore, we recommend using it as a tank in battles.

Drops
Raw Meat
Keratin
Hide

Harvests
Metal, Crystal	■■■
FireStone, Berries	■■■
Rare Mushroom, Oil	■■■
Rare Flower	■■■
Cactus Sap	■■■
Sulfur	■■
Obsidian	■■
Thatch, Wood, Stone	■■

Breeding
Type	Egg
Egg Temp.	16°-20°
Incubation	2h:37m
Maturation	48h:44m

THE ISLAND	SC. EARTH
~~ABERRATION~~	EXTINCTION
GENESIS I	RAGNAROK
THE CENTER	VALGUERO

Level	36
Engram Cost	18
Hide	260
Fiber	140
Metal Ingots	10

CHEAT: *summon Ankylo_Character_BP_C*

CARRYABLE BY: Argentavis, Quetzal, Wyvern, Tusoteuthis

EGG SIZE: Medium

USEFUL TRAPS: Chain Bola, Large Bear Trap, Plant Species Y Trap

TAMING METHOD:
Knockout

SUITABLE FOOD FOR TAMING:
- Regular Kibble
- Crops
- Mejoberries
- Berries

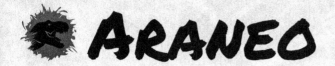

ARANEO

Basic Stats:

Health	150	Food	900	Speed (Land)	200
Stamina	100	Weight	100	Speed (Water)	200
Oxygen	150	Melee Damage	10	Torpidity	80

Habitat: Dark Caves, Underground
Damages: Thatch
Behavior: Highly Aggressive
Type: Invertebrate
Diet: Carnivore
Names: Spider

Attack 1: Melee; increases the victim's torpidity (+10 torpidity for 10 sec.)
Attack 2: Spider Web (-50 % movement speed for 10 sec.)
Attack 3: —

Specifics:
- Warning: it often occurs in groups.
- Can shoot webs that limit the player's mobility. It can, therefore, more easily fall prey to hunters.
- Possesses paralyzing venom.
- We recommend fighting it with ranged weapons.
- Many high-leveled Araneos (150+) can't be tamed.

Utility:
- When you own a tamed Araneo, it's a useful tool for hunting creatures you want to tame (venom and Spider Web).
- Can't be used for harvests.

Drops	Harvests	Breeding
Raw Meat	—	Not breedable
Chitin		

THE ISLAND	SC. EARTH
~~ABERRATION~~	EXTINCTION
GENESIS I	RAGNAROK
THE CENTER	VALGUERO

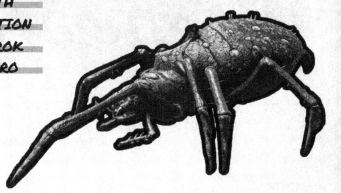

Level	40
Engram Cost	18
Hide	260
Fiber	140
Chitin or Keratin	100

CHEAT: summon SpiderS_Character_BP_C

CARRYABLE BY: Kaprosuchus, Megalosaurus, Argentavis, Quetzal, Wyvern, Tusoteuthis, Karkinos

EGG SIZE: –

USEFUL TRAPS: Bola, Bear Trap, Plant Species Y Trap

TAMING METHOD:
Can be tamed by feeding.

SUITABLE FOOD FOR TAMING:
- Spoiled Meat
- Raw Meat
- Raw Fish Meat

Arthropluera

Basic Stats:

Health	500	Food	1200	Speed (Land)	225
Stamina	200	Weight	100	Speed (Water)	400
Oxygen	-	Melee Damage	18	Torpidity	175

Habitat: Caves, Underground, Desert
Damages: Everything
Behavior: Aggressive
Type: Invertebrate
Diet: Scavenger
Names: -

Attack 1: Melee (increasing the victim's torpidity, x3 torpidity for 10 sec.)
Attack 2: Ranged Attack (reduces the durability of the target's armor by x35)
Attack 3: -

Specifics:
- We recommend attacking it with only long-range weapons (destroys melee weapons).
- Can shoot venom when it turns away from the player.
- Weapons and armor can be destroyed by its acidic blood.
- Can only be tamed by active feeding.
- Can be tamed easier underwater (don't forget to reemerge).
- Attacks the player as soon as he gets too close. Stops attacking when you go away.

Utility:
- Thanks to its ability to attack from a far distance, it's good support in battle.
- Artillery for your base.

Drops	Harvests		Breeding
Raw Meat	Raw Meat	■ ■	Not breedable
Chitin			

THE ISLAND   SC. EARTH
~~ABERRATION~~   EXTINCTION
GENESIS I   RAGNAROK
THE CENTER   VALGUERO

Level	54
Engram Cost	30
Hide	80
Fiber	50
Wood	20
Metal Ingots	30
Flint	8
Cementing Paste	15
Obsidian	35

CHEAT: *summon Arthro_Character_BP_C*

CARRYABLE BY: Megalosaurus, Argentavis, Quetzal, Wyvern, Tusoteuthis, Karkinos

EGG SIZE: –

USEFUL TRAPS: –

TAMING METHOD:
Can be tamed by active feeding.

SUITABLE FOOD FOR TAMING:
- Broth of Enlightenment (10x MejoBerry, 2x Rockarrot, 2x Longrass, 2x Savoroot, 2x Citronal, 5x Deathworm Horn or 5x Woolly Rhino Horn)
- Spoiled Meat
- Raw Meat
- Raw Fish Meat

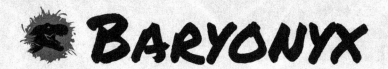

BARYONYX

BASIC STATS:

Health	440	Food	2250	Speed (Land)	400
Stamina	325	Weight	325	Speed (Water)	450
Oxygen	225	Melee Damage	35	Torpidity	400

HABITAT: Near water
DAMAGES: Thatch, Wood
BEHAVIOR: Highly Aggressive
TYPE: Dinosaur
DIET: Piscivore
NAMES: -

ATTACK 1: Melee Bite
ATTACK 2: Tail Attack (only in the water): temporary paralyzes the opponent
ATTACK 3: Taunt

SPECIFICS:
- Can usually be found near water since it feeds on Fish.
- Outside of water, it can be killed quite easily since you can catch it with a Bola.
- Avoid a fight in the water since it can paralyze the attacker.

UTILITY:
- The Spinosaur on a smaller scale. A good mount, fast in the water as well as on land, and able to defend itself (especially in the water). It even fits into many narrow caves. A good mount for exploring caves where there's a lot of water.
- Very good Fish and Meat collector. Fish stored in the Baryonyx spoils significantly slower.

DROPS		HARVESTS		BREEDING	
Raw Meat		Raw Fish Meat	■■■	Type	Egg
Raw Prime Fish		Raw Meat	■■	Egg Temp.	29°-35°
Hide		Hide	■■	Incubation	2h
		Raw Prime Fish	■■	Maturation	46h:18m
		Chitin, Keratin	■■		

~~THE ISLAND~~	~~SE. EARTH~~
~~ABERRATION~~	~~EXTINCTION~~
~~GENESIS I~~	~~RAGNAROK~~
~~THE CENTER~~	~~VALGUERO~~

Level	49
Engram Cost	24
Hide	225
Fiber	350
Metal Ingots	25

CHEAT: *summon Baryonyx_Character_BP_C*

CARRYABLE BY: Megalosaurus, Argentavis, Quetzal, Wyvern, Tusoteuthis, Karkinos

EGG SIZE: Medium

USEFUL TRAPS: Bola, Bear Trap, Large Bear Trap, Plant Species Y Trap

TAMING METHOD:
Knockout

SUITABLE FOOD FOR TAMING:
- Regular Kibble
- Cooked Prime Fish Meat
- Raw Prime Fish Meat
- Raw Fish Meat
- Cooked Fish Meat

BASILISK

Basic Stats:

Health	2750	Food	2500	Speed (Land)	600
Stamina	650	Weight	2200	Speed (Water)	400
Oxygen	∞	Melee Damage	55	Torpidity	175

Habitat: The Spine and Element Falls
Damages: Thatch
Behavior: Highly Aggressive

Type: Fantasy Creature
Diet: Carnivore
Names: -

Attack 1: Melee
Attack 2: Projectile (poison attack that explodes on impact)
Attack 3: -

Specifics:
- Can't drown.
- Impossible to run away from because it's so fast. In order to escape, you can jump off a cliff (the Basilisk then ceases from chasing you).
- We recommend using ranged weapons to attack it.
- Lies in ambush and attacks (buried under the ground).

Utility:
- Due to its high movement speed, it's very useful as mount.
- It can carry a lot.

Drops	Harvests	Breeding
Raw Meat	Raw Meat	Not breedable
Raw Prime Fish		
Hide		
Basilisk Scale		

~~THE ISLAND~~   ~~SE EARTH~~
ABERRATION   ~~EXTINCTION~~
GENESIS I   ~~RAGNAROK~~
~~THE CENTER~~   ~~VALGUERO~~

Level	85
Engram Cost	28
Fiber	150
Cementing Paste	80
Hide	270
Metal Ingots	425
Green Gem	45

CHEAT: summon Basilisk_Character_BP_C

CARRYABLE BY: –
EGG SIZE: –

USEFUL TRAPS: –

TAMING METHOD:
Can be tamed by active feeding. In order to tame it, lay the fertilized egg near the Basilisk (make sure it's not buried in the ground or distracted). Should several eggs be required, the player should retreat to a safe location in the meantime.

SUITABLE FOOD FOR TAMING:
- Fertilized egg of the Rock Drake

BEELZEBUFO

Basic Stats:

Health	220	Food	1500	Speed (Land)	400
Stamina	190	Weight	160	Speed (Water)	700
Oxygen	150	Melee Damage	12	Torpidity	200

Habitat: Swamps
Damages: Thatch
Behavior: Passive

Type: Amphibian
Diet: Carnivore
Names: -

Attack 1: Tongue Attack (increases the victim's torpidity, x3 Torpidity for 10 sec.)
Attack 2: Tongue Swipe (increases the victim's torpidity, x3 Torpidity for 10 sec.)
Attack 3: -

Specifics:
- Has a high attack range (however, only in the area in front of him).
- Poisons his targets and stuns them. Therefore, we recommend attacking it from far away. Consuming Stimberries increases the damage caused by torpidity.

Utility:
- Can knock out creatures with its tongue. Suitable for stunning small creatures.
- Cementing Paste collector: the Beelzebufo automatically transforms insects into Cementing Paste. In addition, it collects Chitin. An amazing mount for swamp caves (collects a lot of Chitin and Cementing Paste there).
- Good mount: fast movement on land and in the water. It can also jump very high and very far.

Drops		Harvests		Breeding	
Raw Meat		Cement. Paste	■■■	Type	Egg
Hide		Chitin	■■■	Egg Temp.	0°-50°
				Incubation	5h
				Maturation	37h:2m

~~THE ISLAND~~ ~~SE. EARTH~~
~~ABERRATION~~ EXTINCTION
GENESIS I RAGNAROK
THE CENTER VALGUERO

Level	40
Engram Cost	16
Hide	170
Fiber	95
Wood	30
Cement. Paste	5

CHEAT: *summon Toad_Character_BP_C*
CARRYABLE BY: Megalosaurus, Argentavis, Quetzal, Wyvern, Tusoteuthis, Karkinos
EGG SIZE: –

USEFUL TRAPS: Bola, Bear Trap, Plant Species Y Trap

TAMING METHOD:
Knockout

SUITABLE FOOD FOR TAMING:
- Regular Kibble
- Raw Mutton
- Cooked Lamb Chop
- Raw Prime Fish
- Cooked Prime Meat
- Raw Meat
- Cooked Prime Fish Meat
- Raw Fish Meat
- Cooked Fish Meat

BLOODSTALKER

BASIC STATS:

Health	450	Food	1200	Speed (Land)	810
Stamina	600	Weight	350	Speed (Water)	810
Oxygen	150	Melee Damage	26	Torpidity	180

HABITAT: Swamp areas
DAMAGES: Thatch, Wood
BEHAVIOR: Aggressive

TYPE: Fantasy Creature
DIET: Sanguivore
NAMES: –

ATTACK 1: Web Left
ATTACK 2: Web Left and Right
ATTACK 3: Stab

SPECIFICS:
- Bloodstalkers are usually found in swamp trees where they lie in wait for their victims.
- Warning: when its health level falls below 40%, it drains its rider's health (or hopefully the blood packs the player is carrying).

UTILITY:
- Very good mount: it can swing forward using its web, double jump, climb, and walk on water.
- Can catch creatures with its webs, pull them close, and hold them.
- Gives its rider spider vision: every creature in the surrounding area is significantly highlighted.

DROPS
Raw Meat
Chitin

HARVESTS
Meat	■

BREEDING
Type	Egg
Egg Temp.	
Incubation	3h
Maturation	51h:10m

~~THE ISLAND~~ ~~SE EARTH~~
~~ABERRATION~~ ~~EXTINCTION~~
GENESIS I ~~RAGNAROK~~
~~THE CENTER~~ ~~VALGUERO~~

Ridable without a saddle

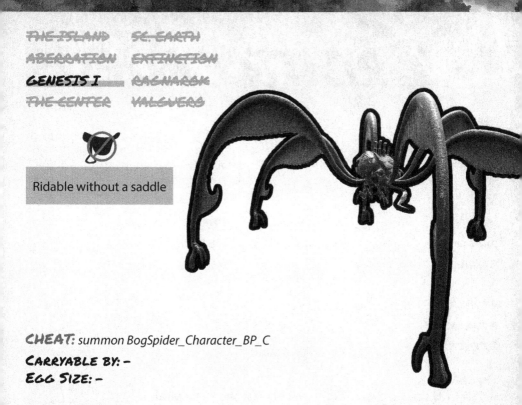

CHEAT: *summon BogSpider_Character_BP_C*
CARRYABLE BY: –
EGG SIZE: –

USEFUL TRAPS: –

TAMING METHOD:
Can be tamed by "feeding".

The Bloodstalker can be tamed when you let him suck blood from blood packs. However, high-leveled Bloodstalkers require a lot of blood packs; sometimes way more than 1000 packs.

You have to have blood packs in your inventory and get caught and sucked by a Bloodstalker. Useful tools you should have during the Bloodstalker's taming process are Bug Repellant (in order to be protected against insect swarms) and a glider suit in case you get released.

BRONTOSAURUS

Basic Stats:

Health	2070	Food	10000	Speed (Land)	150
Stamina	240	Weight	1600	Speed (Water)	300
Oxygen	150	Melee Damage	60	Torpidity	2000

Habitat: Hills, Jungle/Beaches
Damages: Thatch, Wood, Adobe
Behavior: Passive
Type: Dinosaur
Diet: Herbivore
Names: Bronto

Attack 1: Melee/Tail Attack
Attack 2: -
Attack 3: -

Specifics:
- Due to its size, the Bronto drops a lot of Meat and Prime Meat.
- Very slow due to its size. Nevertheless, its tail has a long range when attacking.
- A swipe with its long tail knocks opponents back.

Utility:
- Very good Berry and Thatch collector.
- Can be used as mobile base due to its platform saddle.
- Good mount because of its size, loading capacity, and health.
- Very suitable for transporting a lot of resources.

Drops	Harvests		Breeding	
Raw Meat	Berries	■■■	Type	Egg
Raw Prime Fish	Thatch	■■■	Egg Temp.	28°-31°
Hide	Plant Spec. X Seed	■■■	Incubation	5h
Sauropoden Twist	Wood	■	Maturation	92h:36m

~~THE ISLAND~~ ~~SE-EARTH~~
~~ABERRATION~~ EXTINCTION
GENESIS I RAGNAROK
THE CENTER VALGUERO

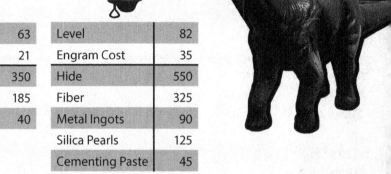

Level	63
Engram Cost	21
Hide	350
Fiber	185
Metal Ingots	40

Level	82
Engram Cost	35
Hide	550
Fiber	325
Metal Ingots	90
Silica Pearls	125
Cementing Paste	45

CHEAT: *summon Sauropod_Character_BP_C*

CARRYABLE BY: –

EGG SIZE: Extra Large

USEFUL TRAPS: Large Bear Trap

TAMING METHOD:
Knockout

SUITABLE FOOD FOR TAMING:
- Exceptional Kibble
- Crops
- Mejoberries
- Berries

BULBDOG

Basic Stats:

Health	145	Food	450	Speed (Land)	50
Stamina	200	Weight	120	Speed (Water)	300
Oxygen	165	Melee Damage	12	Torpidity	60

Habitat: Aberration (almost everywhere)
Damages: Thatch
Behavior: Passive

Type: Fantasy Creature
Diet: Herbivore
Names: Lantern Pug

Attack 1: Melee
Attack 2: –
Attack 3: –

Specifics:
- As a tamed creature, it's an omnivore.

Utility:
- Never use it during a battle since it doesn't fight back.
- Can be tamed quickly (Aquatic Mushroom) and turns on its light when you pet it. The light protects from the Nameless and banishes or weakens them.
- Can be carried on your shoulder. It's light can be enabled via emote (similar to „waving").

Drops
Raw Meat
Hide

Harvests
–

Breeding

Type	Pregnancy
Gestation	4h:11m
Maturation	48h:44m

~~THE ISLAND~~ ~~SE EARTH~~
ABERRATION ~~EXTINCTION~~
GENESIS I ~~RAGNAROK~~
~~THE CENTER~~ **VALGUERO**

CHEAT: summon LanternPug_Character_BP_C
CARRYABLE BY: Pteranodon, Quetzal, Tapejara, Karkinos, Gigantopithecus
EGG SIZE: –

USEFUL TRAPS: Bola, Bear Trap, Plant Species Y Trap

TAMING METHOD:
Can be tamed by active feeding.

SUITABLE FOOD FOR TAMING:
- Plant Species Y Seed
- Aquatic Mushroom
- Cooked Lamb Chop
- Cooked Prime Meat
- Raw Mutton
- Sweet Vegetable Cake
- Cooked Meat
- Raw Prime Fish
- Raw Meat
- Cooked Prime Fish Meat/Cooked Fish Meat
- Raw Prime Fish Meat/Raw Fish Meat
- Amarberry Seeds/Citronal Seeds

CHALICOTHERIUM

Basic Stats:

Health	600	Food	4000	Speed (Land)	210
Stamina	300	Weight	400	Speed (Water)	300
Oxygen	150	Melee Damage	36	Torpidity	500

Habitat: Cold regions
Damages: Thatch, Wood, Stone, Adobe
Behavior: Aggressive

Type: Mammal
Diet: Herbivore
Names: Chalico/Chali

Attack 1: Melee Hand
Attack 2: Stone Throw
Attack 3: Bite

Specifics:
- Can't be tamed with usual narcotics. Instead, you have to use a Beer Jar.
- Warning: the Chalicotherium throws mud on the player which can poison him.
- We recommend using ranged weapons during an attack.

Utility:
- Good mount (fast on land).
- Very suitable for collecting Berries (because of its claws he can collect them very quickly).
- Very effective against enemies because it throws stones on them. For this, no ammunition is required because it grabs the material from the ground on its own.

Drops		Harvests		Breeding	
Raw Meat		Berries	■■■	Type	Pregnancy
Raw Prime Fish		Thatch	■■	Gestation	7h:57m
Hide		Wood	■	Maturation	82h:19m

~~THE ISLAND~~   ~~SE. EARTH~~
ABERRATION   ~~EXTINCTION~~
GENESIS I   ~~RAGNAROK~~
~~THE CENTER~~   **VALGUERO**

Level	42
Engram Cost	30
Hide	265
Fiber	180
Metal Ingots	45

CHEAT: *summon Chalico_Character_BP_C*

CARRYABLE BY: Quetzal, Wyvern, Tusoteuthis

EGG SIZE: –

USEFUL TRAPS: Chain Bola, Large Bear Trap, Plant Species Y Trap

TAMING METHOD:
Can be tamed by feeding.

SUITABLE FOOD FOR TAMING:
- Beer Jar

CARBONEMYS

Basic Stats:

Health	700	Food	3000	Speed (Land)	100
Stamina	200	Weight	270	Speed (Water)	265
Oxygen	150	Melee Damage	13	Torpidity	275

Habitat: Near Rivers, Lakes, Swamp
Damages: Thatch
Behavior: Passive

Type: Reptile
Diet: Herbivore
Names: Turtle

Attack 1: Melee Bite
Attack 2: -
Attack 3: -

Specifics:
- Due to its armor, Melee isn't suggested. Tranquilizer arrows or a large carnivore can better deal with Carbonemys. A battle can take very long due to its high health level.
- In a battle, other nearby Carbonemys come and support their fellows.
- Moves very slowly, which is beneficial for attaining a large amount of Meat at the beginning of the game.

Utility:
- Good pack animal for transport on the water (e.g. on rivers). On land, it's too slow.
- Can be used very well as a tank or blocker during an attack.

Drops	Harvests		Breeding	
Raw Meat	Berries	■ ■	Type	Egg
Hide	Thatch	■ ■	Egg Temp.	30°-34°
Keratin	Wood	■ ■	Incubation	1h:14m
			Maturation	23h:9m

THE ISLAND	~~SC. EARTH~~
~~ABERRATION~~	EXTINCTION
GENESIS I	RAGNAROK
THE CENTER	VALGUERO

Level	10
Engram Cost	12
Hide	170
Fiber	95
Metal Ingots	10

CHEAT: *summon Turtle_Character_BP_C*

CARRYABLE BY: Quetzal, Wyvern, Tusoteuthis, Karkinos

EGG SIZE: Medium

USEFUL TRAPS: Chain Bola, Large Bear Trap, Plant Species Y Trap

TAMING METHOD:
Knockout

SUITABLE FOOD FOR TAMING:
- Regular Kibble
- Crops
- Mejoberries
- Berries

Carnotaurus

Basic Stats:

Health	420	Food	2000	Speed (Land)	425
Stamina	300	Weight	300	Speed (Water)	300
Oxygen	150	Melee Damage	35	Torpidity	350

Habitat:	Everywhere (except swamp areas)	**Type:**	Dinosaur
Damages:	Thatch, Wood	**Diet:**	Carnivore
Behavior:	Highly Aggressive	**Names:**	Carno

Attack 1: Bite
Attack 2: Headbutt
Attack 3: -

Specifics:
- By headbutting the player, it can knock him backwards. Pay attention to what's behind you (maybe an abyss?)
- Also appear in packs.

Utility:
- Very good for collecting Meat.
- Suitable for transporting resources as long as the way isn't too long. It's a good defensive mount with acceptable loading capacity.
- Good fighter and Meat collector until you get a Rex.

Drops	Harvests		Breeding	
Raw Meat	Raw Prime Fish	■■■	Type	Egg
Raw Prime Fish	Raw Meat	■■■	Egg Temp.	26°-32°
Hide	Chitin/Keratin	■■	Incubation	1h:39m
Keratin	Pelt	■■	Maturation	46h:18m
	Hide	■■		

THE ISLAND	SC. EARTH
~~ABERRATION~~	EXTINCTION
GENESIS I	RAGNAROK
THE CENTER	VALGUERO

Level	46
Engram Cost	21
Hide	320
Fiber	170
Metal Ingots	30

CHEAT: *summon Carno_Character_BP_C*
CARRYABLE BY: Quetzal, Wyvern, Tusoteuthis, Karkinos
EGG SIZE: Medium

USEFUL TRAPS: Chain Bola, Large Bear Trap, Plant Species Y Trap

TAMING METHOD:
Knockout

SUITABLE FOOD FOR TAMING:
- Regular Kibble
- Raw Mutton
- Cooked Lamb Chop
- Raw Prime Fish Meat
- Raw Meat
- Cooked Prime Fish Meat
- Cooked Meat
- Raw Fish Meat
- Cooked Fish Meat

CASTOROIDES

Basic Stats:

Health	450	Food	2000	Speed (Land)	160
Stamina	180	Weight	300	Speed (Water)	700
Oxygen	750	Melee Damage	28	Torpidity	350

Habitat: Near Lakes/Rivers **Type:** Mammal
Damages: Thatch, Wood **Diet:** Herbivore
Behavior: Passive **Names:** Giant Beaver

Attack 1: Melee; Bite
Attack 2: –
Attack 3: –

Specifics:
- Their dams are full of useful materials: Wood, Raw Mushrooms and Flowers, Cementing Paste, and Silica Pearls. Since dams don't get replenished, you should loot them completely. They are then destroyed.
- Hunts enemies for a long time, and persistently at that (especially when somebody has looted its dam). Climbs poorly.

Utility:
- One of the best Wood collectors in the game. Wood, Thatch, Stone and Fiber weigh less in its inventory.
- Serves as mobile Forge. You can use it like a Forge.
- Automatically collects Wood and cuts down tress while wandering around.

Drops		Harvests		Breeding	
Raw Meat		Wood	■■■	Type	Pregnancy
Hide		Berries	■■	Gestation	7h:56m
Pelt		Thatch	■■	Maturation	61h:44m

THE ISLAND ~~SC. EARTH~~
~~ABERRATION~~ EXTINCTION
GENESIS I RAGNAROK
THE CENTER VALGUERO

Level	61
Engram Cost	50
Hide	290
Fiber	200
Metal Ingots	100
Thatch	180
Cementing Paste	140

CHEAT: *summon Beaver_Character_BP_C*
CARRYABLE BY: Megalosaurus, Argentavis, Quetzal, Wyvern, Tusoteuthis, Karkinos
EGG SIZE: –

USEFUL TRAPS: Bola, Large Bear Trap, Plant Species Y Trap

TAMING METHOD:
Knockout

SUITABLE FOOD FOR TAMING:
- Superior Kibble
- Crops
- Mejoberries
- Berries

Compsognathus

Basic Stats:

Health	50	Food	450	Speed (Land)	120
Stamina	100	Weight	25	Speed (Water)	200
Oxygen	150	Melee Damage	4	Torpidity	25

Habitat: Jungle, Beaches, Forest
Damages: Thatch
Behavior: Passive/Pack: Aggressive
Type: Dinosaur
Diet: Carnivore
Names: Compy

Attack 1: Melee; Bite
Attack 2: Melee II
Attack 3: -

Specifics:
- Only attacks in groups. A single one doesn't pose any danger. You should, however, make sure that there aren't any more in the proximity.
- Single Compys that find a human being call other Compys. Therefore, you should kill a single one immediately if possible.
- Loses interest when people walk into water.

Utility:
- As soon as it's tamed, it can be carried on your shoulder.

Drops	Harvests	Breeding	
Raw Meat	–	Type	Egg
Hide		Egg Temp.	24°-32°
		Incubation	49m
		Maturation	92h:36m

THE ISLAND ~~SC-EARTH~~
~~ABERRATION~~ **EXTINCTION**
~~GENESIS I~~ **RAGNAROK**
THE CENTER **VALGUERO**

CHEAT: summon Compy_Character_BP_C

CARRYABLE BY: Kaprosuchus, Megalosaurus, Tapejara, Pteranodon, Argentavis, Quetzal, Griffin, Wyvern, Tusoteuthis, Karkinos

EGG SIZE: Small

USEFUL TRAPS: Bola, Bear Trap, Plant Species Y Trap

TAMING METHOD:
Knockout

SUITABLE FOOD FOR TAMING:
- Raw Mutton
- Raw Prime Fish
- Raw Prime Fish Meat

DAEODON

Basic Stats:

Health	900	Food	2500	Speed (Land)	160
Stamina	250	Weight	400	Speed (Water)	300
Oxygen	150	Melee Damage	29	Torpidity	800

HABITAT: Cold areas, Snow biome **TYPE:** Mammal
DAMAGES: Thatch, Wood **DIET:** Carnivore
BEHAVIOR: Highly Aggressive **NAMES:** -

ATTACK 1: Bite
ATTACK 2: Healing (not an attack/carried out automatically)
ATTACK 3: -

Specifics:
- Can heal itself, fellow and allied players, as well as their animals.
- Because of its ability to heal, it needs a lot of food.

Utility:
- Can be used to detect Raw Mushrooms.
- In a group of tamed fighting animals, 1-2 Daeodons are very good support due to their healing skills. Don't forget to supply them with enough food since they consume a lot for healing.
- Cooked Meat or Prime Meat (raw or cooked) are the best types of food and easy to provide.

Drops

Raw Meat
Hide
Keratin

Harvests

Wood	■■
Cactus Sap	■■
Rare Flower	■■
Flint	■■
Obsidian	■■

Breeding

Type	Pregnancy
Gestation	7h:56m
Maturation	48h:44m

THE ISLAND   SC. EARTH
~~ABERRATION~~   EXTINCTION
GENESIS I   RAGNAROK
THE CENTER   VALGUERO

Level	59
Engram Cost	24
Hide	290
Fiber	155
Metal Ingots	20

CHEAT: *summon Daeodon_Character_BP_C*

CARRYABLE BY: Megalosaurus, Argentavis, Quetzal, Wyvern, Tusoteuthis, Karkinos
EGG SIZE: -

USEFUL TRAPS: Bola, Bear Trap, Large Bear Trap, Plant Species Y Trap

TAMING METHOD:
Knockout

SUITABLE FOOD FOR TAMING:
- Superior Kibble
- Raw Mutton
- Cooked Lamb Chop
- Raw Prime Fish
- Cooked Prime Meat
- Raw Meat
- Cooked Prime Fish Meat
- Raw Fish Meat
- Cooked Fish Meat

DEATHWORM

Basic Stats:

Health	20000	Food	100	Unteriridisch	-
Stamina	100	Weight	100	Speed (Water)	300
Oxygen	∞	Melee Damage	225	Torpidity	0

Habitat: Sand Desert around Scorched Earth

Damages: Thatch, Wood, Adobe, Stone

Behavior: Highly Aggressive

Type: Fantasy Creature

Diet: Carnivore

Names: -

Attack 1: Bite
Attack 2: Steal
Attack 3: -

Specifics:
- Suddenly emerges from the sand and attacks.
- Can be defeated with some high-leveled creatures (very difficult alone).

Utility:
- Drops a lot of rare materials.

Drops	Harvests	Breeding
Raw Meat	-	Not breedable
Raw Prime Fish		
Hide, Keratin		
Deathworm Horn		
Leech Blood		
Black Pearls		
Angler Gel		
Organic Polymer		

~~THE ISLAND~~ SC. EARTH
~~ABERRATION~~ ~~EXTINCTION~~
~~GENESIS I~~ RAGNAROK
~~THE CENTER~~ ~~VALGUERO~~

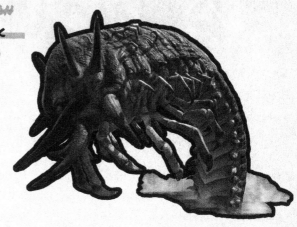

CHEAT: summon Deathworm_Character_BP_C

CARRYABLE BY: –

EGG SIZE: –

USEFUL TRAPS: –

TAMING METHOD: –

SUITABLE FOOD FOR TAMING: –

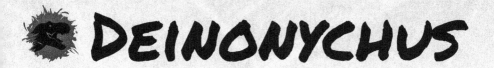

DEINONYCHUS

Basic Stats:

Health	200	Food	1200	Speed (Land)	480
Stamina	150	Weight	140	Speed (Water)	300
Oxygen	150	Melee Damage	30	Torpidity	0

Habitat: Southeastern part of the map
Damages: Thatch, Wood
Behavior: Highly Aggressive
Type: Dinosaur
Diet: Carnivore
Names: -

Attack 1: Melee; Bite and Claw
Attack 2: Pounce Attack
Attack 3: Roar

Specifics:
- Can latch onto walls and even creatures.
- Its attack causes a bleeding wound which, in return, causes melee damage.
- Can climb and jump very high.

Utility:
- It's a kind of a Superraptor. Very useful as mount, fighter, and hunter.
- When you properly utilize its ability to latch onto things, it can even pose a danger for large creatures.

Drops	Harvests		Breeding	
Raw Meat	Raw Prime Fish	■■	Type	Egg
Hide	Raw Meat	■■	Egg Temp.	80°-90°
	Chitin/Keratin	■■	Incubation	5h
	Hide	■■	Maturation	27h:2m
	Pelt	■■		

~~THE ISLAND~~ ~~SC. EARTH~~
~~ABERRATION~~ ~~EXTINCTION~~
~~GENESIS I~~ ~~RAGNAROK~~
~~THE CENTER~~ **VALGUERO**

Level	32
Engram Cost	30
Hide	110
Fiber	65
Wood	20

CHEAT: *summon Deinonychus_Character_BP_C*

CARRYABLE BY: Megalosaurus, Argentavis, Wyvern, Kaprosuchus, Karkinos, Quetzal, Tusoteuthis

EGG SIZE: Special

USEFUL TRAPS: Bear Trap, Large Bear Trap, Plant Species Y Trap

TAMING METHOD:
Can be tamed by breeding.

SUITABLE FOOD FOR TAMING: -

Its eggs can be found in nests located in the southeastern part of the Valguero map. A young Deinonychus can be fed Meat like normal.

DILOPHOSAUR

Basic Stats:

Health	130	Food	450	Speed (Land)	120
Stamina	100	Weight	45	Speed (Water)	300
Oxygen	150	Melee Damage	10	Torpidity	75

Habitat: Beaches (frequently)
Damages: Thatch
Behavior: Highly Aggressive

Type: Dinosaur
Diet: Carnivore
Names: Dilo

Attack 1: Melee; Bite
Attack 2: Poison (spits and decreases the player's movement speed by 50 % for 10 sec.)
Attack 3: –

Specifics:
- Sometimes it doesn't attack the player and flees instead. Then, it can be killed easily because Dilos can't run very fast.
- The poison isn't only dangerous for the player, but also for tames.

Utility:
- Since Dilos are quite small, you can use them as protection in buildings.
- They're also useful when it comes to distracting and slowing down enemies even though its stamina decreases quickly and it doesn't cause a lot of melee damage.
- It's a typical egg-laying dinosaur. Its eggs can be used for the kibble of three different creatures.

Drops	Harvests	Breeding	
Raw Meat	–	Type	Egg
Hide		Egg Temp.	28°-32
Nerdy Glasses Skin		Incubation	1h:8m
		Maturation	21h:3m

THE ISLAND ~~SC. EARTH~~
~~ABERRATION~~ EXTINCTION
GENESIS I RAGNAROK
THE CENTER VALGUERO

CHEAT: summon Dilo_Character_BP_C

CARRYABLE BY: Kaprosuchus, Megalosaurus, Tapejara, Pteranodon, Argentavis, Quetzal, Griffin Wyvern, Tusoteuthis, Karkinos

EGG SIZE: Very Small

USEFUL TRAPS: Bola, Bear Trap, Plant Species Y Trap

TAMING METHOD:
Knockout

SUITABLE FOOD FOR TAMING:
- Basic Kibble
- Raw Mutton
- Cooked Lamb Chop
- Raw Prime Fish
- Cooked Prime Meat
- Raw Prime Fish Meat
- Raw Meat
- Cooked Prime Fish Meat
- Cooked Meat
- Raw Fish Meat
- Cooked Fish Meat

DIMETRODON

Basic Stats:

Health	350	Food	1500	Speed (Land)	110
Stamina	300	Weight	250	Speed (Water)	250
Oxygen	500	Melee Damage	20	Torpidity	750

Habitat: Swamps in The Island's center

Damages: Thatch, Wood

Behavior: Passive

Type: Synapsid

Diet: Carnivore

Names: -

Attack 1: Melee Bite
Attack 2: -
Attack 3: -

Specifics:
- Its eggs are beneath the Dimetrodon. In order to get them, you need to lure it away.
- It's better to move slowly so you can escape. It's also easy to kill it.
- Often, however, there are other dangerous creatures in proximity to the Dimetrodon (in the swamps).

Utility:
- The Dimetrodon is useful for breeding fertilized eggs since it regulates the temperature itself (similar to air conditioning). Just put it near eggs you want to breed (the closer the better).

Drops	Harvests	Breeding	
Raw Meat	-	Type	Egg
Raw Prime Fish		Egg Temp.	30°-34°
Hide		Incubation	2h:29m
		Maturation	46h:18m

THE ISLAND ~~SC. EARTH~~
~~ABERRATION~~ EXTINCTION
GENESIS I RAGNAROK
THE CENTER VALGUERO

CHEAT: *summon Dimetro_Character_BP_C*
CARRYABLE BY: Argentavis, Quetzal, Wyvern, Tusoteuthis, Karkinos
EGG SIZE: Medium

USEFUL TRAPS: Chain Bola, Large Bear Trap, Plant Species Y Trap

TAMING METHOD:
Knockout

SUITABLE FOOD FOR TAMING:
- Regular Kibble
- Raw Mutton
- Cooked Lamb Chop
- Raw Prime Fish
- Cooked Prime Meat
- Raw Prime Fish Meat
- Raw Meat
- Cooked Prime Fish Meat
- Cooked Meat
- Raw Fish Meat
- Cooked Fish Meat

DIPLODOCUS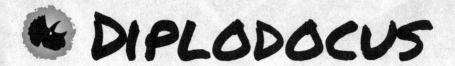

Basic Stats:

Health	1700	Food	10000	Speed (Land)	300
Stamina	550	Weight	800	Speed (Water)	400
Oxygen	300	Melee Damage	0	Torpidity	3000

Habitat:	Woodlands, Plains, Redwoods	**Type:**	Dinosaur
Damages:	-	**Diet:**	Herbivore
Behavior:	Passive	**Names:**	-

Attack 1: Melee; Headbutt
Attack 2: -
Attack 3: -

Specifics:
- Very peaceful and likes cuddling with the player. If it touches the player with its head, the player doesn't suffer any melee damage. However, the knock-back can potentially knock you off a cliff.
- When it attacks, the player suffers hardly any melee damage. Therefore, it's quite easy to kill.

Utility:
- The Diplodocus is a very suitable mount (the omnibus among the transport dinosaurs: up to ten armed players and one rider).
- Since it can be killed more easily than a Brontosaurus, it's a good source for Prime Meat.

Drops	Harvests		Breeding	
Raw Meat	Berries	■■■	Type	Egg
Raw Prime Fish	Thatch	■■■	Egg Temp.	26°-29°
Hide			Incubation	4h:59m
Sauropod Vertebra			Maturation	92h:36m

THE ISLAND   ~~SC EARTH~~
~~ABERRATION~~   EXTINCTION
~~GENESIS I~~   RAGNAROK
THE CENTER   VALGUERO

Level	32
Engram Cost	30
Hide	850
Fiber	600
Metal Ingots	200
Wood	250

CHEAT: summon Diplodocus_Character_BP_C

CARRYABLE BY: Tusoteuthis

EGG SIZE: Medium

USEFUL TRAPS: Chain Bola, Large Bear Trap

TAMING METHOD:
Knockout or Feeding

SUITABLE FOOD FOR TAMING:
- Regular Kibble
- Crops
- Mejoberries
- Berries

DIRE BEAR

Basic Stats:

Health	400	Food	3000	Speed (Land)	190
Stamina	500	Weight	650	Speed (Water)	360
Oxygen	270	Melee Damage	50	Torpidity	1000

Habitat: Redwoods (and neighboring areas)
Damages: Thatch, Wood
Behavior: Aggressive

Type: Mammal
Diet: Carnivore
Names: -

Attack 1: Bite
Attack 2: Swipe
Attack 3: Roar

Specifics:
- Because of its strong territorial behavior, you should avoid this creature unless you want to end up in a battle with it.
- Can feed on Meat as well as Berries.
- By leveling-up, it can become one of the fastest animals on land.

Utility:
- Very fast and versatile mount.
- Useful for collecting Fiber and Meat.
- Due to its high movement speed and great melee damage, we recommend using it as a combat animal.

Drops	Harvests		Breeding	
Raw Meat	Raw Meat	■■■	Type	Pregnancy
Hide	Raw Prime Fish	■■■	Gestation	3h:58m
Pelt	Fiber	■■■	Maturation	46h:18m
	Hide, Berries	■■		
	Chitin	■■		

THE ISLAND	~~SE. EARTH~~
~~ABERRATION~~	EXTINCTION
GENESIS I	RAGNAROK
THE CENTER	VALGUERO

Level	45
Engram Cost	24
Hide	300
Fiber	130
Cementing Paste	100

CHEAT: summon Direbear_Character_BP_C
CARRYABLE BY: Quetzal, Wyvern, Tusoteuthis
EGG SIZE: –

USEFUL TRAPS: Chain Bola, Large Bear Trap

TAMING METHOD:
Knockout

SUITABLE FOOD FOR TAMING:
- Superior Kibble
- Giant Bee Honey
- Raw Mutton
- Cooked Lamb Chop
- Raw Prime Fish
- Cooked Prime Meat
- Raw/Cooked Meat
- Raw/Cooked Prime Fish Meat
- Mejoberries
- Berries
- Raw Fish Meat/Cooked Fish Meat

DIREWOLF

BASIC STATS:

Health	330	Food	1200	Speed (Land)	279
Stamina	260	Weight	170	Speed (Water)	300
Oxygen	150	Melee Damage	33	Torpidity	450

HABITAT: Snow biome, Cold regions
DAMAGES: Thatch
BEHAVIOR: Highly Aggressive
TYPE: Mammal
DIET: Carnivore
NAMES: -

ATTACK 1: Bite
ATTACK 2: Bite II
ATTACK 3: -

SPECIFICS:
- Never strolls around alone. When you see one of them, the pack isn't far away. In packs, Direwolves have a bonus.
- Since it can run very fast, you should keep a far distance from it if you want to avoid a fight.

UTILITY:
- Suitable as a mount since it's ridable without a saddle.
- Good resource collector, companion, and reliable in a battle. It also fits into narrow caves and is a useful companion there.

DROPS	HARVESTS		BREEDING	
Raw Meat	Fiber, Hide	■■■	Type	Pregnancy
Hide	Pelt	■■■	Gestation	4h:10m
Pelt	Angler Gel, Chitin	■■■	Maturation	48h:44m
	Leech Blood	■■■		
	Raw Prime Fish	■■■		
	Raw Meat	■■		
	Organic Polymer	■■		

THE ISLAND **SC. EARTH**
~~ABERRATION~~ **EXTINCTION**
GENESIS I **RAGNAROK**
THE CENTER **VALGUERO**

Ridable without a saddle

CHEAT: *summon Direwolf_Character_BP_C*
CARRYABLE BY: Megalosaurus, Argentavis, Quetzal, Wyvern, Tusoteuthis, Karkinos
EGG SIZE: -

USEFUL TRAPS: Bola, Bear Trap, Large Bear Trap, Plant Species Y Trap

TAMING METHOD:
Knockout

SUITABLE FOOD FOR TAMING:
- Superior Kibble
- Raw Mutton
- Cooked Lamb Chop
- Raw Prime Fish
- Cooked Prime Meat
- Raw Prime Fish Meat
- Raw Meat
- Cooked Prime Fish Meat
- Cooked Meat
- Raw Fish Meat
- Cooked Fish Meat

DODO

Basic Stats:

Health	40	Food	450	Speed (Land)	65
Stamina	100	Weight	50	Speed (Water)	300
Oxygen	150	Melee Damage	5	Torpidity	30

Habitat: Beaches/Open areas **Type:** Bird
Damages: Thatch **Diet:** Herbivore
Behavior: Oblivious **Names:** –

Attack 1: Melee (picking)
Attack 2: –
Attack 3: –

Specifics:
- Harmless and can be defeated easily. Even though they run away when they're being attacked, they're very slow and also not nimble.
- They only attack when you try to steal their eggs.

Utility:
- In PvP, Dodos can transmit Swamp Fever to other players and, consequently, decrease their health (e.g. when sending an infected Dodo to a base of the enemy).
- Since Dodos lay a lot of eggs in a short amount of time, several tamed Dodos are very suitable for an egg farm for kibble and eggs that can be used for taming Oviraptors. Their kibble can be used for three different creatures.
- Also suitable for Meat production due to their short Incubation.

Drops	Harvests	Breeding	
Raw Meat	–	Type	Egg
Hide		Egg Temp.	22°-30°
		Incubation	49m
		Maturation	15h:26m

THE ISLAND ~~SE-EARTH~~
~~ABERRATION~~ EXTINCTION
GENESIS I RAGNAROK
THE CENTER VALGUERO

CHEAT: summon Dodo_Character_BP_C

CARRYABLE BY: Kaprosuchus, Megalosaurus, Tapejara, Pteranodon, Argentavis, Quetzal, Griffin, Wyvern, Tusoteuthis

EGG SIZE: Very Small

USEFUL TRAPS: Bola, Bear Trap, Plant Species Y Trap

TAMING METHOD:
Knockout

SUITABLE FOOD FOR TAMING:
- Basic Kibble
- Crops
- Mejoberries
- Berries

 Doedicurus

Basic Stats:

Health	850	Food	3000	Speed (Land)	86
Stamina	300	Weight	250	Speed (Water)	300
Oxygen	150	Melee Damage	32	Torpidity	800

Habitat: Mountains, Rocky regions
Damages: Thatch, Wood
Behavior: Passive
Type: Mammal
Diet: Herbivore
Names: Doed/Doedic

Attack 1: Tail Attack
Attack 2: Rolling (fast movement)
Attack 3: -

Specifics:
- When it suffers a lot of melee damage, it rolls itself up. By doing so, the melee damage you can do reduces and it begins to heal as well.
- As soon as its health has increased enough, it starts attacking again.

Utility:
- Automatically collects nearby Stones. He also farms other materials quickly.
- The best Stone collector; therefore, it's essential for raw material extraction. Stone weighs only 1/4 in its inventory.
- In order to increase movement speed, the player should use Attack 2 (Rolling). It's also quite fast in the water.

Drops	Harvests		Breeding	
Raw Meat	Stone, Sand	■■■	Type	Pregnancy
Hide	Thatch	■■■	Gestation	4h:57m
Keratin	Wood	■■	Maturation	57h:52m

THE ISLAND	SC. EARTH
ABERRATION	EXTINCTION
GENESIS I	RAGNAROK
THE CENTER	VALGUERO

Level	34
Engram Cost	20
Hide	200
Fiber	110
Stone	15
Metal Ingots	5

CHEAT: *summon Doed_Character_BP_C*

TRAGBAR VON: Megalosaurus, Argentavis, Quetzal, Wyvern, Tusoteuthis, Karkinos

EGG SIZE: –

USEFUL TRAPS: Chain Bola, Large Bear Trap, Plant Species Y Trap

TAMING METHOD:
Knockout

SUITABLE FOOD FOR TAMING:
- Regular Kibble
- Crops
- Mejoberries
- Berries

DUNG BEETLE

Basic Stats:

Health	200	Food	900	Speed (Land)	52
Stamina	100	Weight	5	Speed (Water)	200
Oxygen	150	Melee Damage	5	Torpidity	200

Habitat: Caves, Desert
Damages: Thatch
Behavior: Passive

Type: Invertebrate
Diet: Coprophage
Names: –

Attack 1: Melee
Attack 2: –
Attack 3: –

Specifics:
- This one is quite harmless but can be found in caves. Warning: a lot of other dangerous creatures can lurk there.
- A level 1 Dung Beetle produces just as much as a level 200 Dung Beetle. The only difference is that the high-leveled one has a better loading capacity.
- It can only be tamed as long as they're passive, which means that they don't try to attack the player. Don't touch it, approach from behind, and if possible, wear ghillie Armor.

Utility:
- Can transform Feces into Fertilizer and Oil. The Dung Beetle doesn't collect the Feces on its own, though. You have to put the Feces into its inventory and set it on "wandering around". Therefore, we recommend building a fenced-in area for your Dung Beetles. Make sure it doesn't get overloaded. Give it at least one Feces of each size since it can transform them all at once.

Drops	Harvests	Breeding
Raw Meat	No farming – but produces Fertilizer and Oil (see above)	Not breedable
Chitin		

THE ISLAND **SC. EARTH**
ABERRATION **EXTINCTION**
GENESIS I **RAGNAROK**
THE CENTER **VALGUERO**

CHEAT: *summon DungBeetle_Character_BP_C*

CARRYABLE BY: Kaprosuchus, Megalosaurus, Argentavis, Quetzal, Wyvern, Tusoteuthis, Procoptodon

EGG SIZE: –

USEFUL TRAPS: Bola, Bear Trap, Plant Species Y Trap

TAMING METHOD:
Can be tamed by feeding.

SUITABLE FOOD FOR TAMING:
- Large Animal Feces
- Medium Animal Feces
- Spoiled Meat
- Small Animal Feces
- Human Feces
- Raw Meat
- Raw Fish Meat

ENFORCER

BASIC STATS:

Health	375	Food	1500	Speed (Land)	600
Stamina	450	Weight	800	Speed (Water)	300
Oxygen	150	Melee Damage	34	Torpidity	5000

HABITAT: Sanctuary (in Extinction)
DAMAGES: Thatch
BEHAVIOR: Passive

TYPE: Mechanical Creature
DIET: -
NAMES: -

ATTACK 1: Melee
ATTACK 2: Teleport (has to be charged)
ATTACK 3: Blast

SPECIFICS:
- Can teleport themselves over short distances. With higher levels, they get additional teleport charge (at level 40, 80, 110, and 175).
- When riding an Enforcer, instead of swimming, it will walk on the ground underneath water; just as if there wasn't any there.
- Can't be tamed. Instead, it must be crafted at a City Terminal.

UTILITY:
- Since Enforcers suffer lower melee damage from corrupted creatures and damage them four times more, they're very suitable when you intend on fighting a bunch of them.

DROPS	HARVESTS		BREEDING
Element Dust	Raw Prime Fish	■■■	Not breedable/must be crafted
Scrap Metal	Raw Meat	■■■	
Oil	Chitin/Keratin	■■	
Electronics	Hide	■■	

~~THE ISLAND~~   ~~SE. EARTH~~
~~ABERRATION~~   **EXTINCTION**
~~GENESIS I~~   ~~RAGNAROK~~
~~THE CENTER~~   ~~VALGUERO~~

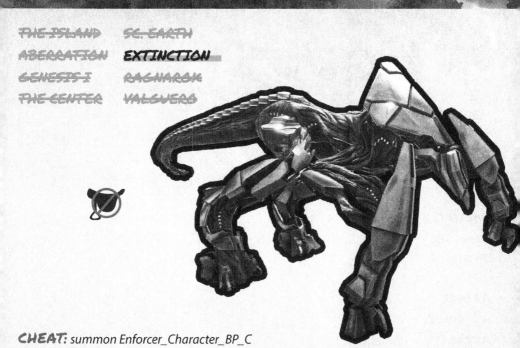

CHEAT: summon Enforcer_Character_BP_C

CARRYABLE BY: Megalosaurus, Quetzal, Wyvern, Tusoteuthis, Pteranodon, Tapejara

EGG SIZE: –

USEFUL TRAPS: Bola, Large Bear Trap

TAMING METHOD:
Can't be tamed; in the case of dead Enforcers, however, construction plans can be found. With those plans, you can build your own new Enforcers at City Terminals.

FUEL: Requires Element as fuel.

SUITABLE FOOD FOR TAMING:
Ð Can't be tamed.

Equus

Basic Stats:

Health	240	Food	1500	Speed (Land)	450
Stamina	560	Weight	350	Speed (Water)	600
Oxygen	150	Melee Damage	9	Torpidity	420

Habitat: Rivers, Open terrain **Type:** Mammal
Damages: Thatch **Diet:** Herbivore
Behavior: loyal **Names:** –

Attack 1: Melee
Attack 2: Buck Kick
Attack 3: Whinny

Specifics:
- In order to tame an Equus, you have to feed and immediately ride it. When breaking it, you have to feed the Equus frequently in order to calm it down. We recommend wearing ghillie armor when approaching the creature.
- Can be mounted with and without a saddle.
- There's also another variant called Unicorn. In that case, the Equus is white and has a horn on its head. On the Island, there can only be one wild Unicorn at any given time.

Utility:
- The second attack is suitable for knocking out other creatures.
- Its saddle can also be used as a Mortar and Pestle.
- Due to its high stamina and movement speed, an Equus is a perfect mount.

Drops	Harvests	Breeding	
Raw Meat	–	Type	Pregnancy
Hide		Gestation	13h:14m
Pelt		Maturation	57h:52m

THE ISLAND   SC. EARTH
~~ABERRATION~~   EXTINCTION
GENESIS I   RAGNAROK
THE CENTER   VALGUERO

Ridable without a saddle

Level	20
Engram Cost	22
Hide	240
Fiber	160
Wood	85
Stone	80

CHEAT: *summon Equus_Character_BP_C*

CARRYABLE BY: Argentavis, Karkinos, Megalosaurus, Quetzal, Wyvern, Tusoteuthis, Karkinos

EGG SIZE: –

USEFUL TRAPS: Bola, Bear Trap, Large Bear Trap, Plant Species Y Trap

TAMING METHOD:
Can be tamed by feeding.

SUITABLE FOOD FOR TAMING:
- Simple Kibble
- Rockarrot
- Crops
- Sweet Vegetable Cake
- Mejoberries
- Berries

Ferox (Small)

Basic Stats:

Health	55	Food	450	Speed (Land)	156
Stamina	100	Weight	55	Speed (Water)	150
Oxygen	150	Melee Damage	6	Torpidity	30

Habitat: Snowy Mountains
Damages: -
Behavior: Cowardly
Type: Fantasy Creature
Diet: Herbivore
Names: Shapeshifter

Attack 1: -
Attack 2: -
Attack 3: -

Specifics:
- Can be carried on the shoulder.
- Transforms into a huge monster by feeding it Element.
- Approaches the player in a curious manner.
- Gets addicted to Element and requires increasing amounts in order to change.

Utility:
- In its small form, it's a cute companion on your shoulder.
- Provides hypothermic as well as hyperthermic insulation when carrying it on your shoulder in its small form and also when riding on the large version.

Drops	Harvests	Breeding	
Raw Meat	-	Type	Pregnancy
		Gestation	9h:55m
		Maturation	92h:34m

~~THE ISLAND~~ ~~SC-EARTH~~
~~ABERRATION~~ ~~EXTINCTION~~
GENESIS I ~~RAGNAROK~~
~~THE CENTER~~ ~~VALGUERO~~

CHEAT: summon Shapeshifter_Small_Character_BP_C

CARRYABLE BY: Kaprosuchus, Megalosaurus, Tapejara, Pteranodon, Argentavis, Quetzal, Griffin, Wyvern, Tusoteuthis

EGG SIZE: –

USEFUL TRAPS: Bola, Bear Trap, Large Bear Trap, Plant Species Y Trap

TAMING METHOD:
Can be tamed by feeding Element.

Feed the small wild Ferox with Element. Consequently, it transforms into its monster version and starts chasing you. Run away or remove yourself from harm's way by using a Crossbow's Zip-line Anchor, for example. Wait until the Ferox has changed back. Then, feed it again and repeat the process until it's tamed. You can buy Element at HLN-A's shop at any time and therefore tame a Ferox even early in the game.

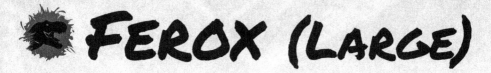

Ferox (Large)

Basic Stats:

Health	1100	Food	1200	Speed (Land)	540
Stamina	1000	Weight	350	Speed (Water)	270
Oxygen	150	Melee Damage	46	Torpidity	180

Habitat: Snowy Mountains
Damages: Thatch, Wood
Behavior: Highly Aggressive
Type: Fantasy Creature
Diet: Herbivore
Names: Shapeshifter

Attack 1: Melee, Paw Swipe
Attack 2: Ranged Attack, Stone Throw
Attack 3: -

Specifics:
- You can feed the Ferox Element to avoid it from changing back.
- In its large form, it can't be placed in a Cryopod.

Utility:
- A very good mount. It can climb, jump over long distances, and even swim a bit. Since it's an animal on top of the food chain, it's ignored by a lot of creatures.
- It's attacks are very intense.

Drops	Harvests	Breeding	
Raw Meat		Type	Pregnancy
		Gestation	
		Maturation	

Cheat: summon Shapeshifter_Small_Character_BP_C

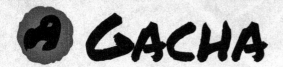
Gacha

Basic Stats:

Health	750	Food	3000	Speed (Land)	300
Stamina	325	Weight	550	Speed (Water)	200
Oxygen	150	Melee Damage	32	Torpidity	600

Habitat: Northwest (Extinction)
Damages: Thatch, Wood, Adobe, Stone
Behavior: Docile

Type: Fantasy Creature
Diet: Carnivore
Names: –

Attack 1: Bite
Attack 2: Melee
Attack 3: –

Specifics:
- Eats almost everything.
- The Crystals on its back contain valuable resources.
- Tamed Gachas can only be reared with at most one other Gacha of the opposite sex; otherwise, they get unhappy.

Utility:
- Tamed Gachas craft resources. In their menu, you can set what type of resources they should produce. Every Gacha can craft resources; even the ones from other add-ons.
- Increase its crafting skill in order to gain more resources.
- Feed it Snow Owl Pellets to buff up its crafting skills.

Drops	Harvests	Breeding	
Raw Meat	Put resources into its inventory and wait until the Crystals drop off its back.	Type	Pregnancy
Raw Prime Fish		Gestation	7h:56m
Hide		Maturation	115h:44m
Stone			

~~THE ISLAND~~   ~~SC. EARTH~~
~~ABERRATION~~   EXTINCTION
~~GENESIS I~~   ~~RAGNAROK~~
~~THE CENTER~~   ~~VALGUERO~~

Level	38
Engram Cost	6
Hide	350
Fiber	185
Chitin/Keratin	150

CHEAT: summon Gacha_Character_BP_C
CARRYABLE BY: Quetzal
EGG SIZE: –

USEFUL TRAPS: Chain Bola, Large Bear Trap

TAMING METHOD:
Can be tamed by active feeding. Wait until the Gacha stops and feed it by placing food in front of its head.

SUITABLE FOOD FOR TAMING:
- Snow Owl Pellets
- TEK or Metal Structures
- Stone or Wood Structures
- Metal tools or Thatch Structures
- Stone
- Berries

Gallimimus

Basic Stats:

Health	150	Food	1000	Speed (Land)	1100
Stamina	300	Weight	270	Speed (Water)	600
Oxygen	150	Melee Damage	8	Torpidity	420

Habitat: Beaches, Rivers, Forests
Damages: Thatch, Wood
Behavior: Skittish

Type: Dinosaur
Diet: Herbivore
Names: -

Attack 1: Melee Bite
Attack 2: -
Attack 3: -

Specifics:
- The taming process can take very long since the Gallimimus flees as soon as it sees the player. We recommend using a Bola.
- Runs away very fast as soon as it's injured.

Utility:
- One of the fastest mounts of the game.
- Can carry two other people in addition to the rider.

Drops	Harvests	Breeding	
Raw Meat	-	Type	Egg
Hide		Egg Temp.	24°-28°
		Incubation	1h:25m
		Maturation	26h:27m

THE ISLAND	SC. EARTH
ABERRATION	EXTINCTION
GENESIS I	RAGNAROK
THE CENTER	VALGUERO

Level	29
Engram Cost	20
Hide	240
Fiber	160
Metal Ingots	25
Wood	120

CHEAT: *summon Galli_Character_BP_C*
CARRYABLE BY: Tusoteuthis
EGG SIZE: Small

USEFUL TRAPS: Bola, Bear Trap, Large Bear Trap, Plant Species Y Trap

TAMING METHOD:
Knockout

SUITABLE FOOD FOR TAMING:
- Simple Kibble
- Crops
- Mejoberries
- Berries

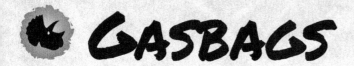

GASBAGS

BASIC STATS:

Health	650	Food	3500	Speed (Land)	490
Stamina	600	Weight	3000	Speed (Water)	300
Oxygen	1000	Melee Damage	5	Torpidity	450

HABITAT: Wasteland (Extinction)   **TYPE:** Fantasy Creature
DAMAGES: Thatch, Wood   **DIET:** Carnivore
BEHAVIOR: Passive   **NAMES:** –

ATTACK 1: Melee
ATTACK 2: Inhale (keep it pressed)
ATTACK 3: Exhale Attack (doesn't work with large opponents)

SPECIFICS:
- Can blow up like a balloon and float away with the aid of jets. These jets are also used during battles to blow the enemy away.
- When inflated, their melee damage decreases to 80%.

UTILITY:
- Due to its tremendous loading capacity and its ability to float, it ranks as the best transport creature in Extinction.
- When floating, you should always make sure that there's a remaining amount of air for slowing down the speed on landing. Otherwise, the Gasbag suffers melee damage.

DROPS	HARVESTS	BREEDING	
Raw Meat	–	Type	Pregnancy
Hide		Gestation	7h:56m
		Maturation	92h:35m

~~THE ISLAND~~   ~~SC. EARTH~~
~~ABERRATION~~   **EXTINCTION**
GENESIS I   ~~RAGNAROK~~
~~THE CENTER~~   ~~VALGUERO~~

Level	43
Engram Cost	6
Hide	350
Fiber	185
Chitin/Keratin	150

Ridable without a saddle

CHEAT: *summon GasBags_Character_BP_C*
CARRYABLE BY: Quetzal, Wyvern
EGG SIZE: –

USEFUL TRAPS: Chain Bola, Large Bear Trap

TAMING METHOD:
Knockout

SUITABLE FOOD FOR TAMING:
- Superior Kibble
- Mejoberries
- Berries
- Crops

GIGANOTOSAURUS

Basic Stats:

Health	80000	Food	4000	Speed (Land)	1500
Stamina	400	Weight	700	Speed (Water)	625
Oxygen	150	Melee Damage	1000	Torpidity	10000

Habitat:	Mountainous/Barren regions	**Type:**	Dinosaur
Damages:	Thatch, Wood, Adobe, Stone	**Diet:**	Carnivore
Behavior:	Highly Aggressive	**Names:**	Gigant/Giga

Attack 1: Bite/Harvests
Attack 2: Roar
Attack 3: Tearing

Specifics:
- A Giganotosaurus enters rage mode when it gets injured. When this is the case, it even throws off the rider and attacks him as well.

Utility:
- Due to its movement speed, torpor, and health, this dinosaur is a mount that can cause a lot of melee damage. It's the largest and strongest Meat collector and a good fighter with good loading capacity.
- Largest predatory dinosaur; therefore, many consider it a "must-have" regarding tames. Warning: tamed Gigas have lower values than wild Gigas.
- One of few creatures that is able to destroy stone structures. Therefore, this dino is of great use when attacking a fort.

Drops	Harvests		Breeding	
Raw Prime Fish	Raw Prime Fish	■■■	Type	Egg
Raw Meat	Raw Meat	■■■	Egg Temp.	43°-44°
Hide	Hide	■■■	Incubation	49h:59m
Giganotosaurus' Heart	Chitin, Keratin	■■	Maturation	280h:35m

THE ISLAND ~~SC. EARTH~~
~~ABERRATION~~ EXTINCTION
~~GENESIS I~~ RAGNAROK
THE CENTER VALGUERO

Level	96
Engram Cost	75
Hide	680
Fiber	350
Metal Ingots	120

CHEAT: *summon Gigant_Character_BP_C*
CARRYABLE BY: –
EGG SIZE: Very Large

USEFUL TRAPS: Large Bear Trap

TAMING METHOD:
Knockout

SUITABLE FOOD FOR TAMING:
- Exceptional Kibble
- Raw Mutton
- Cooked Lamb Chop
- Raw Prime Fish
- Cooked Prime Meat
- Raw Prime Fish Meat
- Raw Meat
- Cooked Prime Fish Meat
- Cooked Meat
- Raw Fish
- Cooked Fish Meat

GIGANTOPITHECUS

Basic Stats:

Health	640	Food	1500	Speed (Land)	195
Stamina	300	Weight	220	Speed (Water)	300
Oxygen	150	Melee Damage	40	Torpidity	1100

Habitat:	Forests	Type:	Mammal
Damages:	Thatch, Wood	Diet:	Herbivore
Behavior:	Aggressive	Names:	-

Attack 1: Melee
Attack 2: Throw Player
Attack 3: -

Specifics:
- The Yeti variant spawns in ice caves. It can't be tamed, though. They're very aggressive as well.

Utility:
- The second attack can be used to get over walls (Gigantopithecus throws the player that's riding on it).
- Gigantopithecus collects Fiber automatically when it's set to "wandering around".
- Good Berry and Fiber collector; especially because a saddle is unnecessary.

Drops
Raw Meat
Hide

Harvests
Fiber	■■■
Berries	■■■
Thatch	■■
Wood	■■

Breeding
Type	Pregnancy
Gestation	6h:36m
Maturation	77h:10m

~~THE ISLAND~~   ~~SE. EARTH~~
~~ABERRATION~~   ~~EXTINCTION~~
GENESIS I   RAGNAROK
THE CENTER   VALGUERO

Ridable without a saddle

Can wear hats

CHEAT: *summon Bigfoot_Character_BP_C*

CARRYABLE BY: Argentavis, Karkinos, Megalosaurus, Quetzal, Wyvern, Tusoteuthis

EGG SIZE: -

USEFUL TRAPS: Chain Bola, Bear Trap, Large Bear Trap, Plant Species Y Trap

TAMING METHOD:
Can be tamed by feeding.

SUITABLE FOOD FOR TAMING:
- Regular Kibble
- Crops
- Mejoberries
- Berries

GLOWTAIL

Basic Stats:

Health	115	Food	450	Speed (Land)	60
Stamina	100	Weight	70	Speed (Water)	300
Oxygen	200	Melee Damage	12	Torpidity	60

Habitat: Caves (Aberration)
Damages: Thatch
Behavior: Cowardly
Type: Fantasy Creature
Diet: Unknown
Names: -

Attack 1: Melee
Attack 2: Projectile
Attack 3: -

Specifics:
- Is a preferred food for a lot of animals.
- Can't be fed when it's in the water.

Utility:
- Its light provides protection against attacks from the Nameless.
- Since it flees when it gets attacked, never start an attack with it.

Drops	Harvests	Breeding	
Raw Prime Fish	-	Type	Egg
Raw Meat		Egg Temp.	30°-34°
Hide		Incubation	2h:30m
		Maturation	48h:44m

~~THE ISLAND~~   ~~SE EARTH~~
ABERRATION   ~~EXTINCTION~~
~~GENESIS I~~   ~~RAGNAROK~~
~~THE CENTER~~   **VALGUERO**

CHEAT: *summon LanternLizard_Character_BP_C*

CARRYABLE BY: Gigantopithecus, Karkinos, Procoptodon, Pteranodon, Quetzal, Tapejara

EGG SIZE: Small

USEFUL TRAPS: Bola, Bear Trap, Plant Species Y Trap

TAMING METHOD:
Can be tamed by active feeding.

SUITABLE FOOD FOR TAMING:
- Plant Species Z Seeds
- Ascerbic Mushroom
- Amarberry Seeds
- Citronal Seeds

 Hyaenodon

Basic Stats:

Health	175	Food	1200	Speed (Land)	140
Stamina	260	Weight	170	Speed (Water)	300
Oxygen	150	Melee Damage	15	Torpidity	450

Habitat: Redwoods, Western Coast, Hills
Damages: Thatch, Wood
Behavior: Highly Aggressive
Type: Mammal
Diet: Carnivore
Names: –

Attack 1: Melee Bite
Attack 2: Claw
Attack 3: Roar

Specifics:
- Usually shows up in packs (bonus points for the pack leader; it's surrounded by a yellow/orange glowing light).

Utility:
- Can't be ridden. Meat stored in its pack saddle lasts twice as long than in other creatures and only weighs half as much.
- Thanks to their bonus, a mixed pack of high-leveled male and female Hyaenodons are a strong battle troop.
- Similar to a pack of wolves, they're good companions for cave exploration.

Drops	Harvests		Breeding	
Raw Meat	Hide	■■■	Type	Pregnancy
Raw Prime Fish	Raw Meat	■■■	Gestation	3h:58m
Hide	Raw Fish Meat	■■	Maturation	46h:18m
Keratin	Pelt	■■		

THE ISLAND   SC. EARTH
~~ABERRATION~~   EXTINCTION
~~GENESIS I~~   RAGNAROK
THE CENTER   VALGUERO

Only pack saddle	
Level	19
Engram Cost	14
Hide	290
Fiber	155
Metal Ingots	20

CHEAT: *summon Hyaenodon_Character_BP_C*

CARRYABLE BY: Kaprosuchus, Megalosaurus, Pteranodon, Argentavis, Quetzal, Griffin, Wyvern, Tusoteuthis, Karkinos

EGG SIZE: –

USEFUL TRAPS: Bola, Large Bear Trap, Plant Species Y Trap

TAMING METHOD:
Can be tamed by petting.

SUITABLE FOOD FOR TAMING:
None; taming by petting (use).

To tame a Hyaenodon, creep up on it from behind. We recommend using ghillie armor to increase your camouflage effect. Creep up as close as you can and press the "use" button as soon as it is requested. You have to pet it about every 30 seconds.

Take care of all the hazards in your area first or lure it to a safe, fenced-in area. Petting only works if the Hyaenodon is far enough away from the pack leader.

IGUANODON

Basic Stats:

Health	250	Food	1800	Speed (Land)	250
Stamina	200	Weight	375	Speed (Water)	450
Oxygen	150	Melee Damage	25	Torpidity	210

Habitat: Forest/Jungle regions
Damages: Thatch, Wood
Behavior: Passive
Type: Dinosaur
Diet: Herbivore
Names: –

Attack 1: Bite/Harvests
Attack 2: Change Stance (changing from walking on two to four legs)
Attack 3: Roar

Specifics:
- A pack animal and, therefore, defends its fellows from getting harmed as soon as they're attacked.
- When walking on four legs, the Iguanodon doesn't use any stamina.

Utility:
- Turns Berries into Seeds. Therefore, the player can grow plants on their own in order to collect (rare) Berries more quickly.
- When using a Bola, it's easy to tame; even at the beginning of the game.
- A very good mount and pack animal, especially because it doesn't require any stamina when walking on four legs.

Drops
- Raw Meat
- Hide

Harvests
Bio Toxin (Mushrooms)	■■■
Berries	■■
Thatch	■■
Wood	■

Breeding
Type	Egg
Egg Temp.	24°-28°
Incubation	1h:26m
Maturation	46h:18m

THE ISLAND   SC. EARTH
~~ABERRATION~~   EXTINCTION
GENESIS I   RAGNAROK
THE CENTER   VALGUERO

Level	30
Engram Cost	12
Hide	80
Fiber	50
Wood	15

CHEAT: *summon Iguanodon_Character_BP_C*

CARRYABLE BY: Argentavis, Megalosaurus, Quetzal, Karkinos, Wyvern, Tusoteuthis

EGG SIZE: Medium

USEFUL TRAPS: Bola, Bear Trap, Large Bear Trap, Plant Species Y Trap

TAMING METHOD:
Knockout

SUITABLE FOOD FOR TAMING:
- Simple Kibble
- Crops
- Mejoberries
- Berries
- Sweet Vegetable Cake

JERBOA

Basic Stats:

Health	55	Food	450	Speed (Land)	156
Stamina	100	Weight	55	Speed (Water)	300
Oxygen	150	Melee Damage	3	Torpidity	30

HABITAT: Scorched Earth
DAMAGES: Thatch
BEHAVIOR: Cowardly
TYPE: Mammal
DIET: Herbivore
NAMES: -

ATTACK 1: Melee
ATTACK 2: -
ATTACK 3: -

Specifics:
- As a tame, it can be carried on the shoulder and equipped it with hats.
- Runs away very quickly as soon as it gets into danger and never attacks.
- Cute pet.

Utility:
- Can warn the player against imminent rain, sand storms, electrical storms, and heat waves.
- Easily and quickly accessible source of Meat and Hide.

Drops	Harvests	Breeding	
Raw Meat	-	Type	Pregnancy
Hide		Gestation	2h:38m
		Maturation	30h:52m

~~THE ISLAND~~ SC. EARTH
~~ABERRATION~~ ~~EXTINCTION~~
~~GENESIS I~~ RAGNAROK
~~THE CENTER~~ VALGUERO

Can wear hats

CHEAT: *summon Jerboa_Character_BP_C*

CARRYABLE BY: Kaprosuchus, Megalosaurus, Tapejara, Pteranodon, Argentavis, Quetzal, Griffin, Gigantopithecus, Wyvern, Karkinos, Tusoteuthis, Megalosaurus, Procoptodon

EGG SIZE: –

USEFUL TRAPS: Bola, Bear Trap, Plant Species Y Trap

TAMING METHOD:
Knockout

SUITABLE FOOD FOR TAMING:
- Plant Species Y Seed
- Crops
- Mejoberries
- Berries

Kairuku

Basic Stats:

Health	95	Food	900	Speed (Land)	70
Stamina	200	Weight	70	Speed (Water)	450
Oxygen	∞	Melee Damage	8	Torpidity	300

Habitat: Snowy areas, Ice islands
Damages: Thatch
Behavior: Cowardly

Type: Birds
Diet: Piscivore
Names: -

Attack 1: Melee Picking
Attack 2: -
Attack 3: -

Specifics:
- In snowy areas where Kairukus live, we recommend wearing warm clothing to avoid suffering melee damage.
- Never attacks. When attacked, it flees.

Utility:
- Because of their peaceful behavior and low health level, Kairukus can be defeated very easily.
- Source for Organic Polymer.
- By using a Wooden Club, you can increase the amount of Organic Polymer dropped.

Drops
Raw Meat
Hide
Organic Polymer

Harvests
-

Breeding
Type	Egg
Egg Temp.	22°-30°
Incubation	1h:30m
Maturation	28h:4m

~~THE ISLAND~~ ~~SE. EARTH~~
~~ABERRATION~~ EXTINCTION
GENESIS I RAGNAROK
THE CENTER VALGUERO

Can wear hats

CHEAT: summon Kairuku_Character_BP_C

CARRYABLE BY: Kaprosuchus, Megalosaurus, Tapejara, Pteranodon, Argentavis, Quetzal, Griffin, Wyvern, Tusoteuthis, Karkinos

EGG SIZE: Very Small

USEFUL TRAPS: Bola, Bear Trap, Plant Species Y Trap

TAMING METHOD:
Knockout

SUITABLE FOOD FOR TAMING:
- Basic Kibble
- Raw Mutton
- Cooked Lamb Chop
- Raw Prime Fish
- Cooked Prime Meat
- Raw Prime Fish Meat
- Raw Meat
- Cooked Prime Fish Meat
- Cooked Meat
- Raw Fish Meat
- Cooked Fish Meat

KAPROSUCHUS

BASIC STATS:

Health	200	Food	1200	Speed (Land)	180
Stamina	350	Weight	140	Speed (Water)	220
Oxygen	150	Melee Damage	25	Torpidity	200

HABITAT: Swamps
DAMAGES: Thatch, Wood
BEHAVIOR: Highly Aggressive
TYPE: Reptile
DIET: Carnivore
NAMES: Kapro/Gator

ATTACK 1: Melee; Bite
ATTACK 2: Leap
ATTACK 3: Grab

SPECIFICS:
- Difficult to recognize between the trees in the swamps.
- We recommend using strong weapons (e.g. swords or pistols). Use Bolas for catching, stunning, and taming.
- Captures opponents with its Bite attack and carries them around. Can take riders off their mounts.

UTILITY:
- Able to carry a lot of creatures using its Bite attack (carrying weight of up to 100).
- Can leap very far; fast movement speed on land and in water.

DROPS	HARVESTS		BREEDING	
Raw Meat	Raw Prime Fish Meat	■■■	Type	Egg
Hide	Raw Meat	■	Egg Temp.	29°-35°
	Hide	■	Incubation	2h
			Maturation	37h:2m

THE ISLAND   SC. EARTH
~~ABERRATION~~   EXTINCTION
GENESIS I   RAGNAROK
THE CENTER   VALGUERO

Level	39
Engram Cost	28
Hide	165
Fiber	120
Chitin/Keratin	65

CHEAT: *summon Kaprosuchus_Character_BP_C*
CARRYABLE BY: Tusoteuthis
EGG SIZE: Medium

USEFUL TRAPS: Bola, Bear Trap, Large Bear Trap, Plant Species Y Trap

TAMING METHOD:
Knockout

SUITABLE FOOD FOR TAMING:
- Regular Kibble
- Raw Mutton
- Cooked Lamb Chop
- Raw Prime Fish
- Cooked Prime Meat
- Raw Prime Fish Meat
- Raw Meat
- Cooked Prime Fish Meat
- Cooked Meat
- Raw Fish Meat
- Cooked Fish Meat

Karkinos

Basic Stats:

Health	1200	Food	5000	Speed (Land)	300
Stamina	600	Weight	800	Speed (Water)	300
Oxygen	∞	Melee Damage	32	Torpidity	800

Habitat: Bodies of water, Rivers in caves
Damages: -
Behavior: Highly Aggressive
Type: Fantasy Creature
Diet: Carnivore
Names: -

Attack 1: Melee (left scissors)
Attack 2: Melee (right scissors)
Attack 3: -

Specifics:
- This aquatic creature can pose a danger when you're fishing. Its attack can pull the player underwater and cause him to drown.
- Can immobilize the player. Therefore, positions behind it or below its belly are recommended.
- Narcotics don't work here. Instead, you have to use a Catapult or Cannon.

Utility:
- Good fighting mount for attacking medium-sized creatures.
- Once killed, it provides a lot of Chitin and Organic Polymer.
- Can carry creatures in its claws and has a great loading capacity. The so-called heavy cargo carrier of Aberration.

Drops	Harvests		Breeding
Raw Meat	Raw Meat	■■■	Not breedable
Chitin			
Organic Polymer			
Raw Prime Fish			

~~THE ISLAND~~   ~~SC. EARTH~~
ABERRATION ~~EXTINCTION~~
GENESIS I   ~~RAGNAROK~~
~~THE CENTER~~ **VALGUERO**

Level	65
Engram Cost	28
Hide	170
Fiber	225
Blue Gem	80
Fungal Wood	200

CHEAT: *summon Crab_Character_BP_C*

CARRYABLE BY: Quetzal

EGG SIZE: ???

USEFUL TRAPS: Chain Bola, Large Bear Trap

TAMING METHOD:
Can be tamed by active feeding.

SUITABLE FOOD FOR TAMING:
- Exceptional Kibble
- Spoiled Meat
- Raw Meat
- Raw Fish Meat

Kentrosaurus

Basic Stats:

Health	650	Food	6000	Speed (Land)	150
Stamina	300	Weight	500	Speed (Water)	300
Oxygen	150	Melee Damage	10	Torpidity	500

Habitat: Mountainous areas, West Coast
Damages: Thatch, Wood
Behavior: Aggressive

Type: Dinosaur
Diet: Herbivore
Names: -

Attack 1: Bite
Attack 2: Tail Attack
Attack 3: -

Specifics:
- Can impale enemies on its spikes and carry them around. In addition, the spikes cause bleeding wounds.
- Reflects melee damage; we recommend attacking it from a far distance.
- Be careful when you're attacking with dinos that cause high melee damage since it gets reflected back to the player sometimes. Especially in the case of Giganotos, this can be very dangerous (high melee damage and chance to make it furious).

Utility:
- Its spikes have a similar effect to a wall made of spines. For this reason, they're very suitable as "guard dinos" for bases.

Drops	Harvests		Breeding	
Raw Meat	Berries	■■	Type	Egg
Hide	Thatch	■	Egg Temp.	24°-30°
Keratin			Incubation	2h:47m
			Maturation	51h:26m

THE ISLAND	SC. EARTH
~~ABERRATION~~	EXTINCTION
GENESIS I	RAGNAROK
THE CENTER	VALGUERO

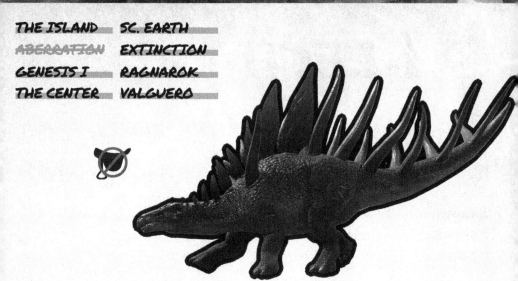

CHEAT: summon Kentro_Character_BP_C

CARRYABLE BY: Tusoteuthis, Wyvern, Quetzal, Karkinos

EGG SIZE: Medium

USEFUL TRAPS: Chain Bola, Bear Trap, Large Bear Trap, Plant Species Y Trap

TAMING METHOD:
Knockout

SUITABLE FOOD FOR TAMING:
- Regular Kibble
- Crops
- Sweet Vegetable Cake
- Mejoberries
- Berries

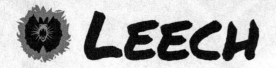
Leech

Basic Stats:

Health	40	Food	450	Speed (Land)	50
Stamina	100	Weight	10	Speed (Water)	70
Oxygen	∞	Melee Damage	7	Torpidity	50

Habitat: Swamps
Damages: Thatch
Behavior: Passive /Aggressive

Type: Invertebrate
Diet: Sanguivore
Names: –

Attack 1: Melee; Bite
Attack 2: –
Attack 3: –

Specifics:
- One variant of the Leech is the Infected Leech. This species transmits Swamp Fever (can be healed with Lesser Antidote).
- When using Bug Repellant, you can even touch Leeches without any danger. However, if you start an attack, it will fight back despite Bug Repellant.
- If attached to the player's skin, they can only be removed by quickly jumping into fire (e.g. Campfires, Cooking Pot).

Utility:
- You can send a Dodo that's infected with Swamp Fever to the enemy's camp (beside humans, it's the only creature that can catch the Swamp Fever).

Drops	Harvests	Breeding
Raw Meat	–	Not breedable
Chitin		
Leech Blood		
Oil		
Silica Pearls		

THE ISLAND ~~SC. EARTH~~
~~ABERRATION~~ ~~EXTINCTION~~
GENESIS I **RAGNAROK**
THE CENTER **VALGUERO**

CHEAT: summon Leech_Character_C

CARRYABLE BY: Kaprosuchus, Megalosaurus, Tusoteuthis

EGG SIZE: –

USEFUL TRAPS: –

TAMING METHOD:
Can't be tamed.

SUITABLE FOOD FOR TAMING:
Ð None since it can't be tamed.

LYSTROSAURUS

Basic Stats:

Health	90	Food	500	Speed (Land)	60
Stamina	100	Weight	90	Speed (Water)	120
Oxygen	215	Melee Damage	6	Torpidity	100

Habitat: Open areas, Sparse forests, Beaches
Damages: Thatch
Behavior: Cowardly
Type: Synapsid
Diet: Herbivore
Names: -

Attack 1: Melee; Bite
Attack 2: -
Attack 3: -

Specifics:
- When attacked, it immediately flees. Nevertheless, it can be defeated easily since its movement speed is very slow.

Utility:
- Since it's very easy to kill, it's a good source for Meat and Hide. However, it's difficult to detect due to its small size and silent movement.
- Once you've tamed it, you can cuddle it. In doing so, nearby players gain experience.

Drops	Harvests	Breeding	
Raw Meat	-	Type	Egg
Hide		Egg Temp.	24°-28°
		Incubation	49m
		Maturation	15h:26m

THE ISLAND | SC. EARTH
~~ABERRATION~~ | EXTINCTION
GENESIS I | RAGNAROK
THE CENTER | VALGUERO

CHEAT: *summon Lystro_Character_BP_C*

CARRYABLE BY: Kaprosuchus, Megalosaurus, Tapejara, Pteranodon, Argentavis, Quetzal, Wyvern, Tusoteuthis, Griffin

EGG SIZE: Very Small

USEFUL TRAPS: Bola, Bear Trap, Plant Species Y Trap

TAMING METHOD:
Can be tamed by feeding.

SUITABLE FOOD FOR TAMING:
- Rare Flower
- Mejoberries
- Berries

MAGMASAUR

Basic Stats:

Health	3000	Food	2000	Speed (Land)	300
Stamina	500	Weight	550	Speed (Water)	150
Oxygen	200	Melee Damage	120	Torpidity	725

Habitat: Volcanic biome
Damages: Thatch, Wood
Behavior: Highly Aggressive

Type: Fantasy Creature
Diet: Carnivore
Names: Cherufe

Attack 1: Melee; Bite
Attack 2: Fire Breathing
Attack 3:

Specifics:
- Very well protected against heat and fire but weak against cold and water.
- Protects its rider against fire, heat, and volcanic eruptions.

Utility:
- In the Magmasaur's inventory, Ambergris weighs half as much and the weight of Metal even reduces to a third.
- Very suitable for fighting Elementals and Golems since their melee damage isn't reduced when doing so.
- Mobile Campfire and Forge: just like a Phoenix, the Magmasaur can melt Metal as well as cook Meat.

Drops
Raw Meat
Raw Prime Fish
Sulfur

Harvests
Stone, Metal	■■■
Raw Prime Fish	■■■
Wood, Obsidian	■■■
Raw Meat	■■
Chitin, Thatch, hide	■■

Breeding
Type	Egg
Egg Temp.	90°-110°
Incubation	5h
Maturation	200h

~~THE ISLAND~~   ~~SE. EARTH~~
~~ABERRATION~~   ~~EXTINCTION~~
GENESIS I   ~~RAGNAROK~~
~~THE CENTER~~   ~~VALGUERO~~

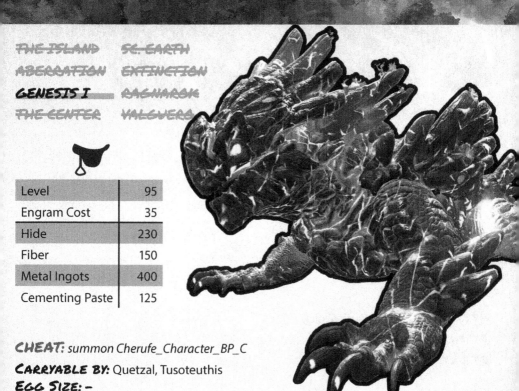

Level	95
Engram Cost	35
Hide	230
Fiber	150
Metal Ingots	400
Cementing Paste	125

CHEAT: summon Cherufe_Character_BP_C

CARRYABLE BY: Quetzal, Tusoteuthis

EGG SIZE: -

USEFUL TRAPS: Chain Bola, Large Bear Trap

TAMING METHOD:
Can be tamed by raising.

In order to get a Magmasaur, you have to steal a Magmasaur's egg and already be in possession of two other Magmasaurs to let them incubate the egg in a lava puddle. Eggs can be found inside a volcano in a lava puddle. Baby Magmasaurs exclusively feed on Ambergris. You can only find it in the moon region of Genesis by harvesting the glowing green stones as well as in the inventory of an Astrocetus.

MAMMOTH

BASIC STATS:

Health	850	Food	5000	Speed (Land)	150
Stamina	330	Weight	500	Speed (Water)	300
Oxygen	150	Melee Damage	48	Torpidity	550

HABITAT: Snow biome
DAMAGES: Thatch, Wood
BEHAVIOR: Passive

TYPE: Mammal
DIET: Herbivore
NAMES: Woolly Mammoth

ATTACK 1: Melee Tusk Attack
ATTACK 2: Stomp
ATTACK 3: -

SPECIFICS:
- Even though Mammoths appear to be easy prey (slow movement speed), you should be careful since Mammoths are pack animals. If you try to go at it with one of them, you have to fight every other pack animal as well.
- Escaping is not very difficult, however. It will stop chasing you after a short distance and won't attack you anymore.

UTILITY:
- Useful for transporting resources (it can carry a lot and is quite fast in regard to its size).
- A very good Wood collector. Wood weighs less than normal in its inventory. In combination with a high loading capacity, it's a good resource collector in the icy north.

DROPS	HARVESTS		BREEDING	
Raw Meat	Wood	■■■	Type	Pregnancy
Raw Prime Fish	Rare Mushrooms	■■■	Gestation	7h:56m
Keratin	Berries	■■■	Maturation	82h:18m
Hide	Rare Flower	■■		
Pelt	Thatch	■		

THE ISLAND ~~SC. EARTH~~
~~ABERRATION~~ EXTINCTION
GENESIS I RAGNAROK
THE CENTER VALGUERO

Level	31
Engram Cost	18
Hide	260
Fiber	140
Metal Ingots	10

CHEAT: *summon Mammoth_Character_BP_C*

CARRYABLE BY: Quetzal, Tusoteuthis

EGG SIZE: –

USEFUL TRAPS: Chain Bola, Large Bear Trap

TAMING METHOD:
Knockout

SUITABLE FOOD FOR TAMING:
- Superior Kibble
- Crops
- Mejoberries
- Berries

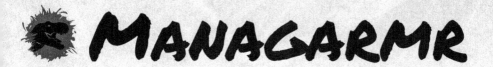

MANAGARMR

Basic Stats:

Health	825	Food	2000	Speed (Land)	1250
Stamina	300	Weight	300	Speed (Water)	1050
Oxygen	150	Melee Damage	0	Torpidity	800

Habitat: Extinction
Damages: Thatch, Wood, Stone, Brick
Behavior: Highly Aggressive

Type: Fantasy Creature
Diet: Carnivore
Names: Mana

Attack 1: Melee Bite
Attack 2: Frigid Breath
Attack 3: -

Specifics:
- Has hind feed which enable it to jump in the air multiple times; it can also hover in place there.
- Can slow down enemies as well as freeze them with its Frigid Breath attack.

Utility:
- One of the fastest mounts. It's very good for reconnaissance and long journeys.
- Its Frigid Breath attack makes it very good support during battles. It can freeze annoying enemies.

Drops
Raw Meat
Raw Prime Fish
Keratin
Hide

Harvests
Raw Fish Meat	■■■
Raw Meat	■■
Hide	■■
Raw Prime Fish	■■
Chitin, Keratin	■■

Breeding
Type	Pregnancy
Gestation	3h:58m
Maturation	92h:35m

~~THE ISLAND~~ ~~SE~~ ~~EARTH~~
~~ABERRATION~~ **EXTINCTION**
~~GENESIS I~~ ~~RAGNAROK~~
~~THE CENTER~~ ~~VALGUERO~~

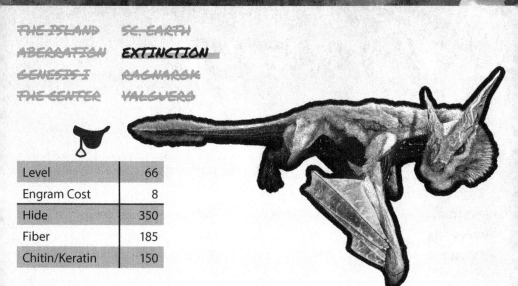

Level	66
Engram Cost	8
Hide	350
Fiber	185
Chitin/Keratin	150

CHEAT: summon IceJumper_Character_BP_C

CARRYABLE BY: –
EGG SIZE: –

USEFUL TRAPS: Chain Bola, Large Bear Trap, Plant Species Y Trap

TAMING METHOD:
Knockout

SUITABLE FOOD FOR TAMING:
- Exceptional Kibble
- Raw Mutton
- Cooked Lamb Chop
- Raw Prime Fish
- Cooked Prime Meat
- Raw Prime Fish Meat
- Cooked Prime Fish Meat
- Raw Meat
- Cooked Meat
- Raw Fish Meat
- Cooked Fish

MANTIS

Basic Stats:

Health	275	Food	900	Speed (Land)	200
Stamina	150	Weight	220	Speed (Water)	175
Oxygen	150	Felee damage	34	Torpidity	350

Habitat: Caves, Dunes, Desert
Damages: Thatch
Behavior: Highly Aggressive
Type: Invertebrate
Diet: Carnivore
Names: -

Attack 1: Bite/Harvests
Attack 2: Leap
Attack 3: -

Specifics:
- Attacks as soon as someone approaches it too closely. Warning: the radius of its attack perimeter is very large and it can jump onto its enemies over long distances.
- You can also equip the Mantis with different items.

Utility:
- The Mantis can use melee weapons on its own (e.g. swords). Therefore, it's a dangerous fighting animal.
- It's perfect for gathering all kinds of materials. Since it's able to handle various tools, for example, axes, pickaxes, or sickles, it farms different materials very quickly.

Drops	Harvests		Breeding
Chitin	Thatch, Flint	■■■	Not breedable
Organic Polymer	Crystal, hide, Wood	■■	
Raw Meat	Raw Meat	■■	
	Chitin, fiber	■■	
	Metal, Keratin, Obsidian, Stone	■■	
	Org. Polymer, Raw Prime Fish	■	

~~THE ISLAND~~   SC. EARTH
~~ABERRATION~~   EXTINCTION
~~GENESIS I~~   RAGNAROK
~~THE CENTER~~   VALGUERO

Level	45
Engram Cost	18
Hide	120
Fiber	75
Metal Ingots	35

CHEAT: *summon Mantis_Character_BP_C*

CARRYABLE BY: Quetzal, Wyvern, Tusoteuthis, Karkinos

EGG SIZE: Large

USEFUL TRAPS: Chain Bola, Bear Trap, Plant Species Y Trap

TAMING METHOD:
Can be tamed by feeding.

SUITABLE FOOD FOR TAMING:
- Deathworm Horn

MEGALANIA

Basic Stats:

Health	480	Food	1500	Speed (Land)	250
Stamina	400	Weight	400	Speed (Water)	300
Oxygen	200	Melee Damage	10	Torpidity	700

Habitat: Caves (primarily)
Damages: Thatch, Wood
Behavior: Highly Aggressive

Type: Reptile
Diet: Carnivore
Names: -

Attack 1: Bite
Attack 2: Claw
Attack 3: -

Specifics:
- Usually spawns on ceilings of caves, therefore, it's quite hard to find.
- Transmit Mega Rabies. An infected person can easily contaminate other players in the proximity (Dodos as well). Mega Rabies can be cured with Antidote.

Utility:
- Good mount for difficult terrain, steep cliffs, and caves, as it can climb up walls and ceilings.
- Use it to infect opponents with Mega Rabies.

Drops	Harvests		Breeding	
Raw Meat	Meat	■■	Type	Egg
Raw Prime Fish	Hide	■	Egg Temp.	29°-35°
Hide			Incubation	2h:00m
Megalania Toxin			Maturation	37h:02m

THE ISLAND   **SC. EARTH**
~~ABERRATION~~   **EXTINCTION**
GENESIS I   **RAGNAROK**
THE CENTER   ~~VALGUERO~~

Level	73
Engram Cost	65
Hide	315
Fiber	215
Metal Ingots	45

CHEAT: *summon Megalania_Character_BP_C*

CARRYABLE BY: Tusoteuthis, Wyvern, Griffin, Quetzal, Argentavis, Megalosaurus, Kaprosuchus, Karkinos, Pteranodon, Tapejara

EGG SIZE: Large

USEFUL TRAPS: Bola, Bear Trap, Plant Species Y Trap

TAMING METHOD:
Knockout

SUITABLE FOOD FOR TAMING:
- Extraordinary Kibble
- Raw Mutton
- Cooked Lamb Chop
- Raw Prime Fish
- Cooked Prime Meat
- Raw Prime Fish Meat
- Raw Meat
- Raw Fish Meat
- Cooked Fish Meat

MEGALOCEROS

BASIC STATS:

Health	300	Food	1200	Speed (Land)	200
Stamina	280	Weight	220	Speed (Water)	300
Oxygen	150	Melee Damage	30	Torpidity	175

HABITAT:	Cold regions	**TYPE:**	Mammal
DAMAGES:	Thatch, Wood	**DIET:**	Herbivore
BEHAVIOR:	Skittish	**NAMES:**	-

ATTACK 1: Melee Bite
ATTACK 2: -
ATTACK 3: -

SPECIFICS:
- The females of this species are one quarter faster than the males.
- There are differences between the males and the females (habitat and skills).

UTILITY:
- Can be used as mount; even in some caves.
- Very suitable for collecting Thatch (only the males with antlers).
- Always keep in mind that tamed female Megaloceros lose their ability to attack as soon as they're wearing a saddle.

DROPS	HARVESTS		BREEDING	
Raw Meat	Thatch	■■■	Type	Pregnancy
Hide	Wood	■	Gestation	6h:6m
Pelt			Maturation	71h:14m
Keratin				

THE ISLAND ~~SE EARTH~~
~~ABERRATION~~ **EXTINCTION**
GENESIS I **RAGNAROK**
THE CENTER **VALGUERO**

Level	30
Engram Cost	20
Hide	200
Fiber	110
Metal Ingots	5

CHEAT: *summon Stag_Character_BP_C*
CARRYABLE BY: Megalosaurus, Argentavis, Quetzal, Wyvern, Tusoteuthis, Karkinos
EGG SIZE: –

USEFUL TRAPS: Bola, Bear Trap, Large Bear Trap, Plant Species Y Trap

TAMING METHOD:
Knockout

SUITABLE FOOD FOR TAMING:
- Simple Kibble
- Crops
- Mejoberries
- Berries

MEGALOSAURUS

Basic Stats:

Health	1025	Food	2000	Speed (Land)	600
Stamina	300	Weight	300	Speed (Water)	300
Oxygen	150	Melee Damage	75	Torpidity	775

Habitat: Caves (primarily)
Damages: Thatch, Wood
Behavior: Highly Aggressive (during the night)

Type: Dinosaur
Diet: Carnivore
Names: -

Attack 1: Bite
Attack 2: Grab
Attack 3: Roar

Specifics:
- Has very different behavior during the day (sleeps if you leave it alone) and during the night (highly aggressive). It wakes up at about 8:30 p.m.
- Better to tame during the day and avoid the alternation of day and night.
- Wakes up when taming it during the alternation of day and night. As a consequence, all the food in its inventory gets lost.
- Warning: as a tame, it isn't able to leave some caves due to its size.

Utility:
- Good nocturnal hunter and a good mount for cave exploration.
- Can carry any creature that weighs 150 or less.

Drops	Harvests		Breeding	
Raw Meat	Raw Meat	■■	Type	Egg
Raw Prime Fish			Egg Temp.	26°-32°
Hide			Incubation	1h:40m
Keratin			Maturation	92h:35m

THE ISLAND   SC. EARTH
~~ABERRATION~~   EXTINCTION
~~GENESIS I~~   RAGNAROK
THE CENTER   ~~VALGUERO~~

Level	57
Engram Cost	50
Hide	320
Fiber	170
Metal Ingots	30

CHEAT: summon Megalosaurus_Character_BP_C

CARRYABLE BY: Tusoteuthis

EGG SIZE: Large

USEFUL TRAPS: Chain Bola, Large Bear Trap, Plant Species Y Trap

TAMING METHOD:
Knockout

SUITABLE FOOD FOR TAMING:
- Superior Kibble
- Raw Mutton
- Cooked Lamb Chop
- Raw Prime Fish
- Cooked Prime Meat
- Raw Prime Fish Meat
- Raw Meat
- Cooked Prime Fish Meat
- Cooked Meat
- Raw Fish Meat
- Cooked Fish Meat

 Mek

Basic Stats:

Health	5500	Food	100	Speed (Air)	1200
Stamina	1000	Weight	1250	Speed (Land)	300
Oxygen	150	Melee Damage	0	Speed (Water)	300
				Torpidity	100

Habitat: Extinction
Damages: Thatch, Wood
Behavior: –

Type: Mechanical Creature
Diet: –
Names: Meki

Attack 1: TEK Sword
Attack 2: TEK Rifle
Attack 3: –

Specifics:
- Meks are robots that can be piloted by the player.
- Meks can be equipped with a shield module (M.D.S.M.), rocket launcher module (M.R.L.M.), or siege cannon module (M.S.C.M.).
- The M.O.M.I module is used with four Meks in order to form a Mega Mek. However, this only works in a boss battle with the Alpha King Titan.

Utility:
- Must be crafted with a TEK replicator.
- Good for fighting Titans. Their add-ons make them very suitable for attacking enemy bases in PvP.

Drops	Harvests		Breeding
Element Dust	Raw Meat	■ ■	Not breedable
Oil	Tribute	■ ■ ■	
Scrap Metal			
Electronics			
Raw Meat			
Hide			

~~THE ISLAND~~ ~~SE. EARTH~~
~~ABERRATION~~ **EXTINCTION**
~~GENESIS I~~ ~~RAGNAROK~~
~~THE CENTER~~ ~~VALGUERO~~

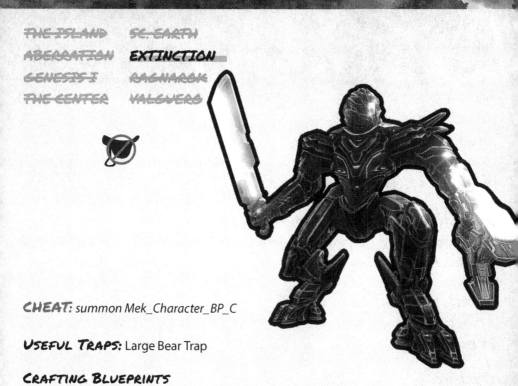

CHEAT: *summon Mek_Character_BP_C*

USEFUL TRAPS: Large Bear Trap

CRAFTING BLUEPRINTS
The Engram for a normal level 51 Mek can be learned from level 91.
You can also find blueprints for high-leveled Meks in Orbital Supply Drops at the bosses.

RESOURCES NEEDED FOR A PRIMITIVE LVL 51 MEK:
- 25 × Black pearl
- 40 × Element
- 225 × Crystal
- 550 × Polymer
- 1000 × Metal Ingots

MEGATHERIUM

BASIC STATS:

Health	740	Food	3000	Speed (Land)	320
Stamina	400	Weight	725	Speed (Water)	300
Oxygen	270	Melee Damage	32	Torpidity	1000

HABITAT: Cold regions, Snow Biome, Redwoods
DAMAGES: Thatch, Wood
BEHAVIOR: Passive

TYPE: Mammal
DIET: Carnivore
NAMES: Giant Sloth

ATTACK 1: Claw or Bite
ATTACK 2: Claw
ATTACK 3: Bite

SPECIFICS:
- Especially strong against insects and obtain a bonus when eating them (they glow red then). Therefore, they're especially good at fighting enemies like Mantis or Deathworms.

UTILITY:
- Suitable for gathering as well as transport. They can gather resources well, have a good loading capacity, and, despite their size, are relatively fast.
- Thanks to its bonus, it's a good hunter for Mantis, Deathworms, and other insects as well.

DROPS	HARVESTS		BREEDING	
Raw Meat	Chitin	■■■	Type	Pregnancy
Raw Prime Fish	Cactus Sap	■■■	Gestation	7h:56m
Hide	Thatch	■■■	Maturation	92h:36m
Pelt	Fiber	■■		
	Berries	■■		
	Hide	■		

THE ISLAND	SC. EARTH
~~ABERRATION~~	EXTINCTION
GENESIS I	RAGNAROK
THE CENTER	VALGUERO

Level	52
Engram Cost	24
Hide	325
Fiber	130
Metal Ingots	55
Cementing Paste	100

CHEAT: *summon Megatherium_Character_BP_C*

CARRYABLE BY: Tusoteuthis, Wyvern, Quezal

EGG SIZE: –

USEFUL TRAPS: Chain Bola, Large Bear Trap

TAMING METHOD:
Knockout

SUITABLE FOOD FOR TAMING:
- Superior Kibble
- Raw Mutton
- Giant Bee Honey
- Cooked Lamb Chop
- Raw Prime Fish
- Cooked Prime Meat
- Raw Meat/Prime Fish Meat
- Cooked Prime Fish Meat
- Cooked Meat
- Raw Fish Meat
- Cooked Fish Meat

Mesopithecus

Basic Stats:

Health	115	Food	450	Speed (Land)	60
Stamina	100	Weight	70	Speed (Water)	300
Oxygen	150	Melee Damage	12	Torpidity	60

Habitat: Beaches, Plains, Forests
Damages: Thatch
Behavior: Cowardly
Type: Mammal
Diet: Carnivore
Names: -

Attack 1: Melee
Attack 2: Throw Poop
Attack 3: -

Specifics:
- Once it's tamed, it can be carried on your shoulder.
- Throws its feces at your enemies from your shoulder.

Utility:
- It doesn't really make sense to kill it since you get just a few drops and it can't harm the player.
- When carrying it on your shoulder, it can warn of danger, carry additional weight (only half of the weight applies to the carrier), and looks cute.
- In PvP, it can open doors (up to Wood) from the inside. Throw it over a wall or into a hole and command it to "attack the target" while aiming at the door you want to open.

Drops
Raw Meat
Raw Prime Fish
Hide

Harvests
Berries	■

Breeding
Type	Pregnancy
Gestation	2h:38m
Maturation	30h:52m

THE ISLAND ~~SC. EARTH~~
~~ABERRATION~~ EXTINCTION
GENESIS I RAGNAROK
THE CENTER VALGUERO

Can wear hats

CHEAT: summon Monkey_Character_BP_C

CARRYABLE BY: Kaprosuchus, Megalosaurus, Tapejara, Pteranodon, Argentavis, Quetzal, Griffin, Wyvern, Tusoteuthis, Gigantopithecus, Karkinos, Procoptodon

EGG SIZE: -

USEFUL TRAPS: Bola, Bear Trap, Plant Species Y Trap

TAMING METHOD:
Can be tamed by feeding.

SUITABLE FOOD FOR TAMING:
- Basic Kibble
- Crops
- Mejoberries
- Berries

Microraptor

Basic Stats:

Health	130	Food	450	Speed (Air)	150
Stamina	100	Weight	45	Speed (Land)	150
Oxygen	150	Melee Damage	8	Speed (Water)	300
				Torpidity	75

Habitat: Rivers with open areas **Type:** Dinosaur
Damages: Thatch **Diet:** Carnivore
Behavior: Highly Aggressive **Names:** –

Attack 1: Bite
Attack 2: Air Attack
Attack 3: Glide Attack
Attack 4: Jump Attack

Specifics:
- A very fast and maneuverable dinosaur.
- In groups, they attack players as well. They also throw the player off its mount.

Utility:
- As soon as it's tamed, it can be carried on your shoulder. As a companion, it can be a good help in a battle.
- In groups, they can also pose a danger (they obtain a group bonus for each one in the group).
- Not able to fly, but due to its enormous jump strength it can stay in the air for several seconds, scout the surrounding area, and attack enemies.

Drops	Harvests	Breeding	
Raw Meat	–	Type	Egg
Hide		Egg Temp.	24°-28°
		Incubation	1h:25m
		Maturation	54h:28m

THE ISLAND   SC. EARTH
~~ABERRATION~~   EXTINCTION
GENESIS I   RAGNAROK
THE CENTER   VALGUERO

CHEAT: summon Microraptor_Character_BP_C
CARRYABLE BY: Kaprosuchus, Megalosaurus, Tusoteuthis, Gigantopithecus, Procoptodon
EGG SIZE: Small

USEFUL TRAPS: Bola, Bear Trap, Plant Species Y Trap

TAMING METHOD:
Knockout

SUITABLE FOOD FOR TAMING:
- Rare Flower
- Rare Mushroom
- Raw Mutton
- Cooked Lamb Chop
- Raw Prime Fish
- Cooked Prime Meat
- Raw Prime Fish Meat
- Raw Meat
- Cooked Prime Fish Meat
- Cooked Meat
- Raw Fish Meat
- Cooked Fish Meat

MORELLATOPS

Basic Stats:

Health	400	Food	6000	Speed (Land)	250
Stamina	220	Weight	440	Speed (Water)	265
Oxygen	150	Melee Damage	32	Torpidity	315

Habitat:	Scorched Earth	**Type:**	Fantasy Creature
Damages:	Thatch, Wood	**Diet:**	Herbivore
Behavior:	Passive	**Names:**	Camelsaurus/Camel

Attack 1: Melee
Attack 2: Melee II
Attack 3: –

Specifics:
- Due to its size, it often gets stuck between rocks. If attacked in such a situation, it will defend itself nevertheless.

Utility:
- Can be tamed easily and is, therefore, an important support at the beginning of Scorched Earth.
- Can store up to 750 units of water. Due to its loading capacity and ability to collect, it's a good mount for your first expeditions.
- Resource gatherer: gathers Berries, Cactus Sap, and Thatch. Very good at gathering Wood from the little mini-trees in Scorched Earth and Cactus Sap from the mini-cacti.

Drops	Harvests		Breeding	
Raw Meat	Berries	■■■	Type	Egg
Hide	Cactus Sap	■■■	Egg Temp.	22°-28°
	Thatch	■■	Incubation	2h:29m
	Wood	■	Maturation	30h:52m

~~THE ISLAND~~ SC. EARTH
~~ABERRATION~~ EXTINCTION
~~GENESIS I~~ RAGNAROK
~~THE CENTER~~ ~~VALGUERO~~

Level	11
Engram Cost	11
Hide	140
Fiber	80
Wood	30

CHEAT: *summon camelsaurus_Character_BP_C*

CARRYABLE BY: Quetzal, Wyvern, Tusoteuthis

EGG SIZE: Small

USEFUL TRAPS: Chain Bola, Large Bear Trap

TAMING METHOD:
Knockout

SUITABLE FOOD FOR TAMING:
- Simple Kibble
- Crops
- Mejoberries
- Berries

Moschops

Basic Stats:

Health	375	Food	300	Speed (Land)	115
Stamina	300	Weight	200	Speed (Water)	220
Oxygen	150	Melee Damage	32	Torpidity	300

Habitat: Beaches and Forests
Type: Synapsid
Damages: Thatch, Wood
Diet: Carnivore
Behavior: Cowardly
Names: -

Attack 1: Bite
Attack 2: -
Attack 3: -

Specifics:
- In order to tame, you must feed it exactly the kind of food it demands. When you look at it from a close distance, the food it wants is indicated.

Utility:
- Gatherer: while the Moschop is wandering around, it automatically gathers a lot resources (including rare ones) on its own.
- You can improve its gathering skills by increasing its level and thereby specialize it.

Drops	Harvests	Breeding	
Raw Meat	See above	Type	Egg
Hide		Egg Temp.	16°-20°
		Incubation	2h:38m
		Maturation	48h:44m

THE ISLAND | SC. EARTH
~~ABERRATION~~ | EXTINCTION
GENESIS I | RAGNAROK
THE CENTER | VALGUERO

CHEAT: *summon Moschops_Character_BP_C*

CARRYABLE BY: Kaprosuchus, Megalosaurus, Argentavis, Quetzal, Wyvern, Tusoteuthis, Karkinos

EGG SIZE: Large

USEFUL TRAPS: Bola, Large Bear Trap, Plant Species Y Trap

TAMING METHOD:
Can be tamed by feeding.

SUITABLE FOOD FOR TAMING:
- Sap
- Leech Blood
- Organic Polymer
- Rare Flower
- Rare Mushroom
- Raw Prime Fish
- Raw Prime Fish Meat

NAMELESS

Basic Stats:

Health	200	Food	1500	Speed (Land)	424
Stamina	150	Weight	180	Speed (Water)	300
Oxygen	150	Melee Damage	10	Torpidity	220

Habitat: All areas except the ones you spawn in
Damages: Thatch
Behavior: Highly Aggressive

Type: Fantasy Creature
Diet: Carnivore
Names: Chupacabra

Attack 1: Melee
Attack 2: —
Attack 3: —

Specifics:
- Attacks in groups of three or more. The strongest one transforms into an Alpha Nameless which constantly calls other Nameless. If you don't have any light or a very strong creature with you, we recommend avoiding fights with them because they will attack you endlessly.
- To protect yourself against attacks, you should always bring some type of light or a glowing animal with you (e.g. Bulbdogs or Glowtails). Set up lamps when you're working in their territory for an extended time. This keeps them away.
- Because of their poison, Basilisks are good for fighting against the Nameless.

Utility:
- The Nameless drop Nameless Venom that can be used for feeding, raising, and imprinting baby Rock Drakes. Their venom is also required in order to reach the bosses.

Drops	Harvests	Breeding
Raw Meat	—	Not breedable
Hide		
Nameless Venom		

~~THE ISLAND~~   ~~SE. EARTH~~
ABERRATION   ~~EXTINCTION~~
~~GENESIS I~~   ~~RAGNAROK~~
~~THE CENTER~~   ~~VALGUERO~~

CHEAT: summon ChupaCabra_Character_BP_C
CARRYABLE BY: Argentavis, Karkinos, Quetzal
EGG SIZE: –

USEFUL TRAPS: –

TAMING METHOD: –

SUITABLE FOOD FOR TAMING: –

Otter

Basic Stats:

Health	40	Food	400	Speed (Land)	170
Stamina	180	Weight	30	Speed (Water)	250
Oxygen	600	Melee Damage	10	Torpidity	350

Habitat: Rivers and Lakes
Damages: Thatch
Behavior: friendly

Type: Mammal
Diet: Carnivore
Names: -

Attack 1: Bite
Attack 2: -
Attack 3: -

Specifics:
- Doesn't attack of its own volition. Only attacks when provoked or attacked first.
- Can be easily killed by Salmon in a shoal or Piranhas.

Utility:
- A cuddly companion you can carry on your shoulder. It increases your heat and cold protection when it's in your proximity (preferably on your shoulder). Thanks to its ample oxygen supply and cold protection, it's very good for diving expeditions in cold waters or caves.
- Catches Fish on command and gathers Silica Pearls or even rare Black Pearls in the process (to make it do this, throw it directly at Fish). The harvest won't be that great, but you can, however, get pearls inland without having to do any deep-sea diving to get them.

Drops
Raw Meat
Raw Prime Fish
Pelt

Harvests
Black Pearls	■■■
Raw Fish Meat	■■■
Silica Pearls	■■

Breeding
Type	Pregnancy
Gestation	7h:56m
Maturation	21h:03m

THE ISLAND ~~SC. EARTH~~
~~ABERRATION~~ **EXTINCTION**
~~GENESIS I~~ **RAGNAROK**
THE CENTER **VALGUERO**

Can wear hats

CHEAT: *summon Otter_Character_BP_C*

CARRYABLE BY: Kaprosuchus, Megalosaurus, Tapejara, Peteranodon, Argentavis, Quetzal, Griffin, Wyvern, Tusoteuthis, Gigantopithecus, Karkinos, Procoptodon

EGG SIZE: -

USEFUL TRAPS: Bola, Bear Trap, Plant Species Y Trap

TAMING METHOD:
Can be tamed by feeding.

SUITABLE FOOD FOR TAMING:
- Sabertooth Salmon
- Piranha
- Coelacanth

Warning: Fish Meat doesn't work for taming here. You have to kill a Fish and carry the Dead Fish. While carrying the Fish, approach the Otter and press the "use" button as soon as it is requested. The bigger the dead Fish, the higher the taming effectiveness. The most difficult task when taming Otters is not to lose sight of the swift little guys.

Oviraptor

Basic Stats:

Health	140	Food	900	Speed (Land)	320
Stamina	120	Weight	100	Speed (Water)	300
Oxygen	150	Melee Damage	12	Torpidity	125

Habitat: Jungle, Forest, Meadows
Damages: Thatch
Behavior: Skittish

Type: Dinosaur
Diet: Carnivore
Names: -

Attack 1: Melee Bite
Attack 2: -
Attack 3: -

Specifics:
- Flees quickly when attacked.
- Can only be tamed with eggs.

Utility:
- Oviraptors can automatically harvest eggs that are lying around (aim at an egg and whistle the command „attack target").
- A tamed Oviraptor accelerates the production of close-by eggs. Mammals get pregnant quicker. To make this happen, set the Oviraptor to "wandering around". Then, you see an egg symbol above every creature whose reproduction is being accelerated.

Drops	Harvests	Breeding	
Raw Meat	See above	Type	Egg
Hide		Egg Temp.	26°-30°
		Incubation	1h:8m
		Maturation	21h:3m

THE ISLAND ~~SC. EARTH~~
~~ABERRATION~~ **EXTINCTION**
GENESIS I RAGNAROK
THE CENTER VALGUERO

CHEAT: *summon Oviraptor_Character_BP_C*

CARRYABLE BY: Kaprosuchus, Megalosaurus, Pteranodon, Argentavis, Quetzal, Griffin, Wyvern, Tusoteuthis, Karkinos,
EGG SIZE: Small

USEFUL TRAPS: Bola, Bear Trap, Plant Species Y Trap

TAMING METHOD:
Can be tamed by feeding.

SUITABLE FOOD FOR TAMING:
- Gigantosaurus Egg
- Quetzal Egg
- Rex Egg
- Spino Egg
- Bronto Egg
- Carno Egg
- All kinds of other Eggs

Despite the fact that you need a relatively large number of Dodo eggs for taming, you can get them the fastest. An alternative would be to opt for eggs you don't necessarily need for the production of other types of kibble.

OVIS

Basic Stats:

Health	100	Food	1200	Speed (Land)	100
Stamina	100	Weight	90	Speed (Water)	300
Oxygen	150	Melee Damage	5	Torpidity	85

Habitat: Forest/Mountains with Meadows
Damages: Thatch
Behavior: Stupid
Type: Mammal
Diet: Herbivore
Names: -

Attack 1: Melee Headbutt
Attack 2: -
Attack 3: -

Specifics:
- Can climb well on rocks.
- Never attacks and flees when being attacked.
- Warning: it often shows up in regions where a lot of predators are.

Utility:
- Can be sheared with scissors. As a result, you obtain Wool, which is a substitute for Pelt.
- Because it's really easy to tame an Ovis, it's a good source of Meat (especially at the beginning of the game). Its Meat is perfect for taming and often better than Raw Prime Meat or even kibble.

THE ISLAND ~~SC EARTH~~
~~ABERRATION~~ **EXTINCTION**
~~GENESIS I~~ **RAGNAROK**
THE CENTER **VALGUERO**

Ridable without a saddle

CHEAT: *summon Sheep_Character_BP_C*

CARRYABLE BY: Kaprosuchus, Megalosaurus, Tapejara, Peteranodon, Argentavis, Quetzal, Griffin, Wyvern, Tusotheuthis, Gigantopithecus, Karkinos, Procoptodon

EGG SIZE: –

USEFUL TRAPS: Bola, Bear Trap, Plant Species Y Trap

TAMING METHOD:
Can be tamed by feeding.

SUITABLE FOOD FOR TAMING:
- Sweet Vegetable Cake

PACHYCEPHALOSAURUS

BASIC STATS:

Health	175	Food	1200	Speed (Land)	200
Stamina	150	Weight	150	Speed (Water)	300
Oxygen	150	Melee Damage	10	Torpidity	160

HABITAT: Forest, Mountain Ranges, Beaches
DAMAGES: Thatch
BEHAVIOR: Passive

TYPE: Dinosaur
DIET: Herbivore
NAMES: Pachy

ATTACK 1: Melee; Ram Attack
ATTACK 2: –
ATTACK 3: –

SPECIFICS:
- Slow unless it starts an attack (Ram Attack).

UTILITY:
- When using it as mount, you can achieve high speeds by using its Ram Attack, but then it can't be steered anymore.
- Warning: it has a very low health level and can, therefore, be very quickly defeated in a fight.
- Useful as a mount and harvest animal at the beginning of the game.

DROPS
Raw Meat
Hide

HARVESTS
Thatch	■
Wood	■

BREEDING
Type	Egg
Egg Temp.	24°-28°
Incubation	1h:25m
Maturation	26h:27m

THE ISLAND ~~SC. EARTH~~
~~ABERRATION~~ EXTINCTION
~~GENESIS I~~ RAGNAROK
THE CENTER VALGUERO

Level	14
Engram Cost	9
Hide	110
Fiber	65
Wood	20

CHEAT: *summon Pachy_Character_BP_C*

CARRYABLE BY: Kaprosuchus, Megalosaurus, Argentavis, Quetzal, Wyvern, Tusoteuthis, Karkinos

EGG SIZE: Small

USEFUL TRAPS: Bola, Bear Trap, Large Bear Trap, Plant Species Y Trap

TAMING METHOD:
Knockout

SUITABLE FOOD FOR TAMING:
- Simple Kibble
- Crops
- Mejoberries
- Berries

PACHYRHINOSAURUS

Basic Stats:

Health	375	Food	3000	Speed (Land)	230
Stamina	150	Weight	365	Speed (Water)	300
Oxygen	150	Melee Damage	28	Torpidity	250

Habitat: Forests and Beaches
Damages: Thatch, Wood
Behavior: Passive

Type: Dinosaur
Diet: Herbivore
Names: -

Attack 1: Headbutt
Attack 2: Camo Cloud
Attack 3: Rage Cloud

Specifics:
- When attacked, not only can this dinosaur fight back, it also releases a chemical that enrages every creature in its surrounding. In doing so, even friendly and peaceful animals can become dangerous.
- Can also release another type of chemical that calms opponents, which makes it possible for the Pachyrhinosaurus to escape. In addition, a whiff of it also induces loss of stamina.

Utility:
- Its chemical can be used in order to hide from enemies or to make them aggressive.
- It's able to carry two players at once.

Drops

Raw Meat
Hide
Keratin

Harvests

Berries	■■■
Thatch	■■■
Wood	■■
Fiber	■

Breeding

Type	Egg
Egg Temp.	22°-28°
Incubation	2h:30m
Maturation	46h:18m

THE ISLAND   ~~SC. EARTH~~
~~ABERRATION~~   EXTINCTION
GENESIS I   RAGNAROK
THE CENTER   VALGUERO

Level	27
Engram Cost	18
Hide	140
Fiber	80
Wood	25

CHEAT: *summon Pachyrhino_Character_BP_C*

CARRYABLE BY: Quetzal, Wyvern, Tusoteuthis, Karkinos

EGG SIZE: Medium

USEFUL TRAPS: Chain Bola, Large Bear Trap, Plant Species Y Trap

TAMING METHOD:
Knockout

SUITABLE FOOD FOR TAMING:
- Bug Repellant
- Crops
- Mejoberries
- Berries

Warning: its head plate protects against head shots. If you want to increase its torpidity, aim at its body.

Paraceratherium

Basic Stats:

Health	1026	Food	6500	Speed (Land)	260
Stamina	300	Weight	850	Speed (Water)	300
Oxygen	150	Melee Damage	45	Torpidity	1300

Habitat: Swamps, Forest edges
Damages: Thatch, Wood, Adobe
Behavior: Passive

Type: Mammal
Diet: Herbivore
Names: Paracer

Attack 1: Melee Stomp
Attack 2: –
Attack 3: –

Specifics:
- Very fast despite its size.
- A friendly creature as long as it isn't attacked. When roaming around in small packs, all pack members defend the one that is being attacked.

Utility:
- Due to its platform saddle, it's a useful mobile base.
- Thanks to its loading capacity, it's perfect for the transportation of many items.
- People like placing weapons such as cannons or ballista on its platform saddle. Thereby, it's transformed into a mobile artillery. With equipment like that, you can even hunt Titanosaurs or Stone Elementals.
- A good source for Raw Prime Meat (one Paracer drops 1-8 Raw Prime Meat).

Drops	Harvests	Breeding	
Raw Meat	–	Type	Pregnancy
Raw Prime Fish		Gestation	7h:56m
Hide		Maturation	92h:36m

THE ISLAND **SC. EARTH**
~~ABERRATION~~ **EXTINCTION**
~~GENESIS I~~ **RAGNAROK**
THE CENTER **VALGUERO**

Level	41
Engram Cost	18
Hide	200
Fiber	110
Metal Ingots	10

Level	50
Engram Cost	24
Hide	320
Fiber	200
Metal Ingots	70
Silica Pearls	45
Cementing Paste	25

CHEAT: summon Paracer_Character_BP_C
CARRYABLE BY: Tusoteuthis
EGG SIZE: –

USEFUL TRAPS: Chain Bola, Large Bear Trap

TAMING METHOD:
Knockout

SUITABLE FOOD FOR TAMING:
- Superior Kibble
- Crops
- Mejoberries
- Berries

PARASAUROLOPHUS

BASIC STATS:

Health	200	Food	1500	Speed (Land)	200
Stamina	450	Weight	480	Speed (Water)	450
Oxygen	150	Melee Damage	12	Torpidity	150

HABITAT: Beaches, Meadows, Forests (very often)
DAMAGES: Thatch
BEHAVIOR: Cowardly

TYPE: Dinosaur
DIET: Herbivore
NAMES: -

ATTACK 1: Melee
ATTACK 2: -
ATTACK 3: -

SPECIFICS:
- Even though it doesn't fight back very well when attacked, it's still a challenge to kill because it escapes very quickly.
- Only attacks when its eggs are being stolen.
- You can quickly catch it with a Bola and quickly tranquilize it as well.

UTILITY:
- We recommend using this animal as a mount, gatherer, and pack animal at the beginning of the game. Since it's easily and quickly tamed, it's one of the first creatures you're going to tame. It's a very helpful aid; especially at the beginning.

DROPS	HARVESTS		BREEDING	
Raw Meat	Berries	■■	Type	Egg
Hide	Thatch	■■	Egg Temp.	24°-28°
	Wood	■	Incubation	1h:25m
	Seeds	■	Maturation	26h:27m

THE ISLAND   SC. EARTH
~~ABERRATION~~   EXTINCTION
GENESIS I   RAGNAROK
THE CENTER   VALGUERO

Level	9
Engram Cost	9
Hide	80
Fiber	50
Wood	15

CHEAT: *summon Para_Character_BP_C*

CARRYABLE BY: Megalosaurus, Quetzal, Wyvern, Tusoteuthis, Karkinos, Argentavis

EGG SIZE: Very Small

USEFUL TRAPS: Bola, Bear Trap, Large Bear Trap, Plant Species Y Trap

TAMING METHOD:
Knockout

SUITABLE FOOD FOR TAMING:
- Basic Kibble
- Crops
- Mejoberries
- Berries

PEGOMASTAX

Basic Stats:

Health	120	Food	450	Speed (Land)	110
Stamina	100	Weight	55	Speed (Water)	300
Oxygen	150	Melee Damage	10	Torpidity	30

Habitat: Beaches, Forest, Redwoods
Damages: Thatch
Behavior: Highly Aggressive (thief)
Type: Dinosaur
Diet: Herbivore
Names: -

Attack 1: Bite
Attack 2: Steal (the Pegomastax steals one item from your inventory)
Attack 3: Leap

Specifics:
- Has the ability to steal single items from your inventory. Once it's stolen, your only chance to get your items back is either to tame, stun, or kill it. The first thing it will steal is Berries, provided you have some. If that's not the case, it steals your equipment.
- Once it's tamed, it can be carried on your shoulders.
- Rather annoying. Try to avoid it completely or kill it on sight.

Utility:
- When you throw it at bushes with Berries, it collects Seeds.
- Use it to steal items from the inventory of enemy players.

Drops	Harvests	Breeding	
Raw Meat	See above	Type	Egg
Hide		Egg Temp.	28°-32°
		Incubation	1h:8m
		Maturation	30h:52m

THE ISLAND   SC. EARTH
~~ABERRATION~~   ~~EXTINCTION~~
GENESIS I   RAGNAROK
THE CENTER   VALGUERO

CHEAT: *summon Pegomastax_Character_BP_C*

CARRYABLE BY: Kaprosuchus, Megalosaurus, Tapejara, Pteranodon, Argentavis, Quetzal, Griffin, Wyvern, Tusoteuthis, Karkinos, Gigantopithecus

EGG SIZE: Small

USEFUL TRAPS: Bola, Bear Trap, Plant Species Y Trap

TAMING METHOD:
Can be tamed by letting it steal something from you.

SUITABLE FOOD FOR TAMING:
- Crops
- Mejoberries
- Berries

Place Berries into the last slot of your inventory. Preferably, only a few (20-25) since the Pegomastax always steals the whole stack. Approach the Pegomastax and let it steal the Berries from your inventory. Repeat this procedure until the Pegomastax has finally been tamed. We recommend luring it into a fenced-in area first since it tends to flee after it has stolen something.

PHIOMIA

Basic Stats:

Health	300	Food	3000	Speed (Land)	150
Stamina	300	Weight	200	Speed (Water)	300
Oxygen	150	Melee Damage	10	Torpidity	240

HABITAT: Beaches, Jungle, Forest (very often) **TYPE:** Mammal
DAMAGES: Thatch **DIET:** Herbivore
BEHAVIOR: Skittish **NAMES:** –

ATTACK 1: Melee
ATTACK 2: –
ATTACK 3: –

Specifics:
- Provided that there are no other creatures in the proximity, you can focus exclusively on hunting the Phiomia.
- Runs away when attacked. Attack it in a rocky region so you have the ability to push it into a corner.

Utility:
- Produces tons of feces. If you need a lot of Fertilizer, it's a very suitable source. Feed it with White Stimberries; this leads to extreme diarrhea, which means lots of feces in return.
- Can't carry as much as other creatures, but it's a good pack animal nevertheless; especially at the beginning of the game.
- Good predator: provides a lot of Meat and Hide considering how easy it is to hunt.

DROPS	HARVESTS		BREEDING	
Raw Meat	Thatch	■■	Type	Pregnancy
Hide	Wood	■■	Gestation	9h:55m
			Maturation	115h:44m

THE ISLAND ~~SE EARTH~~
~~ABERRATION~~ **EXTINCTION**
GENESIS I **RAGNAROK**
THE CENTER **VALGUERO**

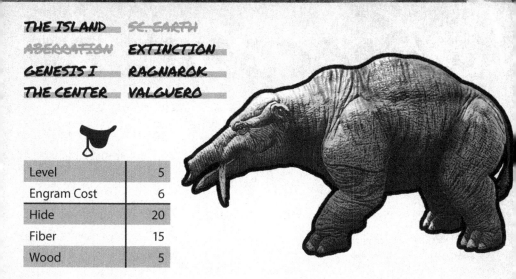

Level	5
Engram Cost	6
Hide	20
Fiber	15
Wood	5

CHEAT: summon Phiomia_Character_BP_C
CARRYABLE BY: Megalosaurus, Argentavis, Quetzal, Wyvern, Tusoteuthis, Karkinos
EGG SIZE: -

USEFUL TRAPS: Bola, Bear Trap, Large Bear Trap, Plant Species Y Trap

TAMING METHOD:
Knockout

SUITABLE FOOD FOR TAMING:
- Basic Kibble
- Crops
- Mejoberries
- Berries

PROCOPTODON

BASIC STATS:

Health	400	Food	1500	Speed (Land)	850
Stamina	350	Weight	550	Speed (Water)	300
Oxygen	150	Melee Damage	20	Torpidity	350

HABITAT: Swamp, Volcano, The Center Island
DAMAGES: Thatch, Wood
BEHAVIOR: Passive

TYPE: Mammal
DIET: Herbivore
NAMES: –

ATTACK 1: Melee
ATTACK 2: –
ATTACK 3: –

SPECIFICS:
- Very rare.
- Usually flees when attacked. Sometimes, it can also happen that it defends itself when its level is higher then the attacker's.
- One member of the same tribe can ride in its pouch while another player rides on the saddle.

UTILITY:
- If a co-player joins you in its pouch, they can easily collect resources while you (the rider) look out for danger.
- It's possible for both players to carry and use weapons. This makes hunting together easy.

DROPS	HARVESTS	BREEDING	
Raw Meat	–	Type	Pregnancy
Hide		Gestation	3h:58m
Pelt		Maturation	46h:18m

THE ISLAND   SC. EARTH
~~ABERRATION~~   EXTINCTION
GENESIS I   RAGNAROK
THE CENTER   VALGUERO

Level	23
Engram Cost	35
Hide	500
Fiber	200
Wool/Hair/Pelt	150
Metal Ingots	70

CHEAT: *summon Procoptodon_Character_BP_C*
CARRYABLE BY: Tusoteuthis
EGG SIZE: –

USEFUL TRAPS: Chain Bola, Large Bear Trap

TAMING METHOD:
Knockout

SUITABLE FOOD FOR TAMING:
- Rare Mushrooms
- Plant Species X Seeds

PULMONOSCORPIUS

Basic Stats:

Health	280	Food	1500	Speed (Land)	300
Stamina	200	Weight	200	Speed (Water)	300
Oxygen	150	Melee Damage	15	Torpidity	150

Habitat: Mountains, Redwoods, Caves **Type:** Invertebrate
Damages: Thatch **Diet:** Carnivore
Behavior: Aggressive **Names:** Scorpion

Attack 1: Melee/Poison (torpidity)
Attack 2: -
Attack 3: -

Specifics:
- Warning: it approaches all creatures because it's curious, but it doesn't attack first. Since it gets very close, it can happen that you touch it accidentally. Then, it attacks.
- Due to its low health, you can easily defeat it when it's alone.
- Since breeding is impossible, an Oviraptor doesn't accelerate its egg production (although its eggs are important to create Kibble for taming the Rex).

Utility:
- Climbs well on rocks.
- Since it needs very little food, it's easy to provide for it.
- Has the ability to stun all other dinosaurs.

Drops	Harvests		Breeding
Raw Meat	Thatch	■■	Not breedable
Chitin	Wood	■■	

THE ISLAND **SC. EARTH**
~~ABERRATION~~ **EXTINCTION**
GENESIS I **RAGNAROK**
THE CENTER **VALGUERO**

Level	22
Engram Cost	12
Hide	170
Fiber	95
Wood	30

CHEAT: *summon Scorpion_Character_BP_C*

CARRYABLE BY: Megalosaurus, Argentavis, Quetzal, Wyvern, Tusoteuthis, Karkinos

EGG SIZE: Medium

USEFUL TRAPS: Bola, Bear Trap, Plant Species Y Trap

TAMING METHOD:
Knockout

SUITABLE FOOD FOR TAMING:
- Regular Kibble
- Spoiled Meat
- Raw Meat
- Raw Fish Meat

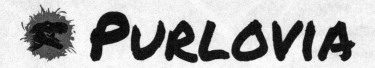

PURLOVIA

Basic Stats:

Health	275	Food	4000	Speed (Land)	230
Stamina	300	Weight	400	Speed (Water)	300
Oxygen	150	Melee Damage	32	Torpidity	500

Habitat: Redwoods, Cold regions
Damages: Thatch, Wood
Behavior: Highly Aggressive
Type: Synapsid
Diet: Carnivore
Names: –

Attack 1: Bite
Attack 2: Surprise Attack (short, medium, or long range)
Attack 3: –

Specifics:
- Attacks unexpectedly since it hides in the ground and jumps out as soon as someone approaches.
- Not very strong but its surprise attacks are very dangerous.
- Its attack knocks enemies back and stuns them for a short period of time.

Utility:
- Very suitable for defending your base or setting up a trap for opponents since it's able to burrow itself in the ground and jumps out unexpectedly.

Drops	Harvests		Breeding	
Raw Meat	Raw Prime Fish	■■	Type	Pregnancy
Hide	Raw Prime Fish	■■	Gestation	4h:11m
			Maturation	48h:44m

THE ISLAND **SC. EARTH**
~~ABERRATION~~ **EXTINCTION**
GENESIS I **RAGNAROK**
THE CENTER **VALGUERO**

CHEAT: summon Purlovia_Character_BP_C
CARRYABLE BY: Quetzal, Wyvern, Tusoteuthis
EGG SIZE: –

USEFUL TRAPS: Chain Bola, Large Bear Trap, Plant Species Y Trap

TAMING METHOD:
Knockout

SUITABLE FOOD FOR TAMING:
- Regular Kibble
- Raw Mutton
- Cooked Lamb Chop
- Raw Prime Fish
- Cooked Prime Meat
- Raw Prime Fish Meat
- Raw Meat
- Cooked Prime Fish Meat
- Cooked Meat
- Raw Fish Meat
- Cooked Fish Meat

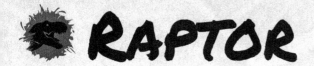
RAPTOR

BASIC STATS:

Health	200	Food	1200	Speed (Land)	480
Stamina	150	Weight	140	Speed (Water)	300
Oxygen	150	Melee Damage	15	Torpidity	180

HABITAT: Almost everywhere **TYPE:** Dinosaur
DAMAGES: Thatch **DIET:** Carnivore
BEHAVIOR: Highly Aggressive **NAMES:** Utahraptor

ATTACK 1: Melee; Bite and Claw
ATTACK 2: –
ATTACK 3: –

SPECIFICS:
- Torpidity is very low. If you have a high melee damage stat, you can try to knock it out it with just a few punches.
- Since it's a dangerous animal anyway, you shouldn't attack it at night or when it appears in a pack.

UTILITY:
- A very fast mount and, therefore, perfect when you want to reach distant places quickly.
- Very suitable for collecting Meat.
- Since it can be knocked out easily and tamed quickly, it's a good first choice for hunting.

DROPS

Raw Meat
Hide

HARVESTS

Raw Prime Fish	■■■
Raw Meat	■■■
Chitin/Keratin	■■
Pelt/Hide	■■

BREEDING

Type	Egg
Egg Temp.	20°-28°
Incubation	1h:59m
Maturation	37h:3m

THE ISLAND   SC. EARTH
ABERRATION   EXTINCTION
GENESIS I   RAGNAROK
THE CENTER   VALGUERO

Level	18
Engram Cost	9
Hide	110
Fiber	65
Wood	20

CHEAT: *summon Raptor_Character_BP_C*

CARRYABLE BY: Mammoth
EGG SIZE: Small

USEFUL TRAPS: Bola, Bear Trap, Large Bear Trap, Plant Species Y Trap

TAMING METHOD:
Knockout

SUITABLE FOOD FOR TAMING:
- Simple Kibble
- Raw Mutton
- Cooked Lamb Chop
- Raw Prime Fish
- Cooked Prime Meat
- Raw Prime Fish Meat
- Raw Meat
- Cooked Prime Fish Meat
- Cooked Meat
- Raw Fish Meat
- Cooked Fish Meat

RAVAGER

Basic Stats:

Health	400	Food	1200	Speed (Land)	300
Stamina	350	Weight	500	Speed (Water)	300
Oxygen	150	Melee Damage	33	Torpidity	500

HABITAT: The Spine (primarily)
DAMAGES: Thatch, Wood
BEHAVIOR: Highly Aggressive
TYPE: Fantasy Creature
DIET: Carnivore
NAMES: -

ATTACK 1: Bite
ATTACK 2: Claw
ATTACK 3: Roar

Specifics:
- Additional attack: Bite Leap.
- Can be easily stopped by using a Bola. Only attack it with ranged weapons.
- Attacks in groups of three to five.
- Doesn't glow in the dark like most of the other animals do. Therefore, it can appear suddenly.

Utility:
- Good mount; it can climb up vines and zip lines.
- Lots of resources only weigh half as much when placed in its inventory. For this reason, it's a versatile predator, explorer, and mount for transport.

Drops		Harvests		Breeding	
Raw Meat		Raw Meat	■■■	Type	Pregnancy
Hide		Raw Prime Fish	■■	Gestation	4h:11m
Pelt		Chitin	■■	Maturation	48h:44m
Raw Prime Fish		Keratin	■■		
		Hide	■■		

~~THE ISLAND~~   ~~SC. EARTH~~
ABERRATION ~~EXTINCTION~~
GENESIS I   ~~RAGNAROK~~
~~THE CENTER~~ **VALGUERO**

Level	47
Engram Cost	20
Hide	285
Fiber	125
Fungal Wood	110

CHEAT: summon CaveWolf_Character_BP_C
CARRYABLE BY: Quetzal, Karkinos
EGG SIZE: -

USEFUL TRAPS: Bola, Bear Trap, Large Bear Trap, Plant Species Y Trap

TAMING METHOD:
Knockout

SUITABLE FOOD FOR TAMING:
- Raw Mutton
- Cooked Lamb Chop
- Raw Prime Fish
- Cooked Prime Meat
- Raw Prime Fish Meat
- Raw Meat
- Cooked Prime Fish Meat
- Cooked Meat
- Raw Fish Meat
- Cooked Fish Meat

REAPER

Basic Stats:

Health	2000	Food	3000	Speed (Land)	466
Stamina	480	Weight	415	Speed (Water)	300
Oxygen	150	Melee Damage	85	Torpidity	925

Habitat: Surface/Element biome
Damages: -
Behavior: Highly Aggressive
Type: Fantasy Creature
Diet: Carnivore
Names: -

Attack 1: Melee/Tail Attack
Attack 2: Acid Projectile
Attack 3: -

Specifics:
- Reapers are very aggressive. Alpha Nameless can call them.
- Can shoot acidic projectiles from its tail. Can also harm players with its tail and knock them back.
- Can't be tamed. Instead, the player must get "impregnated" by the Reaper Queen's tail whip. It takes about twelve hours until the Reaper is born. During this time, the player can't gather experience because the unborn Reaper receives it instead. Right before its "birth", you should use a Pheromone Gland; otherwise the Reaper baby will attack you instantly. Claim the baby immediately after its birth and feed it or it will become wild.

Utility:
- One of the strongest fighting animals in the game.

Drops
Raw Meat
Hide
Reaper Pheromone Gland

Harvests
Raw Meat	■■■

Breeding
Type	Pregnancy
Gestation	12h:00m
Maturation	77h:10m

~~THE ISLAND~~ ~~SE. EARTH~~
ABERRATION ~~EXTINCTION~~
GENESIS I ~~RAGNAROK~~
~~THE CENTER~~ ~~VAL~~

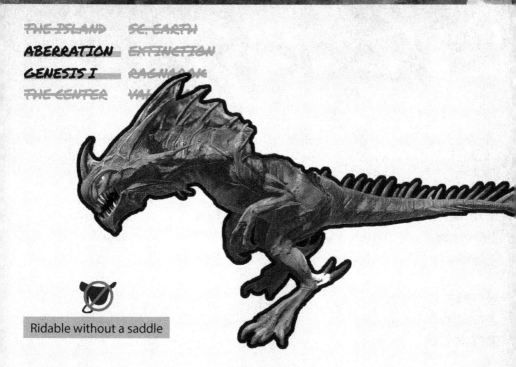

Ridable without a saddle

CHEAT: *summon Xenomorph_Character_BP_Male_C*

There are different variants of Reapers: Elemental Reaper King, Surface Reaper King, Alpha Surface Reaper King, and Reaper Queen.

CARRYABLE BY: –
EGG SIZE: –

USEFUL TRAPS: –

TAMING METHOD:
Can't be tamed. Exception: the player gets „impregnated" by a Reaper Queen and uses a Reaper Pheromone Gland right after its birth (see left).

SUITABLE FOOD FOR TAMING:
- There's no suitable food for taming. You must bear a Reaper baby and raise it.

ROCK DRAKE

BASIC STATS:

Health	1950	Food	2000	Speed (Land)	650
Stamina	450	Weight	400	Speed (Water)	600
Oxygen	150	Melee Damage	60	Torpidity	725

HABITAT: Cave of the Lost (Aberration) **TYPE:** Fantasy Creature
DAMAGES: Thatch, Wood **DIET:** Carnivore
BEHAVIOR: Highly Aggressive **NAMES:** -

ATTACK 1: Bite
ATTACK 2: Toggle
ATTACK 3: Toggle camo

SPECIFICS:
- Able to glide.
- Can turn itself almost invisible. When the player attacks a Rock Drake, it becomes more visible.

UTILITY:
- Good mount for caves, as it can glide and climb. If you want to glide, aim at another rock face and just jump.
- Its feathers glow when Nameless or Reapers are in the proximity.
- Because of its invisibility and climbing skills, you can avoid a lot of danger without being noticed.

DROPS
Raw Meat
Raw Prime Fish
Hide
Rock Drake Feather

HARVESTS
Raw Prime Fish	■■■
Hide	■■■

BREEDING
Type	Egg
Egg Temp.	-90° bis -80°
Incubation	6h:15m
Maturation	92h:36m

~~THE ISLAND~~ ~~SC. EARTH~~
ABERRATION ~~EXTINCTION~~
~~GENESIS I~~ ~~RAGNAROK~~
~~THE CENTER~~ ~~VALGUER~~

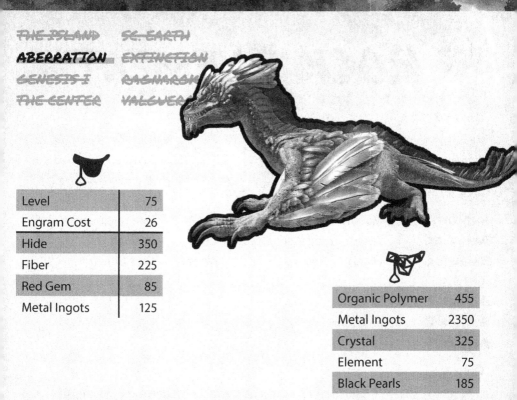

Level	75
Engram Cost	26
Hide	350
Fiber	225
Red Gem	85
Metal Ingots	125

Organic Polymer	455
Metal Ingots	2350
Crystal	325
Element	75
Black Pearls	185

CHEAT: *summon RockDrake_Character_BP_C*

CARRYABLE BY: –

EGG SIZE: Special

USEFUL TRAPS: Chain Bola, Large Bear Trap

TAMING METHOD:
Adult Rock Drakes can't be tamed. You can, however, breed the eggs from a wild Rock Drake. In order to imprint the young animal, you need Nameless Venom.

SUITABLE FOOD FOR TAMING:
There's no suitable food for taming. The procedure is similar to that of Wyverns. They can't be tamed. Instead, the player must steal a Rock Drake egg and breed it. To hatch the eggs, you need at least 24 Air Conditioners because the eggs need a very cold environment. To feed the baby, you need Nameless Venom.

Rock Elemental

Basic Stats:

Health	25000	Food	6000	Speed (Land)	400
Stamina	300	Weight	660	Speed (Water)	300
Oxygen	150	Melee Damage	120	Torpidity	5000

Habitat: Mountains (western areas)
Damages: Thatch, Wood, Adobe, Stone
Behavior: Highly Aggressive
Type: Fantasy Creature
Diet: Minerals
Names: Rock Golem

Attack 1: Melee Punch
Attack 2: Stone Throw
Attack 3: Swipe

Specifics:
- You can easily miss it since it looks like a pile of rocks when it's not moving. Only when you approach it, it starts moving and attacks you.
- When you get far enough away from it, it stops and goes back into its stationary form.
- It can only be stunned by using Cannons, Catapult Turrets, or Rocket Launchers.

Utility:
- Its stone skin reduces the damage caused by enemies by half.
- It's suitable for hunting Deathworms.
- Excellent guard animal for your base, safe mount, and good harvester for Stone and Sulfur.

Drops	Harvests		Breeding
Crystal, Metal	Stone, Sand	■■■	Not breedable
Obsidian	Raw Prime Fish, Raw Meat	■■	
Oil	Chitin, Keratin, Hide	■■	
Stone	Wood, Thatch, Cactus Sap	■	
Sulfur			

~~THE ISLAND~~   SC. EARTH
~~ABERRATION~~   EXTINCTION
~~GENESIS I~~   RAGNAROK
~~THE CENTER~~   ~~VALGUERO~~

Level	70
Engram Cost	40
Hide	270
Fiber	150
Metal Ingots	35

CHEAT: summon RockGolem_Character_BP_C

CARRYABLE BY: –
EGG SIZE: –

USEFUL TRAPS: –

TAMING METHOD:
Knockout

SUITABLE FOOD FOR TAMING:
- Extraordinary Kibble
- Sulfur
- Adobe
- Stone

Chalk Golem

VALGUERO

 # X-Rock Elemental

GENESIS I

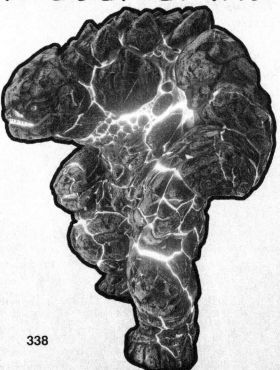

Rubble Golem

EXTINCTION   SC. EARTH

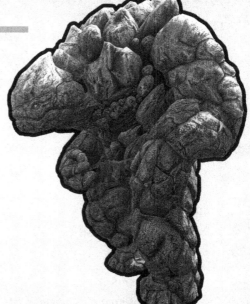

Ice Golem

VALGUERO   GENESIS I

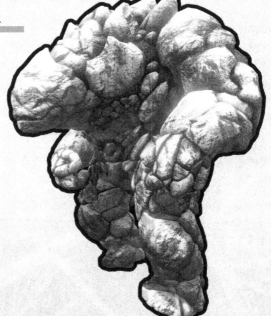

ROLL RAT

Basic Stats:

Health	850	Food	3000	Speed (Land)	250
Stamina	300	Weight	400	Speed (Water)	300
Oxygen	150	Melee Damage	42	Torpidity	800

Habitat: Caves, Swamps
Damages: Thatch, Wood
Behavior: Passive
Type: Reptile
Diet: Carnivore
Names: Boa

Attack 1: Bite
Attack 2: Roll
Attack 3: –

Specifics:
- Rolls up during attacks. Consequently, it can fall off cliffs more easily.
- Burrows into the ground and emerges in the same spot. In doing so, it digs out Gemstones: Red (very rare), Blue (rare), and Green (common). After taming a Roll Rat, it can't dig out Gemstones anymore.

Utility:
- Suitable for collecting Wood and Berries. Wood only weighs a third of the original weight when placed in its inventory.
- Fast mount for up to three people. It becomes very fast during the roll attack; you can still control it, but the saddle takes damage.

Drops	Harvests		Breeding
Raw Meat	Wood	■■■	Not breedable
Hide	Thatch	■	
Keratin	Berries	■	

~~THE ISLAND~~ ~~SC. EARTH~~
ABERRATION ~~EXTINCTION~~
GENESIS I ~~RAGNAROK~~
~~THE CENTER~~ **VALGUERO**

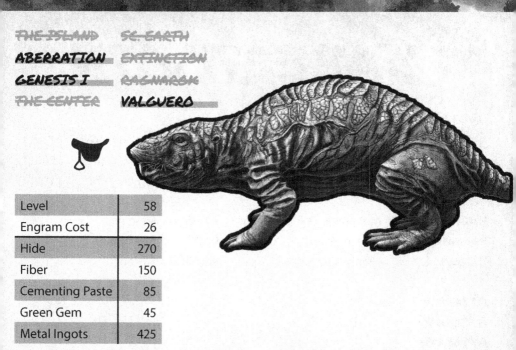

Level	58
Engram Cost	26
Hide	270
Fiber	150
Cementing Paste	85
Green Gem	45
Metal Ingots	425

CHEAT: *summon MoleRat_Character_BP_C*

CARRYABLE BY: Quetzal

EGG SIZE: –

USEFUL TRAPS: Chain Bola, Large Bear Trap, Plant Species Y Trap

TAMING METHOD:
Can be tamed by feeding.

SUITABLE FOOD FOR TAMING:
- Giant Bee Honey

In order to tame it, you have to wait until it has burrowed, then throw food at the hole. Repeat the procedure several times.

Sabertooth

Basic Stats:

Health	250	Food	1200	Speed (Land)	230
Stamina	200	Weight	200	Speed (Water)	300
Oxygen	150	Melee Damage	29	Torpidity	500

Habitat: Mountains, Colder regions
Damages: Thatch, Wood
Behavior: Highly Aggressive

Type: Mammal
Diet: Carnivore
Names: Smilodon

Attack 1: Melee Bite
Attack 2: -
Attack 3: -

Specifics:
- Often appear in pairs or in packs of up to six.
- Immediately attacks when it has spotted the player.

Utility:
- Can be used as mount even in difficult terrain (e.g. caves).
- Very good Keratin and Chitin gatherer (can defend itself in the process).

Drops

Raw Meat
Raw Prime Fish
Keratin
Hide

Harvests

Chitin, Keratin	■■■
Hide, Pelt	■■■
Leech Blood	■■■
Raw Meat	■■
Raw Prime Fish	■■
Organic Polymer	■■
Oil	■

Breeding

Type	Pregnancy
Gestation	4h:10m
Maturation	48h:44m

THE ISLAND   SC. EARTH
~~ABERRATION~~ EXTINCTION
~~GENESIS I~~   RAGNAROK
THE CENTER   VALGUERO

Level	37
Engram Cost	18
Hide	290
Fiber	155
Metal Ingots	20

CHEAT: *summon Saber_Character_BP_C*

CARRYABLE BY: Megalosaurus, Argentavis, Quetzal, Wyvern, Tusoteuthis, Karkinos

EGG SIZE: –

USEFUL TRAPS: Bola, Bear Trap, Large Bear Trap, Plant Species Y Trap

TAMING METHOD:
Knockout

SUITABLE FOOD FOR TAMING:
- Regular Kibble
- Raw Mutton
- Cooked Lamb Chop
- Raw Prime Fish
- Cooked Prime Meat
- Raw Prime Fish Meat
- Raw Meat
- Cooked Prime Fish Meat
- Cooked Meat
- Raw Fish Meat
- Cooked Fish Meat

SHINEHORN

BASIC STATS:

Health	115	Food	450	Speed (Land)	133
Stamina	180	Weight	100	Speed (Water)	300
Oxygen	180	Melee Damage	12	Torpidity	60

HABITAT: Higher altitudes
DAMAGES: Thatch
BEHAVIOR: Cowardly

TYPE: Fantasy Creature
DIET: Herbivore
NAMES: -

ATTACK 1: Melee
ATTACK 2: -
ATTACK 3: -

SPECIFICS:
- This small goat has glowing antlers.
- The glowing antlers can attract Seekers but keep Nameless away.

UTILITY:
- Due to its look and behavior, it's very suitable as pet.
- Should never be used as combat animal.

DROPS	HARVESTS	BREEDING	
Raw Meat	–	Type	Pregnancy
Raw Prime Fish		Gestation	4h:11m
Hide		Maturation	48h:44m

~~THE ISLAND~~   ~~SE. EARTH~~
ABERRATION   ~~EXTINCTION~~
GENESIS I   ~~RAGNAROK~~
~~THE CENTER~~   ~~VALGUERO~~

CHEAT: *summon LanternGoat_Character_BP_C*
CARRYABLE BY: Gigantopithecus, Karkinos, Procoptodon, Pteranodon, Quetzal, Tapejara
EGG SIZE: –

USEFUL TRAPS: Bola, Bear Trap, Plant Species Y Trap

TAMING METHOD:
Can be tamed by feeding.

SUITABLE FOOD FOR TAMING:
- Plant Species Z Seeds
- Aggeravic Mushroom
- Sweet Vegetable Cake
- Amarberry Seeds
- Citronal Seeds

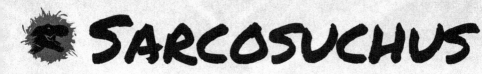

SARCOSUCHUS

BASIC STATS:

Health	400	Food	1500	Speed (Land)	150
Stamina	450	Weight	300	Speed (Water)	750
Oxygen	∞	Melee Damage	35	Torpidity	400

HABITAT: Beaches, Rivers, Swamps
DAMAGES: Thatch, Wood
BEHAVIOR: Highly Aggressive
TYPE: Reptile
DIET: Carnivore
NAMES: Sarco, Kroko

ATTACK 1: Melee; Bite
ATTACK 2: -
ATTACK 3: -

SPECIFICS:
- Since it's very fast in the water, you should be careful when you're in its territory. You shouldn't underestimate it on land either.
- Lies in wait for prey and attacks suddenly.

UTILITY:
- The best diver in the game and therefore suitable for surprise attacks emerging from the water.
- Its good maneuverability on land and high speed underwater (without oxygen problems), make it a good companion and mount for ocean expeditions. It can definitely hold its own against Megalodons.

DROPS

Raw Meat
Raw Prime Fish
Hide
Sarco Skin

HARVESTS

Hide	■■■
Raw Meat	■■■
Keratin	■■■
Chitin	

BREEDING

Type	Egg
Egg Temp.	30°-34°
Incubation	2h:29m
Maturation	46h:18m

THE ISLAND	SC. EARTH
ABERRATION	EXTINCTION
GENESIS I	~~RAGNAROK~~
THE CENTER	VALGUERO

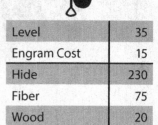

Level	35
Engram Cost	15
Hide	230
Fiber	75
Wood	20

CHEAT: *summon Sarco_Character_BP_C*
CARRYABLE BY: Quetzal, Wyvern, Tusoteuthis
EGG SIZE: Medium

USEFUL TRAPS: Chain Bola, Large Bear Trap, Plant Species Y Trap

TAMING METHOD:
Knockout

SUITABLE FOOD FOR TAMING:
- Regular Kibble
- Raw Mutton
- Cooked Lamb Chop
- Raw Prime Fish
- Cooked Prime Meat
- Raw Prime Fish Meat
- Raw Meat
- Cooked Prime Fish Meat
- Cooked Meat
- Raw Fish Meat
- Cooked Fish Meat

SPINOSAUR

Basic Stats:

Health	700	Food	2600	Speed (Land)	425
Stamina	350	Weight	350	Speed (Water)	1100
Oxygen	650	Melee Damage	40	Torpidity	850

Habitat: Near Water
Damages: Thatch, Wood
Behavior: Highly Aggressive

Type: Dinosaur
Diet: Carnivore
Names: Spino

Attack 1: Melee; Bite
Attack 2: Leap
Attack 3: Grab

Specifics:
- Drops the Fireworks Flaregun Skin among other things.
- Attack range is very low. This means, that you can get quite close to them before it poses a danger.

Utility:
- Perfect for hunting Piranhas and Coelacanths.
- Excellent swimmer and diver and therefore suitable for crossing or exploring the ocean.
- In comparison to an average Rex, it has lower health stats but its attacks are faster, affect more enemies, and knock them back.

Drops	Harvests		Breeding	
Raw Meat	Raw Prime Fish Meat	■■■	Type	Egg
Raw Prime Fish	Raw Fish Meat	■■■	Egg Temp.	30°-32°
Hide	Raw Prime Fish	■■■	Incubation	3h:50m
Spino Fin	Hide	■■	Maturation	71h:14m
Fireworks Flaregun Skin	Pelt	■■		
	Chitin/Keratin	■		

THE ISLAND   SC. EARTH
ABERRATION   EXTINCTION
GENESIS I   RAGNAROK
THE CENTER   VALGUERO

Level	71
Engram Cost	40
Hide	380
Fiber	200
Cementing Paste	45
Silica Pearls	25

CHEAT: summon Spino_Character_BP_C
CARRYABLE BY: Tusoteuthis
EGG SIZE: Large

USEFUL TRAPS: Chain Bola, Large Bear Trap

TAMING METHOD:
Knockout

SUITABLE FOOD FOR TAMING:
- Exceptional Kibble
- Raw Mutton
- Cooked Lamb Chop
- Raw Prime Fish
- Cooked Prime Meat
- Raw Prime Fish Meat
- Raw Meat
- Cooked Prime Fish Meat
- Cooked Meat
- Raw Fish Meat
- Cooked Fish Meat

STEGOSAURUS

Basic Stats:

Health	650	Food	6000	Speed (Land)	170
Stamina	300	Weight	500	Speed (Water)	300
Oxygen	150	Melee Damage	42	Torpidity	500

Habitat: Alomst Everywhere (except for cold regions)
Damages: Thatch, Wood
Behavior: Passive
Type: Dinosaur
Diet: Herbivore
Names: Stego

Attack 1: Melee; Tail Attack
Attack 2: -
Attack 3: -

Specifics:
- Slow movement speed, but you shouldn't underestimate its attacks.
- When it attacks, it swings its tail, which is completely covered by spikes.

Utility:
- Pack animal: it's slow but it can carry a lot.
- Resource gatherer: very suitable for gathering Berries.
- Good Berry harvester until you own a Brontosaurus.

Drops	Harvests		Breeding	
Raw Meat	Berries	■■■	Type	Egg
Raw Prime Fish	Thatch	■■	Egg Temp.	22°-28°
Hide	Wood	■	Incubation	2h:46m
Keratin			Maturation	51h:26m

THE ISLAND **SC. EARTH**
ABERRATION **EXTINCTION**
GENESIS I **RAGNAROK**
THE CENTER **VALGUERO**

Level	26
Engram Cost	15
Hide	200
Fiber	110
Wood	35

CHEAT: *summon Stego_Character_BP_C*

CARRYABLE BY: Quetzal, Wyvern, Tusoteuthis

EGG SIZE: Medium

USEFUL TRAPS: Chain Bola, Large Bear Trap, Plant Species Y Trap

TAMING METHOD:
Knockout

SUITABLE FOOD FOR TAMING:
- Regular Kibble
- Crops
- Mejoberries
- Berries

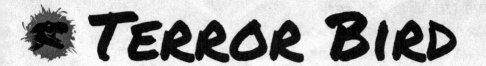

TERROR BIRD

Basic Stats:

Health	270	Food	1500	Speed (Land)	255
Stamina	160	Weight	1500	Speed (Water)	300
Oxygen	150	Melee Damage	18	Torpidity	300

Habitat: Redwoods, Forests
Damages: Thatch, Wood
Behavior: Highly Aggressive

Type: Birds
Diet: Carnivore
Names: Kapro/Gator

Attack 1: Melee; Bite
Attack 2: -
Attack 3: -

Specifics:
- Lives in groups of max. four members. If you want to fight one, you should be able to defeat all the others in the group as well.
- Despite having small wings, it's not able to fly. Its wings do allow it to glide in order to avoid damage caused by falling, though.

Utility:
- Suitable for exploring since it's fast and is able to avoid damage caused by falling.

Drops	Harvests		Breeding	
Raw Meat	Raw Meat	■■■	Type	Egg
Hide	Hide	■■■	Egg Temp.	20°-28°
			Incubation	1h:59m
			Maturation	46h:18m

THE ISLAND **SC. EARTH**
~~ABERRATION~~ **EXTINCTION**
GENESIS I **RAGNAROK**
THE CENTER **VALGUERO**

Level	33
Engram Cost	15
Hide	110
Fiber	65
Wood	20

CHEAT: *summon TerrorBird_Character_BP_C*

CARRYABLE BY: Kaprosuchus, Megalosaurus, Argentavis, Quetzal, Wyvern, Tusoteuthis

EGG SIZE: Medium

USEFUL TRAPS: Bola, Bear Trap, Large Bear Trap, Plant Species Y Trap

TAMING METHOD:
Knockout

SUITABLE FOOD FOR TAMING:
- Regular Kibble
- Raw Mutton
- Cooked Lamb Chop
- Raw Prime Fish
- Cooked Prime Meat
- Raw Prime Fish Meat
- Raw Meat
- Cooked Prime Fish Meat
- Cooked Meat
- Raw Fish Meat
- Cooked Fish Meat

THERIZINOSAUR

Basic Stats:

Health	200	Food	1200	Speed (Land)	180
Stamina	350	Weight	140	Speed (Water)	220
Oxygen	150	Melee Damage	25	Torpidity	200

Habitat: Riverbank, Beaches, Forests
Damages: Thatch, Wood, Adobe, Stone
Behavior: Aggressive
Type: Dinosaur
Diet: Carnivore
Names: Theri, Freddy Krueger

Attack 1: Claw Attack
Attack 2: Leap
Attack 3: Grab

Specifics:
- Heals more quickly when it's being fed Sweet Vegetable Cake.
- Lives alone or in groups. If you attack it, you'll also have to fight the other group members. Its attack destroys armor within seconds.

Utility:
- Very suitable for gathering different materials (see below).

Drops	Harvests		Breeding	
Raw Meat	Wood, Chitin, Keratin, Rare Flower, Hide, Cactus Sap, Silk, Rare Mushroom, Fiber, Plant Species Y Seeds, Berries, Org. Polymer	■■■	Type	Egg
Raw Prime Fish			Egg Temp.	26°-32°
Hide			Incubation	1h:59m
Keratin			Maturation	115h:45m
Therezino claw				
	Thatch, Raw Prime Fish, Raw Meat, Raw Fish Meat, Raw Prime Fish Meat	■■		

THE ISLAND   SC. EARTH
~~ABERRATION~~   EXTINCTION
GENESIS I   RAGNAROK
THE CENTER   VALGUERO

Level	69
Engram Cost	40
Hide	285
Fiber	160
Wood	120
Metal	55

CHEAT: *summon Therizino_Character_BP_C*
CARRYABLE BY: Quetzal, Wyvern, Tusoteuthis
EGG SIZE: Very Large

USEFUL TRAPS: Chain Bola, Large Bear Trap, Plant Species Y Trap

TAMING METHOD:
Knockout

SUITABLE FOOD FOR TAMING:
- Exceptional Kibble
- Crops
- Mejoberries
- Berries

NOTES:
- This creature is often underestimated, but it's a good fighter because of its claws. In addition, it's a serious threat when gathering resources.
- You can improve its resource gathering ability separately.

Thorny Dragon

Basic Stats:

Health	260	Food	1200	Speed (Land)	245
Stamina	350	Weight	300	Speed (Water)	300
Oxygen	150	Melee Damage	40	Torpidity	450

Habitat: Mountains **Type:** Fantasy Creature
Damages: Thatch, Wood **Diet:** Carnivore
Behavior: Highly Aggressive **Names:** Thorny

Attack 1: Claw
Attack 2: Tail Attack
Attack 3: -

Specifics:
- Causes damage as well torpidity with its Tail Attack. Warning: it's able to shoot its spikes.
- Attacks smaller creatures but ignores larger ones.

Utility:
- As a tame equipped with a saddle, you can use it as a mobile Forge.
- Very suitable for collecting large amounts of Wood in a short period of time.
- Can use its tail whip attack to stun small and medium-sized creatures.

Drops	Harvests		Breeding	
Raw Meat	Wood	■■■	Type	Egg
Hide	Thatch	■	Egg Temp.	22°-28°
Keratin			Incubation	2h:29m
			Maturation	48h:44m

~~THE ISLAND~~   SC. EARTH
~~ABERRATION~~   EXTINCTION
GENESIS I   RAGNAROK
~~THE CENTER~~   ~~VALGUERO~~

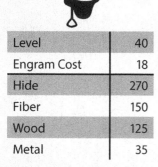

Level	40
Engram Cost	18
Hide	270
Fiber	150
Wood	125
Metal	35

CHEAT: *summon SpineyLizard_Character_BP_C*

CARRYABLE BY: Megalosaurus, Quetzal, Wyvern, Tusoteuthis

EGG SIZE: Medium

USEFUL TRAPS: Bola, Chain Bola, Bear Trap, Large Bear Trap, Plant Species Y Trap

TAMING METHOD:
Knockout

SUITABLE FOOD FOR TAMING:
- Regular Kibble
- Raw Mutton
- Cooked Lamb Chop
- Raw Prime Fish
- Cooked Prime Meat
- Raw Prime Fish Meat
- Raw Meat
- Cooked Prime Fish Meat
- Cooked Meat
- Raw Fish Meat
- Cooked Fish Meat

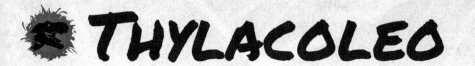

THYLACOLEO

Basic Stats:

Health	700	Food	1500	Speed (Land)	230
Stamina	400	Weight	400	Speed (Water)	600
Oxygen	200	Melee Damage	40	Torpidity	700

Habitat: Swamps
Damages: Thatch, Wood
Behavior: Highly Aggressive

Type: Mammal
Diet: Carnivore
Names: Thyla

Attack 1: Claw
Attack 2: Roar
Attack 3: Pounce

Specifics:
- Usually lurks in trees and jumps at its prey or pulls the rider out of the saddle. This is why the Redwoods are an extremely dangerous place; we recommend avoiding them.
- Warning: when it attacks the player, they won't be able to move anymore, which will cause their death without immediate help.

Utility:
- Due to its melee damage stats, stamina, and it's ability to climb over vertical obstacles, it's a beneficial combat animal.
- A good guard animal for your base.

Drops
Raw Meat
Hide
Keratin
Thylacoleo Claw

Harvests
Raw Meat	■■■
Hide	■■■

Breeding
Type	Pregnancy
Gestation	4h:53m
Maturation	48h:44m

THE ISLAND   **SC. EARTH**
~~ABERRATION~~   **EXTINCTION**
GENESIS I   **RAGNAROK**
THE CENTER   **VALGUERO**

Level	51
Engram Cost	18
Hide	290
Fiber	155
Wood	20

CHEAT: summon Iguanodon_Character_BP_C
CARRYABLE BY: Quetzal, Wyvern, Tusoteuthis
EGG SIZE: -

USEFUL TRAPS: Bola, Bear Trap, Large Bear Trap, Plant Species Y Trap

TAMING METHOD:
Knockout

SUITABLE FOOD FOR TAMING:
- Extraordinary Kibble
- Raw Mutton
- Cooked Lamb Chop
- Raw Prime Fish
- Cooked Prime Meat
- Raw Meat/Prime Fish Meat
- Cooked Prime Fish Meat
- Cooked Meat
- Raw Fish Meat
- Cooked Fish Meat

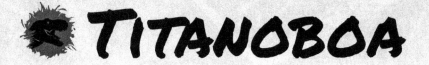
TITANOBOA

Basic Stats:

Health	170	Food	1200	Speed (Land)	225
Stamina	150	Weight	150	Speed (Water)	400
Oxygen	∞	Melee Damage	30	Torpidity	175

Habitat: Caves, Swamps **Type:** Reptile
Damages: Thatch **Diet:** Carnivore
Behavior: Highly Aggressive **Names:** Boa

Attack 1: Bite
Attack 2: -
Attack 3: -

Specifics:
- Has a powerful venom that paralyzes its victims. Should you be poisoned, you won't just fall victim to it, but to all the other predators as well.
- Attacks most creatures as soon as it notices them.
- Warning: it often hides in spots where you can't readily see it.
- We recommend fighting it with ranged weapons.
- Difficult to tame and only feeds on eggs as a tame (fertilized or unfertilized).

Utility:
- Its eggs are white and can be therefore easily recognized in Swamps.

Drops	Harvests	Breeding
Raw Meat	-	Not breedable
Raw Prime Fish		
Filet		
Titanoboa Venom		

THE ISLAND   SC. EARTH
ABERRATION   EXTINCTION
GENESIS I   RAGNAROK
THE CENTER   VALGUERO

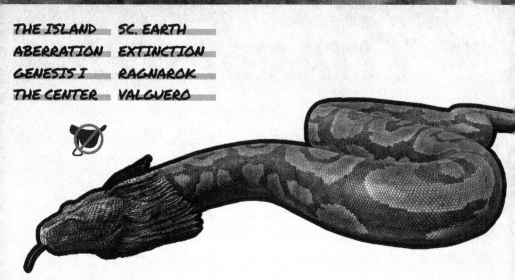

CHEAT: summon BoaFrill_Character_BP_C

CARRYABLE BY: Megalosaurus, Argentavis, Quetzal, Wyvern, Tusoteuthis

EGG SIZE: Large

USEFUL TRAPS: None

TAMING METHOD:
Can be tamed by feeding.

SUITABLE FOOD FOR TAMING:
(All fertilized eggs work. The selection below only shows the best eggs for taming. They are listed according to size).
- Fertilized Giganotosaurus Egg
- Fertilized Bronto Egg
- Fertilized Allosaurus Egg
- Fertilized Baryonyx Egg
- Fertilized Oviraptor Egg
- Fertilized Archaeopteryx Egg

Place the fertilized egg in front of the Boa and let it eat it. Make sure that it isn't aggressive at this point or distracted by you or any other creature in the surroundings. It's preferable to use a flying mount for dropping the eggs. Before you do this, remove all huntable creatures from the Titanboa's surroundings.

TITANOMYRMA

Basic Stats:

Health	35	Food	450	Speed (Land)	67
Stamina	100	Weight	150	Speed (Water)	200
Oxygen	150	Melee Damage	7	Torpidity	50

Habitat: In areas where weeds grow
Damages: Thatch
Behavior: Highly Aggressive
Type: Invertebrate
Diet: Carnivore
Names: –

Attack 1: Melee (drone)
Attack 2: Melee (soldier)
Attack 3: –

Specifics:
- This species exists in two different variants: drone and soldier. Usually two to three soldiers spawn in one group (normally four to six). The rest are drones.
- Drones move on earth. Alternatively, the soldiers have wings.
- Attacks can be dangerous since they attack in swarms and are often unnoticeable in high grass. Their bite is toxic and decreases stamina.

Utility:
- Since it's neither tameable/breedable nor suitable for gathering, you can only collect its drops and gain experience when killing it.
- When they're killed and collected by a Beelzebufo, they drop a considerable amount of Cementing Paste.

Drops	Harvests	Breeding
Raw Meat	–	Not breedable
Chitin		
Cementing Paste		

THE ISLAND	SC. EARTH
~~ABERRATION~~	EXTINCTION
GENESIS I	RAGNAROK
THE CENTER	VALGUERO

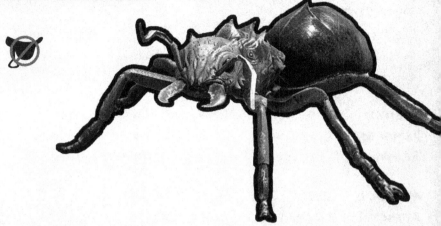

CHEAT: *summon Ant_Character_BP_C*

CARRYABLE BY: Kaprosuchus, Megalosaurus, Tapejara, Pteranodon, Argentavis, Quetzal, Griffin, Wyvern, Tusoteuthis

EGG SIZE: -

USEFUL TRAPS: -

TAMING METHOD: -

SUITABLE FOOD FOR TAMING: -

TITANOSAUR

Basic Stats:

Health	23000	Food	8640	Speed (Land)	700
Stamina	2000	Weight	50000	Speed (Water)	800
Oxygen	600	Melee Damage	1000	Torpidity	25000

Habitat: Forest, Redwoods (very rare)
Damages: Everything
Behavior: Passive
Type: Reptile
Diet: Herbivore
Names: Titano

Attack 1: Stomp
Attack 2: Tail Attack
Attack 3: −

Specifics:
- As long as it's left alone, it's peaceful.
- Because of its high base damage and health stats, a fight with it isn't recommended. Should you fight it nevertheless, heavy ranged weapons and some good large fighting animals are beneficial.

Utility:
- The walking fort: in combination with its ability to destroy large metal structures and climb high walls, it's a dangerous combat animal during tribal warfare due to its platform saddle, which can be equipped with buildings, beds, and stationary weapons and its ability to destroy even metal buildings.
- Warning: once it's tamed, it stops eating and is going to starve to death after some time (you can only use it for about 15-20 hours).

Drops	Harvests	Breeding
Raw Meat	−	Not breedable
Raw Prime Fish		
Hide		
Sauropod Vertebra		

~~THE ISLAND~~   ~~SE. EARTH~~
~~ABERRATION~~   ~~EXTINCTION~~
~~GENESIS I~~   ~~RAGNAROK~~
~~THE CENTER~~   ~~VALGUERO~~

Level	100
Engram Cost	120
Hide	4000
Metal Ingots	4000
Cementing Paste	1600
Fiber	2000

CHEAT: summon Titanosaur_Character_BP_C

CARRYABLE BY: –

EGG SIZE: –

USEFUL TRAPS: Bola, Bear Trap, Large Bear Trap, Plant Species Y Trap

TAMING METHOD:
Knockout (only Cannons, Catapult Turrets, or Rockets; aim for the head). When it's finally been stunned, equip it with a platform saddle and, then it's tamed.

SUITABLE FOOD FOR TAMING: –

TRICERATOPS

Basic Stats:

Health	200	Food	1200	Speed (Land)	180
Stamina	350	Weight	140	Speed (Water)	220
Oxygen	150	Melee Damage	25	Torpidity	200

Habitat: Almost everywhere (normally Mountains)
Damages: Thatch, Wood
Behavior: Passive

Type: Dinosaur
Diet: Herbivore
Names: Trike

Attack 1: Melee (Headbutt)
Attack 2:
Attack 3:

Specifics:
- Sometimes it gets stuck between trees which makes it easier to defeat.
- Its attacks are very dangerous. Its enormous headbutt can knock players off cliffs and mountains. We recommend avoiding this creature.

Utility:
- Suitable for defending your own camp in the beginning.
- Suitable for collecting Berries and Thatch. Just like the Stegosaurus, it's a good resource collector as long as you don't own a Brontosaurus. A Trike is an enormous help in the beginning.

Drops	Harvests		Breeding	
Raw Meat	Cactus Sap	■■■	Type	Egg
Hide	Berries	■■■	Egg Temp.	22°-28°
Keratin	Thatch, Wood	■■	Incubation	2h:29m
	Rare Flower	■	Maturation	46h:18m
	Rare Mushroom	■		

THE ISLAND ~~SC. EARTH~~
ABERRATION EXTINCTION
GENESIS I RAGNAROK
THE CENTER VALGUERO

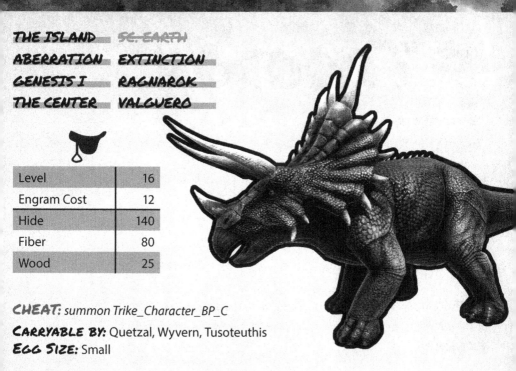

Level	16
Engram Cost	12
Hide	140
Fiber	80
Wood	25

CHEAT: *summon Trike_Character_BP_C*

CARRYABLE BY: Quetzal, Wyvern, Tusoteuthis

EGG SIZE: Small

USEFUL TRAPS: Bola, Bear Trap, Large Bear Trap, Plant Species Y Trap

TAMING METHOD:
Knockout

SUITABLE FOOD FOR TAMING:
- Simple Kibble
- Crops
- Mejoberries
- Berries

WARNING: its head armor protects it against head shots. Aim for its body in order to stun it.

 TROODON

Basic Stats:

Health	200	Food	200	Speed (Land)	480
Stamina	150	Weight	140	Speed (Water)	300
Oxygen	150	Melee Damage	7	Torpidity	180

Habitat: Redwoods, Forest, Banks
Damages: Thatch, Wood
Behavior: Highly Aggressive
Type: Dinosaur
Diet: Carnivore
Names: Trudi, Troodi

Attack 1: Bite (extreme paralysis in humans, decreases a creature's stamina)
Attack 2: Leap
Attack 3: -

Specifics:
- Quite peaceful during the day but very aggressive at night. Its eyes start glowing when it's dark. Attacks in groups. When one of them starts an attack, the others follow.
- Possesses a toxic poison that slowly decreases the victim's movement speed as well as its stamina. If humans are affected by its poison, they are paralyzed very quickly. Therefore, it should only be attacked from a safe distance or when you have a good mount. For players who are exploring by foot, Troodons are nothing but trouble.

Utility:
- Perfect for attacks during the night and to stun enemies.
- Scout feature: in its radial menu, you can select the command „Scout". Then, the nearest selected target is indicated.

Drops	Harvests		Breeding	
Raw Meat	Raw Meat	■ ■	Type	Egg
Hide			Egg Temp.	28°-32°
Nerdy Glasses Skin			Incubation	1h:8m
			Maturation	21h:3m

THE ISLAND	SC. EARTH
~~ABERRATION~~	EXTINCTION
~~GENESIS I~~	RAGNAROK
THE CENTER	VALGUERO

Level	30
Engram Cost	12
Hide	80
Fiber	50
Wood	15

CHEAT: *summon Troodon_Character_BP_C*

CARRYABLE BY: Kaprosuchus, Megalosaurus, Tapejara, Pteranodon, Argentavis, Quetzal, Griffin, Wyvern, Tusoteuthis, Karkinos

EGG SIZE: Medium

USEFUL TRAPS: Bola, Bear Trap, Plant Species Y Trap

TAMING METHOD:
Can be tamed by feeding specific food.

SUITABLE FOOD FOR TAMING:

- In order to tame a Troodon, you must allow it to eat other tamed dinos. Put a tame close to it and allow it to attack and kill it (e.g. you can first set your dino on aggressive and set it back to passive by immediate whistling). As an alternative, you can use other tribe members who are willing to sacrifice themselves. The player that is controlling the taming process, should then stay in the proximity.
- Example: a level 50 Troodon must kill two level 100 Carnos or four level 154 Ankylosaurus in order to be tamed. The higher the level of the sacrificed dino, the more effective the taming.

TYRANNOSAURUS

Basic Stats:

Health	1100	Food	3000	Speed (Land)	515
Stamina	420	Weight	500	Speed (Water)	300
Oxygen	150	Melee Damage	62	Torpidity	1550

Habitat: Snowy regions (more often), Mountains
Damages: Thatch, Wood
Behavior: Highly Aggressive
Type: Dinosaur
Diet: Carnivore
Names: Rex

Attack 1: Bite
Attack 2: Roar
Attack 3: Bite

Specifics:
- Harder to tame since its eggs require a high temperature over a long period of time.
- Attacks every moving creature. If it has the choice between big and small prey, it often opts for the bigger one (lower possibility to flee).

Utility:
- Very good resource collector for Meat, Hide, and Pelt.
- Secure riding and hunting animal.
- Guard and combat animal.
- First choice for many battles against Alpha creatures or bosses.
- Versatile and cool appearance: almost everyone wants to have a Rex.

Drops	Harvests		Breeding	
Raw Meat	Raw Prime Fish	■■■	Type	Egg
Hide	Raw Meat	■■■	Egg Temp.	32°-34°
Raw Prime Fish	Chitin/Keratin	■■	Incubation	4h:59m
Tyrannosaurus Arm	Pelt/Hide	■■	Maturation	92h:35m

THE ISLAND SC. EARTH
~~ABERRATION~~ EXTINCTION
~~GENESIS I~~ RAGNAROK
THE CENTER VALGUERO

Level	74
Engram Cost	40
Hide	380
Fiber	200
Metal Ingots	50

Polymer	350
Metal Ingots	1800
Crystal	250
Element	40
Black Pearls	100

CHEAT: summon Rex_Character_BP_C

CARRYABLE BY: Tusoteuthis

EGG SIZE: Very Large

USEFUL TRAPS: Chain Bola, Large Bear Trap

TAMING METHOD:
Knockout

SUITABLE FOOD FOR TAMING:
- Exceptional Kibble
- Raw Mutton/Cooked Lamb Chop
- Raw Prime Fish/Cooked Prime Meat
- Raw Prime Fish Meat/Cooked Prime Fish Meat
- Raw Meat/Cooked Meat
- Raw Fish Meat/Cooked Fish Meat

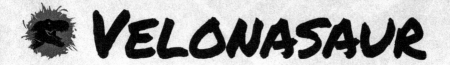
VELONASAUR

Basic Stats:

Health	440	Food	2250	Speed (Land)	505
Stamina	325	Weight	325	Speed (Water)	300
Oxygen	225	Melee Damage	32	Torpidity	400

Habitat: Desert Dome
Damages: Thatch
Behavior: Highly Aggressive

Type: Fantasy Creature
Diet: Carnivore
Names: Velona

Attack 1: Melee/In turret mode: Mini Gun
Attack 2: Tail Attack
Attack 3: Toggle (Turret Mode)

Specifics:
- Normally attacks with claws and teeth. If its opponent is beyond reach, it cocks its spikes and shoots them like a machine gun at its enemies.
- Can be used as turret.

Utility:
- Very good fighting and supporting mount animal that can attack enemies from a distance and is also able to dish it out during melee.
- Even without a rider, you can enable its turret mode via behavior. It works like a turret for your base.

Drops	Harvests		Breeding	
Raw Meat	Raw Prime Fish	■■■	Type	Egg
Hide	Raw Meat	■■■	Egg Temp.	28°-32°
Nerdy glasses	Chitin/Keratin	■■	Incubation	1h:08m
	Hide/Pelt	■■	Maturation	46h:17m

~~THE ISLAND~~　~~SC EARTH~~
~~ABERRATION~~　**EXTINCTION**
~~GENESIS I~~　~~RAGNAROK~~
~~THE CENTER~~　~~VALGUERO~~

Level	27
Engram Cost	8
Hide	350
Fiber	185
Chitin or Keratin	150

CHEAT: summon Spindles_Character_BP_C
CARRYABLE BY: Wyvern, Quetzal
EGG SIZE: Medium

USEFUL TRAPS: Chain Bola, Large Bear Trap, Plant Species Y Trap

TAMING METHOD:
Knockout

SUITABLE FOOD FOR TAMING:
- Regular Kibble
- Raw Mutton
- Cooked Lamb Chop
- Raw Prime Fish
- Cooked Prime Meat
- Raw Prime Fish Meat
- Cooked Prime Fish Meat
- Raw Meat
- Cooked Meat
- Raw Fish Meat
- Cooked Fish Meat

Woolly Rhino

Basic Stats:

Health	500	Food	3000	Speed (Land)	185
Stamina	120	Weight	750	Speed (Water)	300
Oxygen	100	Melee Damage	40	Torpidity	600

Habitat: Colder regions **Type:** Mammal
Damages: Thatch, Wood **Diet:** Herbivore
Behavior: Passive **Names:** –

Attack 1: Melee (Assault/Headbutt)
Attack 2: –
Attack 3: –

Specifics:
- When it employs a charge attack in combat, you should get out of the way because its hit causes a lot of melee damage.
- When it attacks, it's possible that other nearby Woolly Rhinos follow its example.

Utility:
- A good mount that can pull down obstacles like trees. It does, however get, caught on stones sometimes.
- Suitable for attacking enemies (causes a lot of melee damage).

Drops

Hide
Keratin
Pelt
Raw Meat
Woolly Rhino Horn

Harvests

Berries	■■■
Thatch	■■■
Wood	■

Breeding

Type	Pregnancy
Gestation	3h:58m
Maturation	46h:18m

THE ISLAND ~~SC. EARTH~~
~~ABERRATION~~ EXTINCTION
~~GENESIS I~~ RAGNAROK
THE CENTER VALGUERO

Level	53
Engram Cost	24
Hide	250
Fiber	130
Cementing Paste or Achatina Paste	100
Metal Ingots	60

CHEAT: *summon Rhino_Character_BP_C*

CARRYABLE BY: Quetzal, Tusoteuthis

EGG SIZE: -

USEFUL TRAPS: Chain Bola, Large Bear Trap

TAMING METHOD:
Knockout

SUITABLE FOOD FOR TAMING:
- Superior Kibble
- Crops
- Mejoberries
- Berries

YUTYRANNUS

BASIC STATS:

Health	1100	Food	3000	Speed (Land)	700
Stamina	420	Weight	500	Speed (Water)	300
Oxygen	150	Melee Damage	55	Torpidity	1500

HABITAT: The Island (Snow biome) **TYPE:** Dinosaur
DAMAGES: Thatch, Wood **DIET:** Carnivore
BEHAVIOR: Highly Aggressive **NAMES:** -

ATTACK 1: Bite
ATTACK 2: Battle Cry: allies become stronger
ATTACK 3: Fear Roar: induces fear and causes weaker creatures to flee

SPECIFICS:
- Usually appears with two to four Carnos.
- Scares other animals away by using its terrifying roar, which causes them to run away erratically.

UTILITY:
- Strong fighter. When you ride it, take advantage of its roar.
- Good riding mount in a group of combat dinos and very helpful as a part of a battle group against bosses.

DROPS	HARVESTS		BREEDING	
Pelt	Hide	■■■	Type	Egg
Raw Meat	Raw Prime Fish Meat	■■■	Egg Temp.	32°-34°
Raw Prime Fish	Raw Prime Fish	■■	Incubation	5h
Yutyrannus Lungs	Raw Meat	■■	Maturation	185:11m

THE ISLAND   SC. EARTH
~~ABERRATION~~   EXTINCTION
~~GENESIS I~~   RAGNAROK
THE CENTER   VALGUERO

Level	80
Engram Cost	50
Hide	425
Fiber	350
Metal Ingots	135
Silica Pearls or Silicate	125

CHEAT: summon Yutyrannus_Character_BP_C
CARRYABLE BY: Tusoteuthis
EGG SIZE: Special

USEFUL TRAPS: Chain Bola, Large Bear Trap

TAMING METHOD:
Knockout

SUITABLE FOOD FOR TAMING:
- Extraordinary Kibble
- Raw Mutton
- Cooked Lamb Chop
- Raw Prime Fish
- Cooked Prime Meat
- Raw Prime Fish Meat
- Cooked Prime Fish Meat
- Raw Meat
- Cooked Meat
- Raw Fish Meat
- Cooked Fish Meat

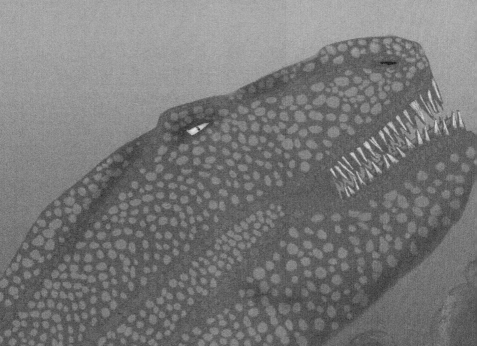

13: Aerial Creatures

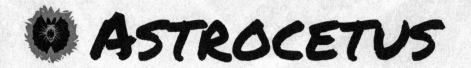

ASTROCETUS

BASIC STATS:

Health	2800	Food	6000	Speed (Air)	600
Stamina	600	Weight	2000	Speed (Water)	300
Oxygen	∞	Melee Damage	88	Torpidity	4200

HABITAT: Lunar biome
DAMAGES: Thatch, Wood
BEHAVIOR: Aggressive

TYPE: Fantasy Creature
DIET: Carnivore
NAMES: -

ATTACK 1: Melee; Bite
ATTACK 2: Melee, Tail Attack
ATTACK 3: -

SPECIFICS:
- Can teleport itself; even through dense matter.
- Slow, and can only be found in the Lunar biome, but can survive everywhere.

UTILITY:
- In addition to the rider, the Tek saddle has three gun turrets that can be manned and require Element as ammunition. Setting it up like this transforms the Astrocetus into a giant aerial battleship.
- The tamed Astrocetus produces Ambergris which is required for raising Magmasaurs.

DROPS	HARVESTS	BREEDING
Ambergris	-	-
Raw Meat		

~~THE ISLAND~~ ~~SE. EARTH~~
~~ABERRATION~~ ~~EXTINCTION~~
GENESIS I ~~RAGNAROK~~
~~THE CENTER~~ ~~VALGUERO~~

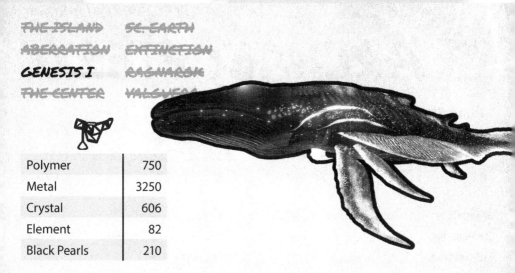

Polymer	750
Metal	3250
Crystal	606
Element	82
Black Pearls	210

CHEAT: summon SpaceWhale_Character_BP_C

CARRYABLE BY: –

EGG SIZE: –

USEFUL TRAPS: –

TAMING METHOD:
Knockout; but only caused by large weapons like a Cannon. We recommend using a Cannon mounted on a Tek Hover Skiff for hunting the Astrocetus.

SUITABLE FOOD FOR TAMING:
- Extraordinary Kibble
- Raw Mutton
- Cooked Lamb Chop
- Raw Prime Fish
- Cooked Prime Meat
- Raw Prime Fish Meat
- Cooked Prime Fish Meat
- Raw Meat
- Cooked Meat
- Raw Fish Meat
- Cooked Fish Meat

Archaeopteryx

Basic Stats:

Health	125	Food	900	Speed (Air)	150
Stamina	150	Weight	30	Speed (Water)	750
Oxygen	150	Melee Damage	5	Torpidity	100

Habitat:	Redwoods	**Type:**	Bird
Damages:	Thatch	**Diet:**	Carnivore
Behavior:	Cowardly	**Names:**	-

Attack 1: Melee
Attack 2: -
Attack 3: -

Specifics:
- As soon as it's tamed, it only feeds on Chitin.
- Before taming, we recommend catching it with a Bola.

Utility:
- Glider: you can use it to glide. By doing this, you can cross canyons or use it as a parachute. Just carry it to make use of this function.
- Collects tree Sap automatically (set to "wandering around").

Drops	Harvests		Breeding	
Raw Meat	Sap	■ ■	Type	Egg
Hide	Raw Meat	■ ■	Egg Temp.	16°-20°
	Raw Fish Meat	■ ■	Incubation	2h:37m
	Chitin	■	Maturation	15h:26m

THE ISLAND SC. EARTH
~~ABERRATION~~ EXTINCTION
GENESIS I RAGNAROK
THE CENTER VALGUERO

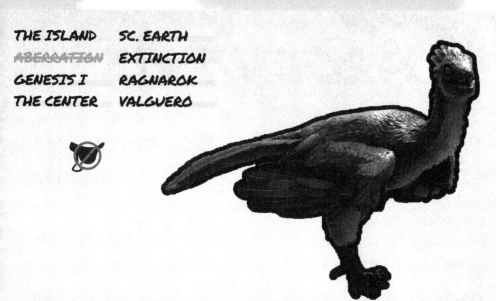

CHEAT: summon Archa_Character_BP_C

CARRYABLE BY: Tusoteuthis, Kaprosuchus, Megalosaurus, Tapejara, Pteranodon, Argentavis, Quetzal, Griffin, Wyvern

EGG SIZE: Small

USEFUL TRAPS: Bola, Bear Trap, Plant Species Y Trap

TAMING METHOD:
Knockout

SUITABLE FOOD FOR TAMING:
- Simple Kibble
- Chitin

ARGENTAVIS

Basic Stats:

Health	365	Food	2000	Torpidity	600
Stamina	400	Weight	400	Speed (Land)	260
Oxygen	150	Melee Damage	25	Speed (Air)	600
				Speed (Water)	300

Habitat: Mountains
Damages: Wood, Thatch
Behavior: Aggressive

Type: Bird
Diet: Scavenger
Names: Argy, Argent, Eagle

Attack 1: Rip (Melee)
Attack 2: Grab and Carry (with its claws)
Attack 3: -

Specifics:
- Becomes aggressive when you approach its prey.
- Very vulnerable to head shots; aim for its head when attempting to tame it.

Utility:
- Air transport: a reliable transport creature due to its great loading capacity and stamina.
- Long-haul aircraft: thanks to its high stamina, it can cover long distances without taking a break.
- Taming animal: you can grab other players or creatures and carry them (Attention: only your own creatures in the official PvE mode).

Drops	Harvests		Breeding	
Raw Prime Fish	Raw Prime Fish	■■■	Type	Egg
Raw Meat	Raw Meat	■■■	Egg Temp.	12°-13,5°
Hide	Chitin, Keratin	■■	Incubation	2h:56m
Argentavis Claw	Hide, Pelt	■■	Maturation	54h:28m
	Organic Polymer	■		

THE ISLAND   SC. EARTH
~~ABERRATION~~   EXTINCTION
GENESIS I   RAGNAROK
THE CENTER   VALGUERO

Level	62
Engram Cost	21
Hide	350
Fiber	185
Chitin	150

CHEAT: summon Argent_Character_BP_C
CARRYABLE BY: Megalosaurus
EGG SIZE: Large

USEFUL TRAPS: Chain Bola, Bear Trap, Large Bear Trap, Plant Species Y Trap

TAMING METHOD:
Knockout

SUITABLE FOOD FOR TAMING:
- Superior Kibble
- Raw Mutton
- Cooked Lamb Chop
- Raw Prime Fish
- Cooked Prime Meat
- Raw Prime Fish Meat
- Cooked Prime Fish Meat
- Raw Meat
- Cooked Meat
- Raw Fish Meat
- Cooked Fish Meat

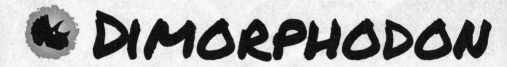
DIMORPHODON

Basic Stats:

				Torpidity	100
Health	125	Food	900	Speed (Land)	80
Stamina	150	Weight	50	Speed (Air)	450
Oxygen	150	Melee Damage	23	Wasser	100

Habitat: Almost everywhere (except for cold regions)
Damages: Thatch
Behavior: Passive

Type: Reptile
Diet: Carnivore
Names: Dimo, Dimorph

Attack 1: Melee
Attack 2: -
Attack 3: -

Specifics:
- Usually appears in groups and can therefore pose a danger.
- Immediately attacks the mount's rider.

Utility:
- Several tamed ones are a good army for protection or attacks. They're small, hard to shoot, and attack with great precision.
- Can be carried on your shoulder.

Drops	Harvests		Breeding	
Raw Meat	Raw Meat	▪▪	Type	Egg
Hide	Raw Prime Fish	▪	Egg Temp.	35°-38°
	Chitin, Keratin	▪	Incubation	1h:20m
	Pelt, Hide	▪	Maturation	25h:02m

THE ISLAND   ~~SE. EARTH~~
ABERRATION   EXTINCTION
GENESIS I   RAGNAROK
THE CENTER   VALGUERO

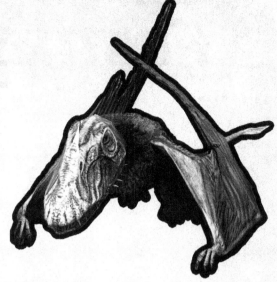

CHEAT: summon Dimorph_Character_BP_C
CARRYABLE BY: Tusoteuthis, Megalosaurus, Kaprosuchus
EGG SIZE: Small

USEFUL TRAPS: Bola, Bear Trap, Plant Species Y Trap

TAMING METHOD:
Knockout

SUITABLE FOOD FOR TAMING:
- Raw Mutton
- Cooked Lamb Chop
- Raw Prime Fish
- Cooked Prime Meat
- Raw Prime Fish Meat
- Cooked Prime Fish Meat
- Raw Meat
- Cooked Meat
- Raw Fish Meat
- Cooked Fish Meat

FEATHERLIGHT

BASIC STATS:

Health	115	Food	450	Speed (Air)	300
Stamina	100	Weight	70	Speed (Land)	60
Oxygen	180	Melee Damage	3	Speed (Water)	100
				Torpidity	60

HABITAT: The Spine/Lost Roads
DAMAGES: Thatch
BEHAVIOR: Cowardly

TYPE: Bird, Fantasy Creature
DIET: Herbivore
NAMES: -

ATTACK 1: Bite attack
ATTACK 2: Melee
ATTACK 3: -

SPECIFICS:
- Glowing feathers on its head.
- Its light can lure other predators (Seeker).

UTILITY:
- Its light prevents Nameless from attacking.
- Can be carried on your shoulder.
- Never start an attack with it since it flees as soon as it's attacked.

DROPS	HARVESTS		BREEDING	
Raw Meat	Raw Meat	■ ■ ■	Type	Egg
Raw Prime Fish			Egg Temp.	29°-32°
Hide			Incubation	1h:40m
			Maturation	48h:44m

~~THE ISLAND~~ ~~SC. EARTH~~
ABERRATION ~~EXTINCTION~~
GENESIS I ~~RAGNAROK~~
~~THE CENTER~~ **VALGUERO**

CHEAT: summon LanternBird_Character_BP_C

CARRYABLE BY: Gigantopithecus, Procoptodon

EGG SIZE: Very Small

USEFUL TRAPS: Bola, Bear Trap, Plant Species Y Trap

TAMING METHOD:
Can be tamed by active feeding.

SUITABLE FOOD FOR TAMING:
- Plant Species Z Seeds
- Auric Mushroom
- Amarberry Seeds
- Citronal Seeds

VULTURE

Basic Stats:

Health	2800	Food	6000	Speed (Air)	600
Stamina	600	Weight	2000	Speed (Water)	300
Oxygen	∞	Melee Damage	88	Torpidity	4200

Habitat: Plains, Edges of Deserts
Damages: Thatch
Behavior: Aggressive

Type: Bird
Diet: Scavenger
Names: -

Attack 1: Bite
Attack 2: -
Attack 3: -

Specifics:
- Immediately attacks in order to defend corpses in the proximity.
- If you want to tame it, eliminate all creatures in the surroundings.

Utility:
- Meat collector: Meat spoils much slower when placed into the Vulture's inventory. Command it to collect Meat; Raw Prime Meat remains fresh for longer.
- In groups, it's a very dangerous opponent: base defense or attack.
- Can be carried on your shoulder and it also attacks from there.

Drops
Raw Meat

Harvests	
Raw Meat	■■■
Raw Prime Fish	■■■
Fiber	■■■
Hide, Berries	■■■
Chitin	■■■

Breeding	
Type	Egg
Egg Temp.	35°-38°
Incubation	1h:21m
Maturation	25h:1m

~~THE ISLAND~~ SC. EARTH
~~ABERRATION~~ ~~EXTINCTION~~
~~GENESIS I~~ RAGNAROK
~~THE CENTER~~ ~~VALGUERO~~

CHEAT: summon Vulture_Character_BP_C
CARRYABLE BY: Tusoeuthis, Procoptodon, Megalosaurus, Kaprosuchus, Gigantopithecus
EGG SIZE: –

USEFUL TRAPS: Bola, Bear Trap, Plant Species Y Trap

TAMING METHOD:
Can be tamed by feeding.

SUITABLE FOOD FOR TAMING:
- Spoiled Meat
- Raw Meat
- Raw Fish Meat

Giant Bee

Basic Stats:

Health	80	Food	450	Speed (Air)	600
Stamina	200	Weight	150	Speed (Water)	200
Oxygen	150	Melee Damage	8	Torpidity	400

Habitat: Redwoods (trees), Cliffs
Damages: -
Behavior: Aggressive

Type: Invertebrate
Diet: Herbivore
Names: -

Attack 1: Melee
Attack 2: -
Attack 3: -

Specifics:
- There are two groups: Drone Bees and Queen Bees. A tamed Queen builds nests and lays Drone eggs. The hatched Drones protect their Queen and produce Honey.
- In order to tame the Queen, you have to find its hive, force it out, and fight off the Drones' dangerous attacks.

Utility:
- When you've finally tamed the Queen, you obtain a hive which can be placed anywhere. As a result, you get fresh Honey regularly. The hive needs to be "fed" with Rare Flowers.
- Even when you own a hive, we recommend approaching it only with ghillie armor when collecting Honey (don't hold anything in your hands or you'll get stung).

Drops	Harvests	Breeding
Raw Meat	Giant Bee Honey ■■■	Not breedable
Chitin		

THE ISLAND   SC. EARTH
ABERRATION   EXTINCTION
GENESIS I   RAGNAROK
THE CENTER   VALGUERO

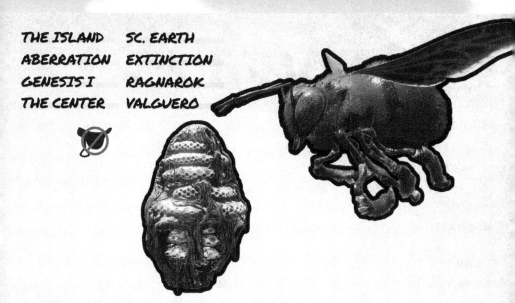

CHEAT: summon Bee_Character_BP_C
CARRYABLE BY: –
EGG SIZE: –

USEFUL TRAPS: Bola

TAMING METHOD:
Can be tamed by feeding.

SUITABLE FOOD FOR TAMING:
- Simple Kibble
- Raw Mutton
- Cooked Lamb Chop
- Raw Prime Fish
- Rare Flower
- Cooked Prime Meat
- Raw Prime Fish Meat
- Cooked Prime Fish Meat
- Raw Meat
- Cooked Meat
- Raw Fish Meat
- Cooked Fish Meat

A GLOWBUG

BASIC STATS:

Health	75	Food	450	Speed (Air)	120
Stamina	100	Weight	50	Speed (Land)	60
Oxygen	150	Melee Damage	18	Speed (Water)	200
				Torpidity	100

HABITAT:	Aberration (almost everywhere)	**TYPE:**	Invertebrate
DAMAGES:	Thatch, Wood	**DIET:**	unknown
BEHAVIOR:	Cowardly	**NAMES:**	-

ATTACK 1: Ground Bite
ATTACK 2: Fly Bite
ATTACK 3: -

SPECIFICS:
- Looks like a giant glow worm.
- You can attack it with any kind of weapon.

UTILITY:
- Since it can be killed easily and also appears in large groups, you can quickly kill a bunch of them.
- Provides Chitin and Raw Meat.
- You can charge dead batteries with them. In order to do so, simply place the dead batteries into your inventory and use the Glowbug.

DROPS	HARVESTS		BREEDING
Raw Meat	Raw Prime Fish	■ ■ ■	Not breedable
Chitin			
Raw Prime Fish			
Cementing Paste			

~~THE ISLAND~~ ~~SE. EARTH~~
ABERRATION ~~EXTINCTION~~
GENESIS I ~~RAGNAROK~~
~~THE CENTER~~ **VALGUERO**

CHEAT: summon Lightbug_Character_BaseBP_C
CARRYABLE BY: –
EGG SIZE: –

USEFUL TRAPS: Bola, Bear Trap, Plant Species Y Trap

TAMING METHOD: –

SUITABLE FOOD FOR TAMING: –

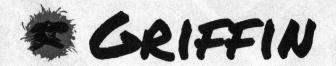

GRIFFIN

Basic Stats:

Health	950	Food	1600	Speed (Air)	750
Stamina	225	Weight	280	Speed (Water)	300
Oxygen	150	Melee Damage	27	Torpidity	1500

Habitat: Ragnarok (only)
Damages: Thatch, Wood
Behavior: Highly Aggressive

Type: Fantasy Creature
Diet: Carnivore
Names: –

Attack 1: Claw
Attack 2: Grab
Attack 3: Dive-bomb (touch + pitch); no button necessary

Specifics:
- Due to the fact that it's a fast (flying) mount, it's a strong and versatile creature.
- To tame it, you can lure it into a cave or a covered dino trap so that it can't fly away.
- Tamed, it can carry two players who can both use their weapons.

Utility:
- During its Dive-bomb, it moves very fast and can cause a lot of damage.
- Due to its speed (especially while dive-bombing), it's a very suitable mount for stealing Wyvern eggs and is able to then flee quickly.

Drops	Harvests		Breeding
Raw Meat	Keratin, Hide	■■■	Not breedable
Hide	Organic Polymer	■■■	
Raw Prime Fish	Raw Fish Meat/Meat	■■	
	Raw Prime Fish Meat	■■■	
	Chitin, Thatch	■■■	

~~THE ISLAND~~ ~~SE. EARTH~~
~~ABERRATION~~ ~~EXTINCTION~~
~~GENESIS I~~ RAGNAROK
~~THE CENTER~~ ~~VALGUERO~~

CHEAT: summon Griffin_Character_BP_C
CARRYABLE BY: –
EGG SIZE: –

USEFUL TRAPS: Chain Bola, Bear Trap, Large Bear Trap, Plant Species Y Trap

TAMING METHOD:
Knockout

SUITABLE FOOD FOR TAMING:
- Extraordinary Kibble
- Raw Mutton
- Cooked Lamb Chop
- Raw Prime Fish
- Cooked Prime Meat
- Raw Prime Fish Meat
- Cooked Prime Fish Meat
- Raw Meat
- Cooked Meat
- Raw Fish Meat
- Cooked Fish Meat

ICHTHYORNIS

BASIC STATS:

Health	50	Food	1000	Speed (Land)	75
Stamina	150	Weight	55	Speed (Air)	600
Oxygen	150	Melee Damage	1	Torpidity	120

HABITAT:	Shores	TYPE:	Bird
DAMAGES:	Thatch	DIET:	Carnivore
BEHAVIOR:	Skittish	NAMES:	-

ATTACK 1:	Rip
ATTACK 2:	Bite
ATTACK 3:	Rob

SPECIFICS:
- The Pegomastax of the aerial world. It robs players as well as other creatures, stealing mainly food.

UTILITY:
- You can set a tamed one to "hunt and retrieve". it will then bring you small Fish, Dodos, or Compys for harvesting.
- Creatures hunted by the Ichthyornis, drop Raw Prime Meat even though they wouldn't usually do that (e.g. Raw Prime Meat from Dodos or Compys). This makes it a great supplier of Raw Prime Meat.

DROPS	HARVESTS		BREEDING	
Raw Meat	Raw Prime Fish	■■■	Type	Egg
Hide	Raw Meat	■■	Egg Temp.	29°-32°
	Raw Prime Fish Meat	■■■	Incubation	1h:40m
	Raw Fish Meat	■■	Maturation	37h:02m

THE ISLAND   SC. EARTH
ABERRATION   EXTINCTION
GENESIS I   RAGNAROK
~~THE CENTER~~   VALGUERO

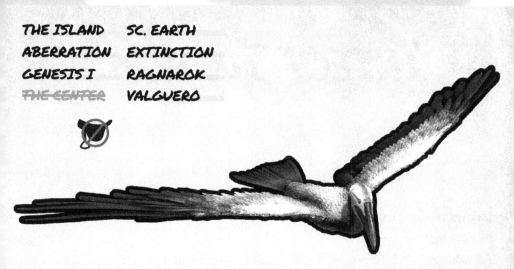

CHEAT: summon Ichthyornis_Character_BP_C
CARRYABLE BY: Tusoteuthis, Megalosaurus
EGG SIZE: Medium

USEFUL TRAPS: Chain Bola, Bear Trap, Large Bear Trap, Plant Species Y Trap

TAMING METHOD:
Knockout

SUITABLE FOOD FOR TAMING:
- Regular Kibble
- Raw Prime Fish Meat
- Cooked Prime Fish Meat
- Raw Fish Meat
- Cooked Fish Meat

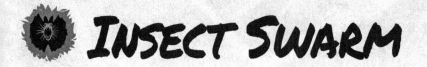
INSECT SWARM

Basic Stats:

Health	500	Food	100	Speed (Air)	300
Stamina	100	Weight	100	Speed (Water)	400
Oxygen	150	Melee Damage	23	Torpidity	100

Habitat: Swamps
Damages: -
Behavior: Aggressive

Type: Invertebrate
Diet: -
Names: -

Attack 1: Bite
Attack 2: -
Attack 3: -

Specifics:
- An individual Insect Swarm isn't that dangerous but can definitely be annoying. The best way to get rid of it is to use a Torch. It also retreats as soon as you're standing in at least knee-deep water.
- It's also possible to kill an Insect Swarm by luring them over a Campfire.
- Destroys plants you've planted in plots.
- Drains the player's stamina. Therefore, it becomes especially annoying when you're in the middle of a fight against other creatures.
- Sometimes, it can even attack through walls.

Drops	Harvests	Breeding
Raw Meat	-	Not breedable
Hide		

~~THE ISLAND~~   ~~SE. EARTH~~
~~ABERRATION~~   ~~EXTINCTION~~
GENESIS I   ~~RAGNAROK~~
~~THE CENTER~~   ~~VALGUERO~~

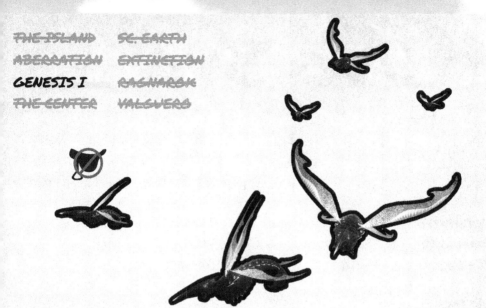

CHEAT: summon InsectSwarmChar_BP_C

CARRYABLE BY: –

EGG SIZE: –

USEFUL TRAPS: –

TAMING METHOD: –

SUITABLE FOOD FOR TAMING: –

JUG BUG

BASIC STATS:

Health	75	Food	450	Speed (Land)	60
Stamina	100	Weight	50	Speed (Air)	120
Oxygen	150	Melee Damage	18	Torpidity	100

HABITAT: Everzwhere
DAMAGES: Thatch, Wood
BEHAVIOR: Passive

TYPE: Invertebrate
DIET: Carnivore
NAMES: -

ATTACK 1: -
ATTACK 2: -
ATTACK 3: -

SPECIFICS:
- There are two variants: one filled with Water (blue) and the other one filled with Oil (purple).
- You can obtain Water or Oil by pressing the "use" button.

UTILITY:
- A real lifesaver when there's no Water in the vicinity.
- Quick source for Oil.

DROPS	HARVESTS	BREEDING
Raw Meat	-	Not breedable
Chitin		

~~THE ISLAND~~ SC. EARTH
~~ABERRATION~~ ~~EXTINCTION~~
~~GENESIS I~~ ~~RAGNAROK~~
~~THE CENTER~~ ~~VALGUERO~~

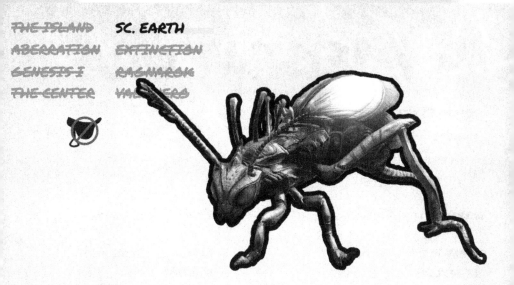

CHEAT: summon Jugbug_Character_BP_C
CARRYABLE BY: Tusoteuthis, Megalosaurus, Kaprosuchus
EGG SIZE: -

USEFUL TRAPS: Bola, Bear Trap, Plant Species Y Trap

TAMING METHOD: -

SUITABLE FOOD FOR TAMING: -

MEGANEURA

BASIC STATS:

Health	45	Food	450	Speed (Land)	175
Stamina	100	Weight	50	Speed (Air)	185
Oxygen	150	Melee Damage	10	Torpidity	100

HABITAT: Swamp, Forests by the water
DAMAGES: Thatch
BEHAVIOR: Passive

TYPE: Invertebrate
DIET: Carnivore
NAMES: -

ATTACK 1: Bite (Suck Attack) – stamina decreases
ATTACK 2: -
ATTACK 3: -

SPECIFICS:
- Attacks you as soon as you get too close to a corpse it has claimed for itself.

UTILITY:
- A good source for Chitin and Cementing Paste (with a Beelzebufo).
- Kill a creature in the swamp and leave it. The corpse will attract a lot of Meganeuras.

DROPS	HARVESTS	BREEDING
Raw Meat	–	Not breedable
Chitin		

THE ISLAND   SC. EARTH
~~ABERRATION~~   EXTINCTION
GENESIS I   RAGNAROK
THE CENTER   VALGUERO

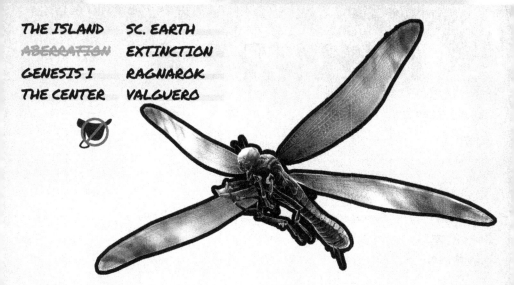

CHEAT: summon Dragonfly_Character_BP_C
CARRYABLE BY: Tusoteuthis, Megalosaurus, Kaprosuchus
EGG SIZE: -

USEFUL TRAPS: Chain Bola, Large Bear Trap, Plant Species Y Trap

TAMING METHOD: -

SUITABLE FOOD FOR TAMING: -

 Lymantria

Basic Stats:

Health	260	Food	2000	Speed (Land)	110
Stamina	150	Weight	175	Speed (Air)	600
Oxygen	150	Melee Damage	18	Torpidity	550

Habitat: Everywhere (except for the Desert)
Damages: Thatch, Wood
Behavior: Cowardly

Type: Invertebrate
Diet: Carnivore
Names: Lyma

Attack 1: Spore Cloud (slows down enemies)
Attack 2: -
Attack 3: -

Specifics:
- When it flees, it releases a cloud of spores, which slows down pursuers.

Utility:
- Produces Silk.
- A slow flying mount for beginners who don't have other flying mounts.
- The Spore Cloud slows down players and creatures: taming, attack, and defense support.

Drops	Harvests	Breeding
Silk	–	Not breedable
Raw Meat		
Chitin		

~~THE ISLAND~~ SC. EARTH
~~ABERRATION~~ EXTINCTION
~~GENESIS I~~   RAGNAROK
~~THE CENTER~~ VALGUERO

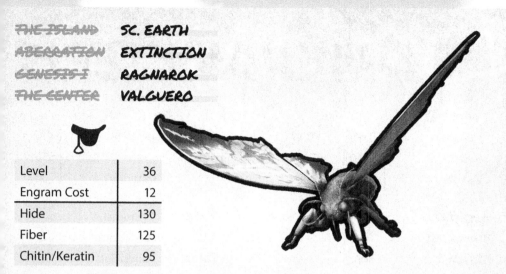

Level	36
Engram Cost	12
Hide	130
Fiber	125
Chitin/Keratin	95

CHEAT: *summon Moth_Character_BP_C*
CARRYABLE BY: Megalosaurus
EGG SIZE: –

USEFUL TRAPS: Bola, Chain Bola, Bear Trap, Large Bear Trap, Plant Species Y Trap

TAMING METHOD:
Knockout

SUITABLE FOOD FOR TAMING:
- Regular Kibble
- Crops
- Mejoberries
- Berries

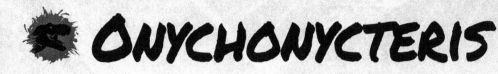

ONYCHONYCTERIS

BASIC STATS:

Health	250	Food	1500	Speed (Air)	350
Stamina	100	Weight	50	Speed (Water)	350
Oxygen	150	Melee Damage	35	Torpidity	200

HABITAT: Caves
DAMAGES: Thatch
BEHAVIOR: Highly Aggressive

TYPE: Mammal
DIET: Carnivore
NAMES: Onyc/Bat

ATTACK 1: Bite / Claw (quickly and heavily damages armor)
ATTACK 2: -
ATTACK 3: -

SPECIFICS:
- It's absolutely necessary to use Bug Repellant when approaching to tame it.
- A dangerous hunter and opponent in The Island's caves.

UTILITY:
- Protects your base well.
- Useful during attacks since it destroys armor quickly.

DROPS	HARVESTS	BREEDING
Raw Meat	-	Not breedable
Hide		

THE ISLAND	SC. EARTH
~~ABERRATION~~	EXTINCTION
GENESIS I	RAGNAROK
THE CENTER	VALGUERO

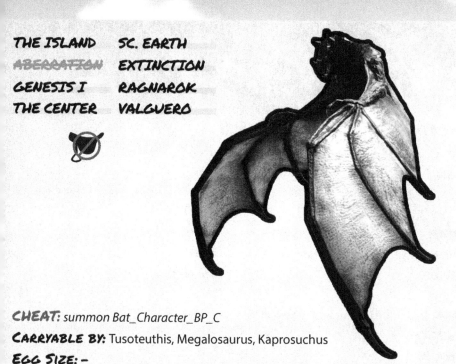

CHEAT: summon Bat_Character_BP_C
CARRYABLE BY: Tusoteuthis, Megalosaurus, Kaprosuchus
EGG SIZE: -

USEFUL TRAPS: Chain Bola, Large Bear Trap, Plant Species Y Trap

TAMING METHOD:
Can be tamed by feeding.

SUITABLE FOOD FOR TAMING:
- Raw Mutton
- Cooked Lamb Chop
- Raw Prime Fish
- Cooked Prime Meat
- Raw Prime Fish Meat
- Cooked Prime Fish Meat
- Raw Meat
- Cooked Meat
- Raw Fish Meat
- Cooked Fish Meat

PELAGORNIS

BASIC STATS:

Health	240	Food	1200	Speed (Land)	132
Stamina	180	Weight	150	Speed (Air)	600
Oxygen	150	Melee Damage	16	Torpidity	120

HABITAT: Ocean and Coasts **TYPE:** Bird
DAMAGES: Thatch, Wood **DIET:** Carnivore
BEHAVIOR: Cowardly **NAMES:** Pela

ATTACK 1: Bite (bonus against small fish)
ATTACK 2: -
ATTACK 3: -

SPECIFICS:
- As a riding mount, you can use it on shore, by sea, and in the air. It doesn't throw off its rider in the water and lands on/swims in the water elegantly.
- Has a damage bonus for smaller fish as well as Piranhas and Coels.

UTILITY:
- Resource gatherer: Organic Polymer. The Pelagornis collects valuable resources from the Kairukus it's able to kill very quickly.
- Collects Fish Meat.
- Universal riding mount with high stamina but, unfortunately, low loading capacity.

DROPS	HARVESTS		BREEDING	
Raw Meat	Raw Fish Meat	■■■	Type	Egg
Hide	Organic Polymer	■■■	Egg Temp.	29°-32°
	Raw Meat	■■	Incubation	1h39m
	Hide	■■	Maturation	37h03m
	Chitin/Keratin	■■		

THE ISLAND   SC. EARTH
~~ABERRATION~~ ~~EXTINCTION~~
GENESIS I   RAGNAROK
THE CENTER   VALGUERO

Level	43
Engram Cost	30
Hide	230
Fiber	125
Chitin/Keratin	75

CHEAT: summon Pela_Character_BP_C
CARRYABLE BY: Megalosaurus
EGG SIZE: Medium

USEFUL TRAPS: Bola, Bear Trap, Large Bear Trap, Plant Species Y Trap

TAMING METHOD:
Knockout

SUITABLE FOOD FOR TAMING:
- Regular Kibble
- Raw Prime Fish Meat
- Cooked Prime Fish Meat
- Raw Fish Meat
- Cooked Fish Meat

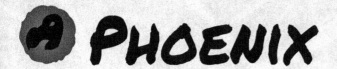

PHOENIX

Basic Stats:

Health	640	Food	1500	Speed (Land)	260
Stamina	352	Weight	324	Speed (Air)	600
Oxygen	150	Melee Damage	14	Torpidity	200

Habitat: Desert
Damages: Thatch, Wood
Behavior: Cowardly

Type: Fantasy Creature
Diet: flame eater
Names: Firebird

Attack 1: Bite
Attack 2: Fire Ball
Attack 3: Claw Attack

Specifics:
- Only spawns in heatwaves and can therefore only be tamed during them. After the heatwave, it turns to ash when it's untamed. However, it will be reborn from said ashes during the next heatwave.
- In order to tame a Phoenix, you must shoot it with fire, which takes quite some time.
- Despite its flames, it's no heat source.

Utility:
- Can be used as a Forge or Campfire; it refines Metal and cooks Meat in its inventory.
- Its feces contain Silica Pearls.
- By using its first and third attack, it can harvest a lot of resources. When using its Claw Attack, it can even collect Stone and Metal.

Drops	Harvests		Breeding
Raw Meat	Silica Pearls	■■■	No breeding
Hide	Almost everything	■■■	

~~THE ISLAND~~   SC. EARTH
~~ABERRATION~~   ~~EXTINCTION~~
~~GENESIS I~~   ~~RAGNAROK~~
~~THE CENTER~~   ~~VALGUERO~~

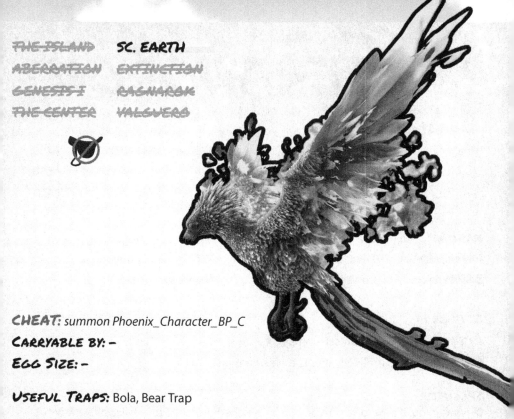

CHEAT: summon Phoenix_Character_BP_C
CARRYABLE BY: –
EGG SIZE: –

USEFUL TRAPS: Bola, Bear Trap

TAMING METHOD:
Can be tamed with fire.

SUITABLE FOOD FOR TAMING: –

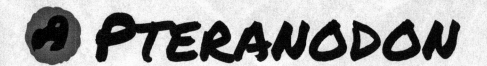

PTERANODON

Basic Stats:

Health	210	Food	1200	Speed (Land)	260
Stamina	150	Weight	120	Speed (Air)	600
Skittish	150	Melee Damage	18	Torpidity	120

Habitat: Everywhere
Damages: Thatch, Wood
Behavior: Cowardly
Type: Dinosaur
Diet: Carnivore
Names: Ptera

Attack 1: Bite
Attack 2: Grab (can carry small creatures)
Attack 3: Barrel Roll (affects melee damage)

Specifics:
- For taming, it's important to bring a Bola. Otherwise, the Ptera will just fly away.
- Very vulnerable to head hits.
- Lands very often and is therefore a good target for Bolas.

Utility:
- For many players, it's the first tamed flying mount. You can tame it very quickly with Dodo Kibble, which is easily procured.
- Fast short distance scout: due to its stamina, it has to take a lot of breaks during its flights but is suitable for short distance flights.
- The first transport mount, but will later be outperformed by the Argentavis.

Drops	Harvests		Breeding	
Raw Meat	Raw Meat	■■	Type	Egg
Hide	Organic Polymer	■■	Egg Temp.	29°-32°
	Hide	■■	Incubation	1h:39m
	Chitin/Keratin	■	Maturation	37h:02m
	Raw Prime Fish	■		

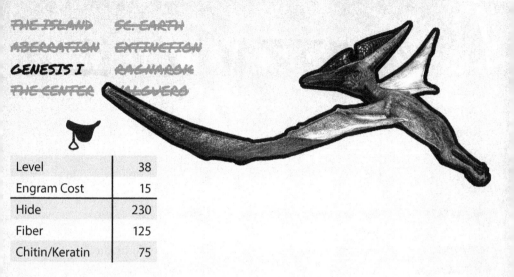

~~THE ISLAND~~   ~~SE EARTH~~
~~ABERRATION~~   ~~EXTINCTION~~
GENESIS I   ~~RAGNAROK~~
~~THE CENTER~~   ~~VALGUERO~~

Level	38
Engram Cost	15
Hide	230
Fiber	125
Chitin/Keratin	75

CHEAT: *summon Ptero_Character_BP_C*
CARRYABLE BY: Megalosaurus
EGG SIZE: –

USEFUL TRAPS: Bola, Chain Bola, Bear Trap, Large Bear Trap, Plant Species Y Trap

TAMING METHOD:
Knockout

SUITABLE FOOD FOR TAMING:
- Regular Kibble
- Raw Mutton
- Cooked Lamb Chop
- Raw Prime Fish
- Cooked Prime Meat
- Raw Prime Fish Meat
- Cooked Prime Fish Meat
- Raw Meat
- Cooked Meat
- Raw Fish Meat
- Cooked Fish Meat

QUETZALCOATLUS

BASIC STATS:

Health	1200	Food	1200	Speed (Land)	360
Stamina	800	Weight	800	Speed (Air)	500
Oxygen	150	Melee Damage	32	Torpidity	1850

HABITAT: Almost everywhere (very rare)
TYPE: Dinosaur
DAMAGES: Adobe, Wood, Thatch
DIET: Carnivore
BEHAVIOR: Cowardly
NAMES: Quetzal, Quetz

ATTACK 1: Bite
ATTACK 2: Grab (can also carry larger dinos, e.g. Carnos)
ATTACK 3: -

SPECIFICS:
- Wild ones never land, therefore, it's hard to tame it on your own.
- Always flees when its attacked; usually towards the center of "The Island" (Lat. 50 Lon. 50).

UTILITY:
- Long-distance transport: high stamina and loading capacity - able to fly.
- Mobile base with platform saddle: attacking platform, crafting resources.
- Gathering resources: place an Ankylo on its platform and collect Metal.
- Taming cage for aerial creatures: build a taming trap on its platform.

DROPS	HARVESTS		BREEDING	
Raw Meat	Raw Prime Fish	■ ■	Type	Egg
Raw Prime Fish	Raw Meat	■ ■	Egg Temp.	5°-6°
Hide	Chitin/Keratin	■ ■	Incubation	16h:40m
	Hide	■ ■	Maturation	185h:11m
	Organic Polymer	■ ■		

THE ISLAND ~~SE. EARTH~~
~~ABERRATION~~ EXTINCTION
~~GENESIS I~~ RAGNAROK
THE CENTER VALGUERO

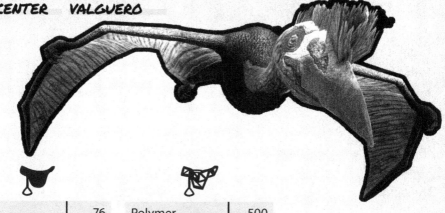

Level	76	Polymer	500
Engram Cost	44	Metal Ingots	2500
Hide	750	Crystal	370
Fiber	500	Element	55
Cementing Paste	100	Black Pearls	140
Silica Pearls	85		

CHEAT: summon Quetz_Character_BP_C

CARRYABLE BY: abc

EGG SIZE: Extra Large

USEFUL TRAPS: Chain Bola, Bear Trap, Large Bear Trap, Plant Species Y Trap

TAMING METHOD:
Knockout

SUITABLE FOOD FOR TAMING:

- Exceptional Kibble
- Raw Mutton
- Cooked Lamb Chop
- Raw Prime Fish
- Cooked Prime Meat
- Raw Prime Fish Meat
- Cooked Prime Fish Meat
- Raw Meat
- Cooked Meat
- Raw Fish Meat/Cooked Fish Meat

SCOUT

Basic Stats:

Health	3	Food	7	Speed (Land)	245
Stamina	90	Weight	0	Speed (Water)	300
Oxygen	∞	Melee Damage	0	Geschw. Fliegen	600

Habitat: Sanctuary
Damages: -
Behavior: Passive

Type: Mechanical Creature
Diet: -
Names: -

Attack 1: Laser Marking
Attack 2: Speed Boost
Attack 3: Descent

Specifics:
- Not a challenging opponent itself. It marks enemies and creatures and as a consequence, Enforcers and Defense Units attack the marked enemy.
- Can't be tamed. You can craft your own Scout at a City Terminal or with a Tek replicator.

Utility:
- Once it's built, it can be equipped just like a weapon in your inventory and then be thrown. You control it with a remote control, which remains in your inventory and can be re-used even after you've stopped using it.
- Can be used for surveillance and scouting.

Drops	Harvests		Breeding
Raw Meat	Raw Meat	■■■	Not breedable
	Raw Prime Fish	■■■	
	Fiber	■■■	

~~THE ISLAND~~ ~~SE-EARTH~~
~~ABERRATION~~ **EXTINCTION**
~~GENESIS I~~ ~~RAGNAROK~~
~~THE CENTER~~ ~~VALGUERO~~

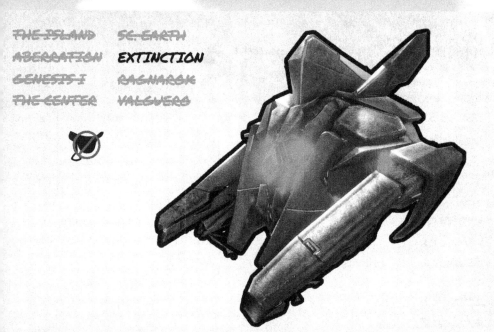

CHEAT: *summon Scout_Character_BP_C*
CARRYABLE BY: abc
EGG SIZE: –

USEFUL TRAPS: Bola, Chain Bola, Bear Trap, Plant Species Y Trap

TAMING METHOD: –

SUITABLE FOOD FOR TAMING: –

SEEKER

BASIC STATS:

Health	250	Food	1500	Speed (Air)	525
Stamina	100	Weight	50	Speed (Land)	350
Oxygen	150	Melee Damage	10	Speed (Water)	240
				Torpidity	200

HABITAT: Surface, The Spine
DAMAGES: Thatch, Wood
BEHAVIOR: Highly Aggressive

TYPE: Fantasy Creature
DIET: Carnivore
NAMES: –

ATTACK 1: Bite
ATTACK 2: Claw
ATTACK 3: Charge Breath

SPECIFICS:
- Small wings.
- Stronger when there's a charge source in the proximity (e.g. Bulbdog); therefore, turn off every light when Seekers are approaching.
- Targets easy/weak prey (this also includes the player).

UTILITY:
- Since it can't be tamed, you should kill it to get drops.

DROPS	HARVESTS	BREEDING
Raw Meat	–	Not breedable
Hide		
Oil		

~~THE ISLAND~~ ~~SE. EARTH~~
ABERRATION ~~EXTINCTION~~
GENESIS I ~~RAGNAROK~~
~~THE CENTER~~ VALGUERO

CHEAT: summon Pteroteuthis_Char_BP_C
CARRYABLE BY: –
EGG SIZE: –

USEFUL TRAPS: –

TAMING METHOD: –

SUITABLE FOOD FOR TAMING: –

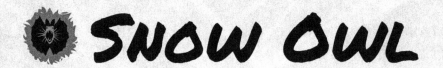
Snow Owl

Basic Stats:

Health	325	Food	2000	Speed (Air)	600
Stamina	350	Weight	375	Speed (Water)	300
Oxygen	150	Melee Damage	25	Speed (Land)	260
Torpidity	600				

Habitat:	Snow Dome (northeast)	**Type:**	Bird
Damages:	Thatch, Wood, Greenhouse	**Diet:**	Carnivore
Behavior:	Aggressive	**Names:**	Owl

Attack 1: Melee
Attack 2: Dive-bomb/Freeze & Heal (keep the "use" button pressed down all the way)
Attack 3: Predator Vision (on/off)

Specifics:
- Using its Predator Vision, you can easily spot creatures and Element veins.
- Warning: its healing features also heal enemies.

Utility:
- Good choice for transport.
- Effective during fights and can freeze nearby opponents.
- Very good support due to its healing ability.
- Its feces (Snow Owl Pellets) are an excellent Fertilizer and a popular boost food for Gachas.

Drops	Harvests		Breeding	
Raw Meat	Raw Meat	■■	Type	Egg
Hide			Egg Temp.	12°-13,5°
			Incubation	2h:56m
			Maturation	54h:27m

~~THE ISLAND~~ ~~SE, EARTH~~
~~ABERRATION~~ EXTINCTION
~~GENESIS I-I~~ ~~RAGNAROK~~
~~THE CENTER~~ ~~VALGUERO~~

Level	61
Engram Cost	6
Hide	350
Fiber	185
Chitin/Keratin	150

CHEAT: *summon Owl_Character_BP_C*

CARRYABLE BY: –

EGG SIZE: Large

USEFUL TRAPS: Chain Bola, Large Bear Trap, Plant Species Y Trap

TAMING METHOD:
Knockout

SUITABLE FOOD FOR TAMING:
- Superior Kibble
- Raw Mutton
- Cooked Lamb Chop
- Raw Prime Fish
- Cooked Prime Meat
- Raw Prime Fish Meat
- Cooked Prime Fish Meat
- Raw Meat
- Cooked Meat
- Raw Fish Meat
- Cooked Fish Meat

Tapejara

Basic Stats:

Health	325	Food	1600	Speed (Air)	700
Stamina	250	Weight	280	Speed (Water)	300
Oxygen	150	Melee Damage	18	Torpidity	450

Habitat: Almost everywhere (Forests, primarily)
Damages: Thatch, Wood
Behavior: Cowardly
Type: Reptile
Diet: Carnivore
Names: Tape

Attack 1: Bite
Attack 2: Grab (can grab other creatures)
Attack 3: Mock

Specifics:
- Immediately flees with high speed when approached.
- Lands very rarely; use ghillie armor and a Bola to catch it on the ground.
- Can cling to trees and walls as well as land on them.

Utility:
- Very good flying mount: three people fit on the saddle and can use their weapons from it too.
- Taming method: two people – one steers and the other one shoots.
- Air transport: appropriate speed and stamina, average loading capacity.
- Generally, a better version of the Pteranodon.

Drops
Raw Meat

Harvests
Raw Meat	■■
Raw Prime Fish	■■
Chitin/Keratin	■■
Hide	■■

Breeding
Type	Egg
Egg Temp.	29°-32°
Incubation	1h:39m
Maturation	54h:28m

THE ISLAND SC. EARTH
~~ABERRATION~~ EXTINCTION
~~GENESIS I~~ RAGNAROK
THE CENTER VALGUERO

Level	55
Engram Cost	21
Hide	260
Fiber	180
Cementing Paste	120
Metal Ingots	45

CHEAT: *summon Tapejara_Character_BP_C*
CARRYABLE BY: Megalosaurus
EGG SIZE: Large
USEFUL TRAPS: Bola, Chain Bola, Bear Trap, Large Bear Trap, Plant Species Y Trap

TAMING METHOD:
Knockout

SUITABLE FOOD FOR TAMING:
- Superior Kibble
- Raw Mutton
- Cooked Lamb Chop
- Raw Prime Fish
- Cooked Prime Meat
- Raw Prime Fish Meat
- Cooked Prime Fish Meat
- Raw Meat
- Cooked Meat
- Raw Fish Meat
- Cooked Fish Meat

WYVERN (FIRE)

BASIC STATS:

Health	1725	Food	2000	Speed (Air)	690
Stamina	275	Weight	400	Speed (Water)	1100
Oxygen	150	Melee Damage	80	Torpidity	3000
Torpidity	725				

HABITAT: Dragonmalte Trench (esp.)
DAMAGES: Thatch, Wood
BEHAVIOR: Highly Aggressive
TYPE: Fantasy Creature
DIET: Carnivore
NAMES: -

ATTACK 1: Bite
ATTACK 2: Fire Breath
ATTACK 3: Grab (can grab other creatures an carry them)

SPECIFICS:
- There are four variants: Fire (red), Lightning (blue), and Poison Wyvern (green). Ice Wyverns only exist on the Ragnarok and Valguero map. In order to catch them (and tranquilize them to get Wyvern Milk), you should build a huge stone cage.

UTILITY:
- Flying attacks: its "breath" attacks are very effective.
- Efficiently gathers a lot of resources.
- Warning: a tamed Wyvern has less health than a wild one.

DROPS	HARVESTS		BREEDING	
Raw Prime Fish	Raw Meat/Prime Meat	■■■	Type	Egg
Sulfur	Chitin/Keratin	■■	Egg Temp.	80°-90°
Hide	Hide, Thatch	■■	Incubation	4h:59m
Wyvern Claws	Organic Polymer	■■	Maturation	92h:35m
Wyvern Milk	Cactus Sap	■■		

~~THE ISLAND~~ SC. EARTH
~~ABERRATION~~ ~~EXTINCTION~~
~~GENESIS I~~ RAGNAROK
~~THE CENTER~~ VALGUERO

CHEAT: summon Wyvern_Character_BP_Base_C
CARRYABLE BY: abc
EGG SIZE: -

USEFUL TRAPS: Chain Bola, Large Bear Trap

TAMING METHOD:
Can by tamed by breeding.

SUITABLE FOOD FOR TAMING: Wyvern Milk

You can't tame a grown Wyvern. You have to fly to the Dragonmalte Trench in the western part of the Scorched Earth map where their nests are and steal a fertilized Wyvern egg. Flee as fast as you can because every Wyvern will then start to hunt you. Then, you can breed the egg and raise a tamed Wyvern. You will need multiple Air Conditioners or constantly burning Campfires to keep the required high temperatures.

Warning:
Wyvern babies only drink Wyvern Milk, which can only obtained from **tranquilized, wild,** female Wyverns. Tamed Wyverns do not produce any Wyvern Milk. Dead Alpha Wyverns provide a lot of milk. If a baby Wyvern has a lower food value than 1200, you must force-feed it with Wyvern Milk (place it into its inventory and press use).

WYVERN (POISON)

HABITAT: Dragon Trench (western desert edge) - otherwise, rather rare
SPECIAL ATTACK: Spits poisonous acid that explodes on impact.
SC. EARTH
RAGNAROK
VALGUERO

 # WYVERN (LIGHTNING)

HABITAT: Dragon Trench (western desert edge)- otherwise, rather rare
SPECIAL ATTACK: Breathes a beam of lighting at its target.
SC. EARTH
RAGNAROK
VALGUERO

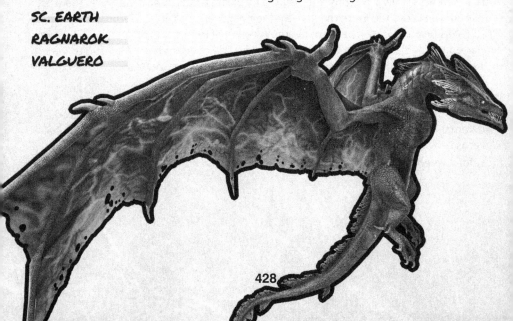

WYVERN (FOREST)

HABITAT: Only spawns in the boss battle against Forest Titan.
SPECIAL ATTACK: Fire Breath
EXTINCTION

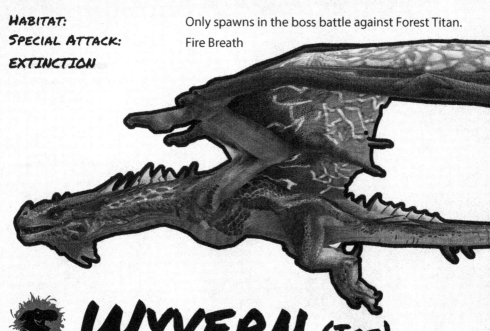

WYVERN (ICE)

HABITAT: Ragnarok: Mountaintops; Valguero: The Great Trench
SPECIAL ATTACK: Ice Breath (decreases movement speed)
VALGUERO
RAGNAROK

AMMONITE

Basic Stats:

Health	165	Food	450	Speed (Air)	120
Stamina	100	Weight	150	Speed (Water)	40
Oxygen	∞	Melee Damage	0	Torpidity	50

HABITAT: Caves (underwater)
DAMAGES: –
BEHAVIOR: Passive

TYPE: Invertebrate
DIET: bottom feeder
NAMES: –

ATTACK 1: Call for Help (releases pheromone)
ATTACK 2: –
ATTACK 3: –

SPECIFICS:
- When attacked, it releases a pheromone in the form of a green substance.
- Consequently, other aquatic creatures come to its defense.

UTILITY:
- It's worth it to hunt this creature: you can craft Pheromone Darts from the Ammonite Bile you've obtained. If you shoot an animal with a Pheromone Dart, it becomes aggressive.
- Drops rare Black Pearls.

Drops	Harvests	Breeding
Ammonite Bile	–	Not breedable
Black Pearls		
Silica Pearls		
Chitin		
Oil		
Raw Meat		

THE ISLAND   ~~SC-EARTH~~
~~ABERRATION~~ ~~EXTINCTION~~
GENESIS I   RAGNAROK
THE CENTER   VALGUERO

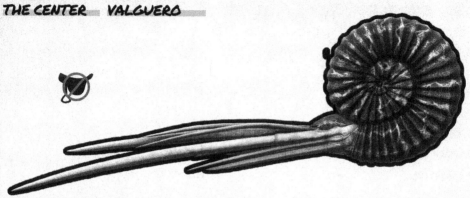

CHEAT: summon Ammonite_Character_C
CARRYABLE BY: Kaprosuchus, Megalosaurus, Tusoteuthis
EGG SIZE: -

USEFUL TRAPS: -

TAMING METHOD: -

SUITABLE FOOD FOR TAMING: -

ANGLERFISH

Basic Stats:

Health	450	Food	1500	Speed (Land)	400
Stamina	240	Weight	350	Speed (Water)	330
Oxygen	150	Melee Damage	30	Torpidity	900

Habitat: Deep Sea
Damages: Thatch, Wood
Behavior: Aggressive

Type: Fish
Diet: Carnivore
Names: Angler

Attack 1: Bite
Attack 2: -
Attack 3: -

Specifics:
- Illuminates its environment with its "bulb".
- Aggressive, and immediately attacks nearby creatures.

Utility:
- Very suitable mount for exploring the ocean. Its light illuminates the depths and you can ride it without a saddle.
- Attracts fellow species and is therefore perfect for hunting them and collecting Angler Gel.
- Use a Metal Hatchet to collect the Angler Gel from other dead animals.

Drops	Harvests		Breeding	
Angler Gel	Silica Pearls	■■	Type	Egg
Raw Fish Meat	Raw Meat	■■	Egg Temp.	10°-50°
	Chitin/Keratin	■■	Incubation	5h
	Pelt	■■	Maturation	37h:2m
	Raw Prime Fish	■■		

THE ISLAND ~~SC. EARTH~~
~~ABERRATION~~ ~~EXTINCTION~~
GENESIS I **RAGNAROK**
THE CENTER **VALGUERO**

Ridable without a saddle

CHEAT: summon Angler_Character_BP_C
CARRYABLE BY: Tusoteuthis
EGG SIZE: –

USEFUL TRAPS: –

TAMING METHOD:
Knockout

SUITABLE FOOD FOR TAMING:
Regular Kibble
Raw Mutton
Cooked Lamb Chop
Raw Prime Fish
Cooked Prime Meat
Raw Prime Fish Meat
Raw Meat
Cooked Prime Fish Meat
Cooked Meat
Raw Fish Meat
Cooked Fish Meat

BASILOSAURUS

BASIC STATS:

Health	2400	Food	8000	Speed (Air)	300
Stamina	300	Weight	700	Speed (Water)	300
Oxygen	150	Melee Damage	47	Torpidity	2000

HABITAT: Ocean (avoids deep water) **TYPE:** Mammal
DAMAGES: Thatch, Wood, Greenhouse **DIET:** Piscivore
BEHAVIOR: Passive **NAMES:** -

ATTACK 1: Lunge
ATTACK 2: Spout
ATTACK 3: -

SPECIFICS:
- Stays close to the surface and suffers melee damage in deep water. Don't dive too deep with it.
- Generates Oil (max. 20) over time, which you can find in its inventory.

UTILITY:
- Suitable mount for underwater caves since it's able to take a lot of damage, heals quickly, and can carry many things. In addition, it protects the rider against cold.
- It's immune to torpidity induced by Cnidarias and doesn't suffer any melee damage. Therefore, it's a good resource gatherer for Bio Toxin.

DROPS	HARVESTS		BREEDING	
Hide	Bio Toxin	■■■	Type	Pregnancy
Oil	Raw Fish Meat	■■	Gestation	7h:56m
Raw Prime Fish	Chitin	■■	Maturation	185h:35m
Basilosaurus Bacon	Pelt	■■		
	Raw Prime Fish	■■		

THE ISLAND ~~SC-EARTH~~
~~ABERRATION~~ ~~EXTINCTION~~
~~GENESIS I~~ RAGNAROK
THE CENTER VALGUERO

Level	60
Engram Cost	30
Hide	200
Fiber	250
Cementing Paste	55

CHEAT: summon Basilosaurus_Character_BP_C
CARRYABLE BY: Tusoteuthis
EGG SIZE: -

USEFUL TRAPS: -

TAMING METHOD:
Can be tamed by feeding.

SUITABLE FOOD FOR TAMING:

Exceptional Kibble
Raw Mutton
Cooked Lamb Chop
Raw Prime Fish
Cooked Prime Meat
Raw Prime Fish Meat
Raw Meat
Cooked Prime Fish Meat
Cooked Meat
Raw Fish Meat
Cooked Fish Meat

CNIDARIA

BASIC STATS:

Health	180	Food	1200	Speed (Air)	250
Stamina	120	Weight	25	Speed (Water)	250
Oxygen	∞	Melee Damage	30	Torpidity	250

HABITAT: Ocean (everywhere) **TYPE:** Invertebrate
DAMAGES: Thatch **DIET:** Herbivore
BEHAVIOR: Aggressive **NAMES:** Jellyfish

ATTACK 1: Spike
ATTACK 2: -
ATTACK 3: -

SPECIFICS:
- Becomes aggressive as soon as you approach it.
- Its toxin is very dangerous and can knock out enemies very quickly. It paralyzes the opponent; the rider gets thrown of immediately.
- Completely avoid it unless you want to hunt it.
- To hunt it, lure it to the beach and kill it from a safe distance or use a Basilosaurus to hunt it.
- The Basilosaurus is immune to its toxin.

UTILITY:
- Its Bio Toxin is a very good anesthetic with which you can craft enhanced Tranquilizer Darts for rifles.

DROPS	HARVESTS	BREEDING
Bio Toxin	-	Not breedable

THE ISLAND   ~~SE-EARTH~~
~~ABERRATION~~ ~~EXTINCTION~~
GENESIS I   RAGNAROK
THE CENTER   VALGUERO

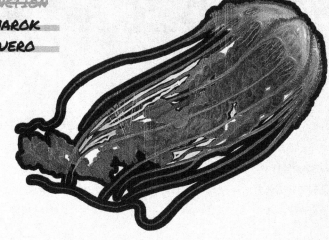

CHEAT: *summon Cnidaria_Character_BP_C*

CARRYABLE BY: Tusoteuthis, Kaprosuchus, Megalosaurus

EGG SIZE: -

USEFUL TRAPS: -

TAMING METHOD: -

SUITABLE FOOD FOR TAMING: -

COELACANTH

BASIC STATS:

Health	30	Food	100	Speed (Air)	120
Stamina	100	Weight	8	Speed (Water)	150
Oxygen	∞	Melee Damage	5	Torpidity	15

HABITAT: Rivers, Ponds, Seashore
DAMAGES: Thatch, Greenhouse
BEHAVIOR: Cowardly

TYPE: Fish
DIET: Carnivore
NAMES: Coel

ATTACK 1: Bite
ATTACK 2: -
ATTACK 3: -

SPECIFICS:
- Exists in many different sizes.
- Under certain circumstances, it's responsible for lags since it can spawn in large groups and overload a weak server.

UTILITY:
- You can simply hunt it to get Fish Meat, but it doesn't drop Prime fish Meat.

DROPS	HARVESTS	BREEDING
Raw Fish Meat	-	Not breedable

THE ISLAND   SC. EARTH
ABERRATION   EXTINCTION
GENESIS I   RAGNAROK
THE CENTER   VALGUERO

CHEAT: summon Coel_Character_BP_C

CARRYABLE BY: Tusoteuthis, Kaprosuchus, Megalosaurus

EGG SIZE: –

USEFUL TRAPS: –

TAMING METHOD:
Can be tamed by feeding.

SUITABLE FOOD FOR TAMING: –

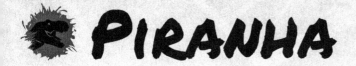
PIRANHA

BASIC STATS:

Health	150	Food	1200	Speed (Air)	250
Stamina	120	Weight	15	Speed (Water)	250
Oxygen	∞	Melee Damage	22	Torpidity	250

HABITAT: Rivers (warm), Seashores (warm)
DAMAGES: Thatch, Greenhouse
BEHAVIOR: Highly Aggressive

TYPE: Fish
DIET: Carnivore
NAMES: -

ATTACK 1: Bite
ATTACK 2: -
ATTACK 3: -

SPECIFICS:
- Very aggressive behavior.
- Usually occurs in shoals and is, therefore, dangerous. A single one can be killed easily.
- Poses a danger for low level players without armor.

UTILITY:
- Provide Fish Meat. Apart from that, they're kind of annoying.

DROPS	HARVESTS	BREEDING
Raw Fish Meat	-	Not breedable

THE ISLAND   ~~SE-EARTH~~
~~ABERRATION~~   EXTINCTION
GENESIS I   RAGNAROK
THE CENTER   VALGUERO

CHEAT: summon Piranha_Character_BP_C

CARRYABLE BY: Tusoteuthis, Kaprosuchus, Megalosaurus

EGG SIZE: -

USEFUL TRAPS: -

TAMING METHOD:
Can be tamed by feeding.

SUITABLE FOOD FOR TAMING: -

DIPLOCAULUS

Basic Stats:

Health	190	Food	1500	Speed (Air)	70
Stamina	165	Weight	150	Speed (Water)	267
Oxygen	1050	Melee Damage	10	Torpidity	220

Habitat:	Swamps	**Type:**	Amphibian
Damages:	Thatch, Greenhouse	**Diet:**	Piscivore
Behavior:	Skittish	**Names:**	Diplo, Newt

Attack 1: Bite
Attack 2: -
Attack 3: -

Specifics:
- Flight animal.
- We recommend catching it with a Bola and stunning it afterwards.
- Provides the player with oxygen.

Utility:
- Can be ridden in the water without a saddle and provides the player with oxygen. A good companion when exploring the ocean if you don't have a diving suit.
- Suitable for hunting Trilo Bites. The Diplocaulus kills and harvests Trilo Bites very quickly and effectively (their Oil and Silica Pearls as well).
- Due to both application possibilities, it's a good animal for your first ocean expeditions and for collecting Oil and Silica Pearls.

Drops	Harvests		Breeding	
Raw Meat	Chitin	■■■	Type	Egg
Hide	Thatch	■■	Egg Temp.	0°-50°
	Fiber	■■	Incubation	5h
	Raw Meat	■■	Maturation	37h:2m

THE ISLAND ~~SC. EARTH~~
~~ABERRATION~~ **EXTINCTION**
GENESIS I ~~RAGNAROK~~
THE CENTER ~~VALGUERO~~

Ridable without a saddle (only in the water)

CHEAT: summon Diplocaulus_Character_BP_C

CARRYABLE BY: Tusoteuthis, Kaprosuchus, Megalosaurus, Tapejara, Pteranodon, Argentavis, Quetzal, Griffin, Wyvern

EGG SIZE: –

USEFUL TRAPS: Bola, Bear Trap, Plant Species Y Trap

TAMING METHOD:
Knockout

SUITABLE FOOD FOR TAMING:
Simple Kibble
Raw Mutton
Cooked Lamb Chop
Raw Prime Fish
Cooked Prime Meat
Raw Prime Fish Meat
Raw Meat
Cooked Prime Fish Meat
Cooked Meat
Raw Fish Meat
Cooked Fish Meat

DUNKLEOSTEUS

Basic Stats:

Health	710	Food	2000	Speed (Air)	650
Stamina	200	Weight	910	Speed (Water)	650
Oxygen	150	Melee Damage	60	Torpidity	1150

Habitat: Deep Sea
Damages: Thatch, Wood, Stone
Behavior: Aggressive

Type: Fish
Diet: Carnivore
Names: Dunkle

Attack 1: Bite
Attack 2: -
Attack 3: -

Specifics:
- Can take a lot of damage, but isn't very mobile.

Utility:
- Very good resource gatherer for Oil, Stone, and Black Pearls (the latter from the Eurypterid).
- Good transport mount in the water.
- Serves as a combat animal and distraction during battles. It can damage stone bases and is able to take a lot of damage.
- Use it as distraction when taming other dangerous sea creatures.

Drops	Harvests		Breeding	
Raw Fish Meat	Oil	■■■	Type	Pregnancy
Raw Prime Fish Meat	Stone	■■■	Gestation	7h:56m
Chitin	Metal	■■	Maturation	92h:35m
	Raw Meat	■■		
	Chitin/Keratin	■■		
	Black Pearls	■■		

THE ISLAND ~~SC-EARTH~~
~~ABERRATION~~ ~~EXTINCTION~~
~~GENESIS I~~ **RAGNAROK**
THE CENTER **VALGUERO**

Level	44
Engram Cost	20
Hide	300
Fiber	180
Cementing Paste	120
Metal Ingots	80

CHEAT: *summon Dunkle_Character_BP_C*
CARRYABLE BY: Tusoteuthis
EGG SIZE: –

USEFUL TRAPS: –

TAMING METHOD:
Knockout

SUITABLE FOOD FOR TAMING:

Superior Kibble
Raw Mutton
Cooked Lamb Chop
Raw Prime Fish
Cooked Prime Meat
Raw Meat/Prime Fish Meat
Cooked Prime Fish Meat
Cooked Meat
Raw Fish Meat
Cooked Fish Meat

ELECTROPHORUS

BASIC STATS:

Health	180	Food	1500	Speed (Air)	400
Stamina	165	Weight	150	Speed (Water)	330
Oxygen	1050	Melee Damage	3	Torpidity	175

HABITAT: Ocean
DAMAGES: Thatch, Wood
BEHAVIOR: highly Aggressive
TYPE: Fish
DIET: Carnivore
NAMES: –

ATTACK 1: Bite
ATTACK 2: Electric Shock
ATTACK 3: –

SPECIFICS:
- Very aggressive and chases the player for a relatively long time.
- Riot armor is the best protection against its electric shocks.
- As an alternative, you can use a Basilosaurus. This creature is immune to electric shocks.
- Difficult to tame without getting shocked.

UTILITY:
- Can be used (in schools) for stunning and taming other creatures.
- Very useful combat support.

DROPS	HARVESTS	BREEDING	
Raw Prime Fish Meat	–	Type	Egg
Raw Fish Meat		Egg Temp.	0°-50°
		Incubation	5h
		Maturation	46h:18m

THE ISLAND ~~SC. EARTH~~
~~ABERRATION~~ ~~EXTINCTION~~
GENESIS I **RAGNAROK**
THE CENTER **VALGUERO**

CHEAT: *summon Eel_Character_BP_C*
CARRYABLE BY: Tusoteuthis
EGG SIZE: -

USEFUL TRAPS: -

TAMING METHOD:
Can be tamed by feeding.

SUITABLE FOOD FOR TAMING:

Raw Mutton
Cooked Lamb Chop
Bio Toxin
Raw Prime Fish
Cooked Prime Meat
Raw Prime Fish Meat
Raw Meat
Cooked Prime Fish Meat
Cooked Meat
Raw Fish Meat/Cooked Fish Meat

EURYPTERID

BASIC STATS:

Health	160	Food	450	Speed (Air)	90
Stamina	100	Weight	150	Speed (Water)	200
Oxygen	∞	Melee Damage	7	Torpidity	50

HABITAT: Deep Sea (bottom) - rare
DAMAGES: Thatch
BEHAVIOR: Aggressive

TYPE: Invertebrate
DIET: Carnivore
NAMES: -

ATTACK 1: Melee (Poison: stuns and decreases stamina)
ATTACK 2: -
ATTACK 3: -

SPECIFICS:
- Becomes aggressive when approaching it.
- You'll usually encounter it in packs.
- Can't swim and can therefore only be found on the ocean floor.

UTILITY:
- One of the rare sources of Black Pearls. Use a Metal Pick to collect Black Pearls from its dead body.
- Should you rather harvest Chitin, use an axe.

DROPS	HARVESTS	BREEDING
Raw Meat	-	Not breedable
Chitin		
Silica Pearls		
Black Pearls		
Oil		

THE ISLAND ~~SC. EARTH~~
~~ABERRATION~~ ~~EXTINCTION~~
GENESIS I RAGNAROK
THE CENTER VALGUERO

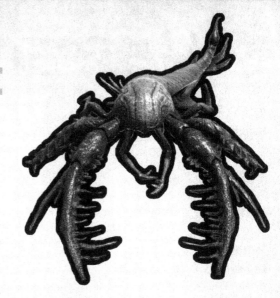

CHEAT: summon Euryp_Character_C

CARRYABLE BY: Tusoteuthis, Kaprosuchus, Megalosaurus

EGG SIZE: -

USEFUL TRAPS: -

TAMING METHOD: -

SUITABLE FOOD FOR TAMING: -

HESPERORNIS

BASIC STATS:

Health	95	Food	900	Speed (Air)	125
Stamina	200	Weight	70	Speed (Water)	200
Oxygen	∞	Melee Damage	1	Torpidity	300

HABITAT: Rivers, Lakes, Shores or Lagoons (shallow)
DAMAGES: Thatch, Greenhouse, Wood
BEHAVIOR: Cowardly

TYPE: Bird
DIET: Piscivore
NAMES: -

ATTACK 1: Bite (on shore, in the water, and on the surface)
ATTACK 2: -
ATTACK 3: -

SPECIFICS:
- Unable to fly. You can usually find it on the surface of the water. Due to its short legs, it doesn't pose a danger to terrestrial creatures.
- Fast glider in and on the water.

UTILITY:
- Drops Organic Polymer.
- Lays both normal and Golden Hesperornis eggs, which are ingredients for the extraordinary kibble with which you can tame the Yutyrannus. Let it hunt and eat 25 fish (to do so, throw it at a fish), and after some time it will lay an egg. This can be a normal or a Golden Hesperornis egg.
- You can cook its normal Hesperornis egg in a Cooking Pot in order to transform it into Oil.

DROPS
Raw Meat
Hide
Organic Polymer

HARVESTS	
Raw Fish Meat	■

BREEDING	
Type	Egg
Egg Temp.	22°-30°
Incubation	1h:31m
Maturation	28h:3m

THE ISLAND ~~SC. EARTH~~
~~ABERRATION~~ **EXTINCTION**
GENESIS I **RAGNAROK**
THE CENTER **VALGUERO**

CHEAT: summon Hesperornis_Character_BP_C

CARRYABLE BY: Tusoteuthis, Megalosaurus

EGG SIZE:
Small (Hesperornis egg) for simple kibble
Special (Golden Hesperornis egg) for extraordinary kibble

USEFUL TRAPS: -

TAMING METHOD:
Can be tamed by feeding.

SUITABLE FOOD FOR TAMING:
- Sabertooth Salmon
- Piranha
- Coelacanth

WARNING: Fish Meat doesn't work for taming here. You have to kill a Fish and carry it. To do this, approach the Hesperornis and press the "use" button as soon as it's requested. The bigger the dead Fish, the more it benefits the taming process. Fish killed by the Ichthyornis (Bird), have a way more effective impact on the taming process.

ICHTHYOSAURUS

BASIC STATS:

Health	275	Food	1000	Speed (Air)	600
Stamina	300	Weight	250	Speed (Water)	600
Oxygen	150	Melee Damage	15	Torpidity	300

HABITAT: Ocean
DAMAGES: Thatch, Greenhouse, Wood
BEHAVIOR: Cowardly

TYPE: Reptile
DIET: Carnivore
NAMES: Ichthy

ATTACK 1: Bite
ATTACK 2: -
ATTACK 3: -

SPECIFICS:
- When wild, it's very curious and approaches the player.
- Often accompanies Megalodons and other large fish.
- Warning: it attacks wild terrestrial creatures in the water. If you accidentally drop a stunned creature in the water, it will definitely attack it.

UTILITY:
- Easily tamable first mount for expeditions in the water.
- Very good for harvesting Eurypterids.
- You can increase its movement speed very easily and then you have a fast mount for reconnaissance and long trips in the water.

DROPS

Raw Meat

HARVESTS

Raw Meat	■ ■
Raw Prime Fish	■
Chitin/Keratin	■
Pelt	■

BREEDING

Type	Pregnancy
Gestation	7h:56m
Maturation	92h:35m

THE ISLAND ~~SC. EARTH~~
~~ABERRATION~~ ~~EXTINCTION~~
~~GENESIS I~~ RAGNAROK
THE CENTER VALGUERO

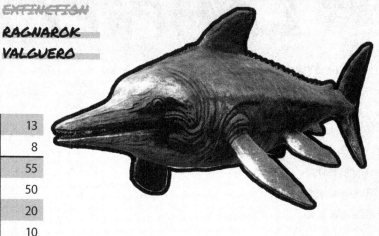

Level	13
Engram Cost	8
Hide	55
Fiber	50
Wood	20
Metal	10
Flint	8

CHEAT: summon Dolphin_Character_BP_C

CARRYABLE BY: Tusoteuthis, Kaprosuchus, Megalosaurus

EGG SIZE: -

USEFUL TRAPS: -

TAMING METHOD:
Can be tamed by feeding.

SUITABLE FOOD FOR TAMING:

Simple Kibble
Raw Mutton
Cooked Lamb Chop
Raw Prime Fish
Cooked Prime Meat
Raw Meat/Prime Fish Meat
Cooked Prime (Fish) Meat
Raw Fish Meat /Cooked Fish Meat

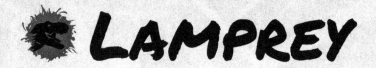
LAMPREY

BASIC STATS:

Health	40	Food	450	Speed (Air)	75
Stamina	100	Weight	10	Speed (Water)	70
Oxygen	∞	Melee Damage	7	Torpidity	50

HABITAT: Water
DAMAGES: -
BEHAVIOR: Highly Aggressive

TYPE: Fish
DIET: Carnivore
NAMES: -

ATTACK 1: Melee
ATTACK 2: -
ATTACK 3: -

SPECIFICS:
- Poisonous.
- Can't be tamed. You can, however, catch it with a Fish Trap (and release it again).

UTILITY:
- Drops a lot of items; for instance, Silica Pearls and Oil.
- If it attaches itself to something, it glows. Therefore, it can be used as light source. It also releases a substance that protects the victim against radiation when it's attached to something.

DROPS	HARVESTS	BREEDING
Raw Meat	-	Not breedable
Silica Pearls		
Oil		
Chitin		
Leech Blood		

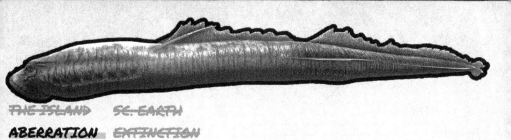

~~THE ISLAND~~   ~~SC. EARTH~~
ABERRATION   ~~EXTINCTION~~
GENESIS I   ~~RAGNAROK~~
~~THE CENTER~~   **VALGUERO**

CHEAT: *summon Lamprey_Character_C*
CARRYABLE BY: –
EGG SIZE: –

USEFUL TRAPS: Fish Trap
TAMING METHOD: –

SUITABLE FOOD FOR TAMING: –

LEEDSICHTHYS

BASIC STATS:

Health	4400	Food	8000	Speed (Air)	900
Stamina	500	Weight	1800	Speed (Water)	900
Oxygen	∞	Melee Damage	115	Torpidity	4500

HABITAT: Ocean **TYPE:** Fish
DAMAGES: Thatch, Greenhouse, Wood **DIET:** Piscivore
BEHAVIOR: Aggressive (attacks rafts) **NAMES:** −

ATTACK 1: Bite
ATTACK 2: −
ATTACK 3: −

SPECIFICS:
- Hates rafts. It attacks them immediately and destroys them after a few attempts. Its attack even reaches through Metal Foundations; no matter how securely you've built the raft.
- We, therefore, recommend avoiding being on a raft in the open sea. Instead, stay in shallow waters. You can throw Giant Bee Honey in the water in order to calm down an aggressive Leedsichthys for a very short amount of time in order to get away with your raft.

UTILITY:
- You can harvest Fish Meat and Prime fish Meat from Leedsichthys without killing it. Swim to the Leedsichthys and press the "use" button (E) while aiming at it.

DROPS	HARVESTS	BREEDING
Raw Fish Meat	−	Not breedable
Raw Prime Fish Meat		
Hide		

THE ISLAND   ~~SC. EARTH~~
~~ABERRATION~~   ~~EXTINCTION~~
GENESIS I   ~~RAGNAROK~~
THE CENTER   **VALGUERO**

CHEAT: summon Leedsichthys_Character_BP_C
CARRYABLE BY: –
EGG SIZE: –

USEFUL TRAPS: –

TAMING METHOD: –

SUITABLE FOOD FOR TAMING: –

LIOPLEURODON

BASIC STATS:

Health	3200	Food	2000	Speed (Air)	400
Stamina	800	Weight	1000	Speed (Water)	200
Oxygen	∞	Melee Damage	40	Torpidity	800

HABITAT: Deep Sea (very rarely)
DAMAGES: Thatch, Greenhouse, Wood
BEHAVIOR: Elusive
TYPE: Reptile
DIET: sweet tooth
NAMES: -

ATTACK 1: Lunge Attack
ATTACK 2: -
ATTACK 3: -

SPECIFICS:
- Behavior towards swimmers is aways passive, but may attack mounts that approach too closely.
- Can only be tamed for 30 minutes, then it disappears.
- Teleports to another place when harmed.

UTILITY:
- As soon as it has been tamed, the person that is taming it gets a bonus for opening crates. For the next 30 minutes, the quality of the crates' content is significantly better. During this time the player is surrounded by sparkles.
- The bonus is not dependent on the animal's level. Therefore, it's better to find and tame a low-level Liopleurodon since it's faster and cheaper.

DROPS	HARVESTS	BREEDING
Raw Fish Meat	-	Not breedable
Raw Prime Fish Meat		
Hide		
Megalodon Tooth		

THE ISLAND ~~SC-EARTH~~
~~ABERRATION~~ ~~EXTINCTION~~
~~GENESIS I~~ RAGNAROK
THE CENTER VALGUERO

Ridable without a saddle

CHEAT: summon Liopleurodon_Character_BP_C
CARRYABLE BY: –
EGG SIZE: –

USEFUL TRAPS: –

TAMING METHOD:
Can be tamed by feeding.

SUITABLE FOOD FOR TAMING:
Giant Bee Honey from the Giant Bee

MANTA

Basic Stats:

Health	320	Food	1000	Speed (Air)	600
Stamina	270	Weight	200	Speed (Water)	600
Oxygen	∞	Melee Damage	28	Torpidity	700

Habitat: Ocean
Damages: Thatch, Greenhouse, Wood
Behavior: Aggressive

Type: Fish
Diet: Carnivore
Names: -

Attack 1: Tail Sting
Attack 2: -
Attack 3: -

Specifics:
- Difficult to tame: it only eats Angler Gel and is aggressive.
- Lure it to very shallow water, wait a little bit, then use Bug Repellant. Then, approach it from behind in order to feed it.

Utility:
- A very fast and defensive aquatic creature.

Drops
Raw Fish Meat

Harvests	
Raw Prime Fish	■■
Raw Meat	■■
Chitin	■■
Pelt	■■

Breeding	
Type	Pregnancy
Gestation	7h:56m
Maturation	37m:2h

THE ISLAND ~~SC. EARTH~~
~~ABERRATION~~ ~~EXTINCTION~~
GENESIS I RAGNAROK
THE CENTER VALGUERO

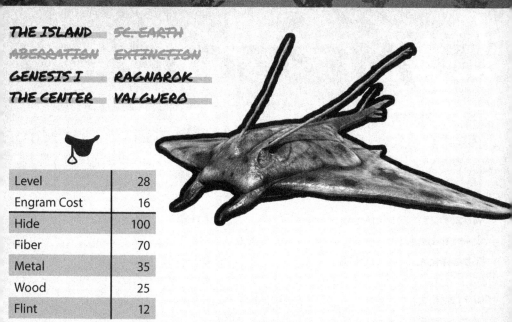

Level	28
Engram Cost	16
Hide	100
Fiber	70
Metal	35
Wood	25
Flint	12

CHEAT: summon Manta_Character_BP_C

CARRYABLE BY: Tusoteuthis, Kaprosuchus, Megalosaurus

EGG SIZE: –

USEFUL TRAPS: –

TAMING METHOD:
Can be tamed by feeding.

SUITABLE FOOD FOR TAMING:
Angler Gel

MEGACHELON

BASIC STATS:

Health	1920	Food	8800	Speed (Land)	235
Stamina	100	Weight	2500	Speed (Water)	650
Oxygen	∞	Melee Damage	40	Torpidity	10000

HABITAT: Ocean
DAMAGES: -
BEHAVIOR: Docile

TYPE: Fantasy Creature
DIET: Carnivore
NAMES: -

ATTACK 1: Bite
ATTACK 2: -
ATTACK 3: -

SPECIFICS:
- Emits oxygen, enabling you to stay at an underwater base.

UTILITY:
- Its back doesn't just provide enough space for a base, but also supplies said space with oxygen.
- Produces Rare Mushrooms and Rare Flowers.

DROPS	HARVESTS	BREEDING
Raw Meat	-	-
Raw Prime Fish		
Shell Fragment		

~~THE ISLAND~~   ~~SC. EARTH~~
~~ABERRATION~~ ~~EXTINCTION~~
GENESIS I   ~~RAGNAROK~~
~~THE CENTER~~ ~~VALGUERO~~

Level	45
Engram Cost	35
Hide	312
Fiber	260
Metal	76
Silica Pearls	42
Cementing Paste	28
Shell Fragment	22

CHEAT: summon GiantTurtle_Character_BP_C
CARRYABLE BY: –
EGG SIZE: –

USEFUL TRAPS: –

TAMING METHOD:
In order to tame a Megachelon, you have to lure a Microbe Swarm to it.

SUITABLE FOOD FOR TAMING: –

MEGALODON

Basic Stats:

Health	600	Food	2000	Speed (Air)	400
Stamina	320	Weight	250	Speed (Water)	400
Oxygen	150	Melee Damage	40	Torpidity	800

Habitat:	Ocean	**Type:**	Fish
Damages:	Thatch, Wood	**Diet:**	Carnivore
Behavior:	Highly Aggressive	**Names:**	-

Attack 1: Bite
Attack 2: -
Attack 3: -

Specifics:
- Very aggressive.
- Has a very long range and hunts players for a long time.

Utility:
- A very defensive aquatic creature.
- You can also use it as resource gatherer in the water. It can hold its own against many aquatic creatures as well. Just avoid the largest aquatic creatures and Cnidarias.
- Two to three of them are a good escort in the water.

Drops	Harvests		Breeding	
Raw Fish Meat	Raw Fish Meat	▪▪	Type	Pregnancy
Raw Prime Fish Meat	Raw Meat	▪▪	Gestation	7h:56m
Megalodon Tooth	Chitin	▪▪	Maturation	92h:35m
	Pelt	▪▪		
	Raw Prime Fish	▪▪		

THE ISLAND ~~SC EARTH~~
~~ABERRATION~~ ~~EXTINCTION~~
~~GENESIS I~~ RAGNAROK
THE CENTER VALGUERO

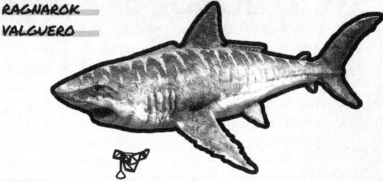

Level	47
Engram Cost	18
Hide	290
Fiber	155
Cementing Paste	30

Polymer	500
Metal Ingots	2500
Crystal	370
Element	55
Black Pearls	140

CHEAT: *summon Megalodon_Character_BP_C*
CARRYABLE BY: Tusoteuthis
EGG SIZE: -

USEFUL TRAPS: -

TAMING METHOD:
Knockout

SUITABLE FOOD FOR TAMING:
Superior Kibble
Raw Mutton
Cooked Lamb Chop
Raw Prime Fish
Cooked Prime Meat
Raw Meat/Prime Fish Meat
Cooked Meat/Prime fish Meat
Raw Fish Meat
Cooked Fish Meat

Microbe Swarm

Basic Stats:

Health		Food		Speed (Air)	
Stamina		Weight		Speed (Water)	
Oxygen		Melee Damage		Torpidity	

Habitat: Ocean
Damages: -
Behavior: Aggressive

Type: Fish
Diet: -
Names: Parakeet fish school

Attack 1: Melee, Bite
Attack 2: -
Attack 3: -

Specifics:
- These Parrot Fish attack the player all at once and can be just as annoying as an Insect Swarm in the swamp.

Utility:
- Lure the swarm into the proximity of a Megachelons in order to feed them to the Megachelon and thereby tame it.
- Other than this, it's just an annoying danger in the ocean.

Drops	Harvests	Breeding
Raw Fish Meat	-	Not breedable

~~THE ISLAND~~   ~~SE. EARTH~~
~~ABERRATION~~   ~~EXTINCTION~~
GENESIS I   ~~RAGNAROK~~
~~THE CENTER~~   ~~VALGUERO~~

CHEAT: summon MicrobeSwarmChar_BP_Escort_C

CARRYABLE BY: –

EGG SIZE: –

USEFUL TRAPS: –

TAMING METHOD: –

SUITABLE FOOD FOR TAMING: –

MOSASAURUS

BASIC STATS:

Health	3600	Food	8000	Speed (Air)	1100
Stamina	400	Weight	1300	Speed (Water)	1100
Oxygen	∞	Melee Damage	100	Torpidity	3000

HABITAT: Deep Sea
DAMAGES: Thatch, Greenhouse, Wood
BEHAVIOR: Highly Aggressive
TYPE: Reptile
DIET: Carnivore
NAMES: Mosa

ATTACK 1: Bite
ATTACK 2: -
ATTACK 3: -

SPECIFICS:
- Very aggressive.
- You can only find it in the deep sea and it avoids the surface.
- Chases you until a certain depth is reached. Use this to your advantage to get away or to stun it with a Crossbow.

UTILITY:
- Thanks to its platform saddle, you can use it as a mobile base.
- Use it as a battleship: high health and melee damage stats are reasons why it's the number one aquatic fighter. In addition, you can mount artillery (e.g. Cannons or Ballista Turrets) on the platform.
- We recommend using it as transport mount and resource base (e.g. build a Forge on the platform).

DROPS	HARVESTS		BREEDING	
Raw Prime Fish	Raw Prime Fish	■■■	Type	Pregnancy
Hide	Raw Meat	■■■	Gestation	7h:56m
Fireworks Flare-Gun Skin	Chitin/Keratin	■■	Maturation	280h:35m
	Pelt	■■		

THE ISLAND ~~SC. EARTH~~
~~ABERRATION~~ ~~EXTINCTION~~
~~GENESIS I~~ RAGNAROK
THE CENTER VALGUERO

Level	78
Engram Cost	60
Hide	800
Fiber	600
Cementing Paste	140
Silica Pearls	100
Metal Ingots	400

Level	93
Engram Cost	80
Hide	960
Fiber	720
Cementing Paste	180
Silica Pearls	320
Metal Ingots	1200

Defeat to learn:
Alpha Broodmother Lysrix

Polymer	500
Metal Ingots	2500
Crystal	370
Element	55
Black Pearls	140

CHEAT: *summon Mosa_Character_BP_C*
CARRYABLE BY: Tusoteuthis
EGG SIZE: -

USEFUL TRAPS: -

TAMING METHOD:
Knockout

SUITABLE FOOD FOR TAMING:
Exceptional Kibble
Raw Mutton
Cooked Lamb Chop
Raw Prime Fish
Cooked Prime Meat

PLESIOSAUR

Basic Stats:

Health	2400	Food	5000	Speed (Air)	800
Stamina	800	Weight	800	Speed (Water)	800
Oxygen	150	Melee Damage	75	Torpidity	1600

Habitat: Deep Sea (often in front of caves)
Damages: Thatch, Greenhouse, Wood
Behavior: Highly Aggressive

Type: Reptile
Diet: Carnivore
Names: Plesio

Attack 1: Bite
Attack 2: -
Attack 3: -

Specifics:
- Often found in front of underwater caves. **Warning:** it's likely to happen that you'll find several creatures of this kind.
- Avoids the surface.

Utility:
- Use it as a mobile base with platform saddle.
- Use it as a resource gatherer and crafter (crafting stations on a platform) or as a transport mount.
- Good combat platform: it's is very strong and its platform can be individually upgraded with Cannons and Catapult Turrets.

Drops

Raw Prime Fish
Hide
Fireworks Fare Gun Skin

Harvests

Raw Prime Fish	■■
Raw Meat	■■
Chitin	■■
Pelt	■■
Keratin	■

Breeding

Type	Birth
Gestation	7h:56m
Maturation	185h:11m

THE ISLAND ~~SC. EARTH~~
~~ABERRATION~~ ~~EXTINCTION~~
GENESIS I RAGNAROK
THE CENTER VALGUERO

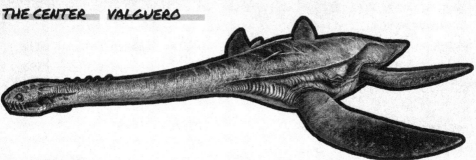

Level	64
Engram Cost	40
Hide	400
Fiber	250
Cementing Paste	65
Silica Pearls	40

Level	84
Engram Cost	50
Hide	680
Fiber	405
Cementing Paste	55
Silica Pearls	155
Metal Ingots	112

CHEAT: *summon Plesiosaur_Character_BP_C*
CARRYABLE BY: Tusoteuthis
EGG SIZE: -

USEFUL TRAPS: -

TAMING METHOD:
Knockout

SUITABLE FOOD FOR TAMING:
Superior Kibble
Raw Mutton
Cooked Lamb Chop
Raw Prime Fish
Cooked Prime Meat

Sabertooth Salmon

Basic Stats:

Health	65	Food	100	Speed (Air)	190
Stamina	100	Weight	18	Speed (Water)	190
Oxygen	∞	Melee Damage	4	Torpidity	15

Habitat: Rivers, Shores
Damages: Thatch, Greenhouse
Behavior: Passive

Type: Fish
Diet: Carnivore
Names: -

Attack 1: Bite
Attack 2: -
Attack 3: -

Specifics:
- Peaceful, but attacks as soon as it's attacked.
- Occurs in shoals.
- Flee as soon as a player approaches them. If one of them is attacked, the other ones fight back as well.
- Can be caught with a Fish Trap.

Utility:
- Source for Fish and Prime Fish Meat.

Drops	Harvests	Breeding
Raw Fish Meat Raw Prime Fish Meat	-	Not breedable

THE ISLAND   ~~SC. EARTH~~
~~ABERRATION~~   EXTINCTION
GENESIS I   RAGNAROK
THE CENTER   VALGUERO

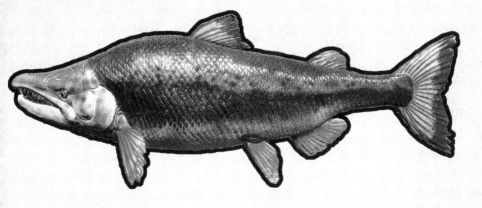

CHEAT: summon Salmon_Character_BP_C

CARRYABLE BY: Tusoteuthis, Kaprosuchus, Megalosaurus

EGG SIZE: -

USEFUL TRAPS: Fish Trap

TAMING METHOD: -

SUITABLE FOOD FOR TAMING: -

TRILOBITE

BASIC STATS:

Health	160	Food	450	Speed (Air)	70
Stamina	100	Weight	150	Speed (Water)	200
Oxygen	∞	Melee Damage	0	Torpidity	50

HABITAT: Shores/Beaches
DAMAGES: -
BEHAVIOR: Cowardly

TYPE: Invertebrate
DIET: Carnivore
NAMES: -

ATTACK 1: -
ATTACK 2: -
ATTACK 3: -

SPECIFICS:
- Peaceful, and flees when its attacked. All nearby Trilobites flee as soon as one of them is attacked.
- Occur in small groups.
- Can break through obstacles well.

UTILITY:
- Good source for Chitin. Use an axe, a Wolf, or Sabertooth to harvest the Chitin.
- Sometimes you obtain Silica Pearls and Oil as well. For lower level players, it's a good option for getting these resources without having to go to dangerous regions.

DROPS	HARVESTS	BREEDING
Raw Meat	–	Not breedable
Chitin		
Silica Pearls		
Oil		
Black Pearls		

THE ISLAND ~~SC EARTH~~
~~ABERRATION~~ ~~EXTINCTION~~
GENESIS I RAGNAROK
THE CENTER VALGUERO

CHEAT: *summon TriloBite_Character_C*
CARRYABLE BY: Tusoteuthis, Kaprosuchus, Megalosaurus
EGG SIZE: –

USEFUL TRAPS: –

TAMING METHOD: –

SUITABLE FOOD FOR TAMING: –

TUSOTEUTHIS

Basic Stats:

Health	2700	Food	3200	Speed (Air)	7500
Stamina	300	Weight	800	Speed (Water)	1500
Oxygen	215	Melee Damage	65	Torpidity	1800

Habitat: Deep Sea
Damages: Thatch, Greenhouse, Wood
Behavior: Highly Aggressive
Type: Invertebrate
Diet: Carnivore
Names: -

Attack 1: Tentacle Slap
Attack 2: Grab
Attack 3: Ink

Specifics:
- Produces Oil, which you can find in its inventory.
- Taming procedure is difficult. See instructions on the next page.

Utility:
- Can even carry a Rex or Mosasaurus with its tentacles.
- Good resource collector. It has a great range with its tentacles.
- Use it as taming support: animals caught in its tentacles become stunned over time (however, when stunned, the Tusoteuthis drops them).

Drops	Harvests		Breeding	
Raw Fish Meat	Oil	■ ■ ■	Type	Egg
Raw Prime Fish Meat	Raw Meat	■ ■ ■	Egg Temp.	0°-50°
Keratin	Metal	■ ■	Incubation	5h
Oil	Fiber	■ ■	Maturation	280h:35m
Black Pearls	Thatch	■ ■		
Tusoteuthis Tentacle				

THE ISLAND ~~SC. EARTH~~
~~ABERRATION~~ ~~EXTINCTION~~
GENESIS I RAGNAROK
THE CENTER VALGUERO

Level	91
Engram Cost	40
Hide	320
Fiber	795
Cementing Paste	45
Metal Ingots	30

CHEAT: summon Tusoteuthis_Character_BP_C

CARRYABLE BY: –

EGG SIZE: –

USEFUL TRAPS: –

TAMING METHOD:
Can be tamed by feeding.

SUITABLE FOOD FOR TAMING:

50x Black Pearls   30x Cooked Prime Fish Meat
20x Raw Meat   30x Cooked Meat

WARNING: the data above relates to one feeding interval, for example, 50x Black Pearls: you'll need way more than that (hundreds of pearls and thousands of Meat).

HOW TO TAME THE TUSOTEUTHIS:
- In order for you to be able to feed it, it needs to hold an animal in its tentacles.
- Put the food close to its mouth (right at the roots of its tentacles).
- It loves Black Pearls. Other food is significantly less effective, so it's best to only use Black Pearls.
- Use a tamed Carbonemys, for example (since it has a lot of health, it can take a lot of damage and it doesn't need any oxygen): put food for healing (preferably Sweet Vegetable Cake) and Stimberries for restoring torpidity in its inventory. Then, put it in front of the Tusoteuthis and wait until it catches it.
- Now, you can feed the Tusoteuthis with Black Pearls in order to tame it.
- You might have to put more animals in front of the Tusoteuthis because it immediately releases stunned animals.

15.1 General Info about Bosses

Every ARK offers one or more boss fights. Every time you defeat one of the bosses, you win trophies, a certain amount of Element, and you learn new Tek Engrams.

Tek Engrams and Element can only be obtained when defeating one of the bosses. For all Tek items and buildings, you need Element. Therefore, you have to fight bosses frequently in order to acquire a sufficient amount of it.

Every boss has a different level of difficulty and, depending on the level, drops different amounts of Tek Engrams and Element.

Bosses can have three different levels of difficulty:

- **Gamma Boss**: green (easiest boss); drops a small amount of Element as reward and only a few Tek Engrams.
- **Beta Boss:** yellow (way more difficult); you obtain a fair amount of Element and usually a lot of Tek Engrams.
- **Alpha Boss:** red (the most difficult boss and a real challenge); you obtain a large amount of Element and some of the rare Tek Engrams.

Should you manage to defeat high-level bosses first, you learn every Tek Engram from the low-leveled bosses as well.

In order to be able to get to the bosses, you need the following items as tribute:

- Artifacts: *artifacts* can usually be found in the caves from the ARKs. You need certain kinds of artifacts for each boss.
- Trophies: when you defeat the stronger animals from the ARK, you sometimes receive trophies, for example, a *Tyrannosaurus Arm* or a *Argentavis Claw*. You need some of those trophies for Beta and Alpha bosses as well.

Keep all the artifacts and trophies from animals that you've gained during the game – you're going to need them for the bosses.

In order to get access to one of the three ARK obelisks (no matter which one) or to a Supply Crate, open the console by pressing *use*. Since obelisks are available constantly, we recommend using them.

Place every creature and co-player you want as support during the battle into the obelisk's circle.

Above, you can see the blue obelisk's platform on the ARK Ragnarok. The console is located in the center and sends up a beam of light into the sky.

You need artifacts from the caves and a certain amount of trophies (e.g. Rex Arms), in order to teleport to the bosses.

Place all „tributes" into the console and click on the boss you want to conjure. Now, a portal appears that leads to the bosses. Every creature and player located under the dome is sent to the boss arena after 30 to 40 seconds. A maximum of 10 players and 20 tamed creatures can be sent to the boss arena. All players have to dismount and are not allowed to ride.

> Bosses are generally a great challenge. We recommend going into battle with the support of other players and with high-leveled fighting mounts.

You can join a boss fight as long as the dome is building up and you enter the teleportation circle within the allotted time. The color of the dome shows you the difficulty of the boss and you can see the corresponding boss arena in the dome's reflection.

In the picture above, you can see the green obelisk's portal in the Ragnarok ARK opening and giving access to the boss arena where the Alpha bosses are (recognizable by the red dome). The player accompanied by a single Rex in the picture above probably has no chance.

A maximum of 10 players and 20 tamed dinos on the obelisk's platform can be teleported to the respective boss arena.

You can only bring specific dinos with you:

- Only creatures that weigh less than 560. The Rex is the largest dino you're allowed to take with you. Bronto, Giganoto, or Paracer, for example, are not allowed to accompany you.
- Bringing flying mounts is not allowed. The only exception is *Scorched Earth*: there, aerial creatures are allowed and make sense; especially Wyverns.
- You can't bring any creatures that are able to climb.

The countdown, which indicates the time you have to defeat the enemy, starts as soon as the first player enters the arena.

> When the first player has entered the boss arena, the boss has to be defeated in a certain period of time. Otherwise, all players and creatures in the arena will die. Your equipment and tamed dinos are lost forever as well.

When every player in the boss arena dies, every tamed creature and item in the arena is lost. Your co-players should collect valuable drops from dead players and take them with them.

When you've defeated the boss, you should quickly loot its body because as soon as one minute has passed, every survivor and creature is going to be teleported back to their spawn point. **Important: you aren't allowed to ride when being teleported back.**

> The boss is empty? Then, one of your tames has already collected the items or they're in your inventory; take a look!

Basic equipment for fighting bosses:
- Good personal equipment: very good armor, a very good rifle or shotgun with sufficient munition, enough food, water, remedies, buff possibilities (specific food and troughs).
- Several high-leveled and enhanced fighting dinos with good saddles (even though you aren't riding them; saddles provide armor protection). They need high health stats and good fighting power. A Rex is often used as a fighting dino.
- Dinos to support you: a Yutyrannus, for example, whose scream strengthens fellow dinos and weakens the enemies. Bring one to two Daeodons loaded with meat; they heal your damaged creatures.

15.2 Broodmother Lysrix

Type: Giant Spider

Attack 1: Bite
- strong venom

Attack 2: Web Attack
- paralyzes

Conjures up to 20 Araneo spiders as support.

Arena: Underground spider cave; natural pillars provide protection.

	Item	Easy	Medium	Hard
Portal Costs	Minimum Player Level	30	50	70
	Artifact Of The Hunter	1	1	1
	Artifact Of The Massive	1	1	1
	Artifact Of The Clever	1	1	1
	Argentavis Talon	-	5	10
	Sauropod Vertebra	-	5	10
	Sarcosuchus Skin	-	5	10
	Titanoboa Venom	-	5	10

Tactic:
Keep a safe distance and avoid melee attacks. Stay away from the Araneos; some of the good fighting animals should be able to defeat them very quickly and keep them away from you. Bring stimberries as stimulants in order to protect yourself from being paralyzed by Araneos.

Reward:

- **Gamma**: 10x Element, Gamma Broodmother, Trophy, Broodmother Flag, Tek Foundation.

- **Beta**: 28x Element, Beta Broodmother Trophy, Broodmother Flag, Tek Boots, Tek Ceiling, Sloped Tek Roof, Sloped Tek Wall (left & right), Tek Catwalk, Tek Fence Foundation, Tek Ladder, Tek Pillar, Tek Railing, Tek Ramp, Tek Staircase, Tek Wall.

- **Alpha**: 74x Element, Alpha Broodmother Trophy, Broodmother Flag, Mosasaur Tek Saddle, Tek Helmet, Tek Turret.

15.3 Megapithecus

Type: Giant Gorilla/Yeti

Attack 1: Melee
- a lot of damage

Attack 2: Stone Throw
- high range

Conjures numerous Gigantopithecus as support.

Arena: Destroyed monastery in an icy mountain landscape; bring sufficient cold protection.

	Item	Easy	Medium	Hard
Portal Costs	Minimum Player Level	45	65	85
	Artifact Of The Pack	1	1	1
	Artifact Of The Devourer	1	1	1
	Artifact Of The Brute	1	1	1
	Spinosaurus Sail	-	5	10
	Megalania Toxin	-	5	10
	Thylacoleo Hook-Claw	-	5	10
	Megalodon Tooth	-	5	10
	Therizino Claws	-	5	10

Tactic:
Keep a safe distance and avoid the rocks it throws. Command some fighting dinos to take care of the smaller apes. The other dinos should attack the Megapithecus while you support and command your dinos from a safe distance. Be aware that there are more apes coming.

Reward:

- **Gamma**: 20x Element, Gamma Megapithecus Trophy, Megapithecus Flag, Tek Gauntlets, Tek Hatchframe, Tek Trapdoor, Tek Window, Tek Window Frame.

- **Beta**: 55x Element, Beta Megapithecus Trophy, Megapithecus Flag, Tek Dinosaur Gate, Tek Dinosaur Gateway, Tek Door, Tek Doorframe, Tek Generator, Tek Rifle, Tek Trough.

- **Alpha**: 110x Element, Alpha Megapithecus Trophy, Megapithecus Flag, Rex Tek Saddle, Tek Grenade.

15.4 Dragon

Type: Dragon

Attack 1: Bite & Claws

Attack 2: Fire Ball

Attack 3: Flame Breath

Conjures a bunch of Pteranodons (beta and alpha difficulty) as support.

Arena: Burnt world without much cover. An active volcano is seething in the background. Bring sufficient heat protection.

Portal Costs

Item	Easy	Medium	Hard
Minimum Player Level	55	75	100
Artifact Of The Skylord	1	1	1
Artifact Of The Immune	1	1	1
Artifact Of The Strong	1	1	1
Artifact Of The Cunning	1	1	1
Tusoteuthis Tentacle	-	5	10
Basilosaurus Blubber	-	5	10
Giganotosaurus Heart	-	1	2
Tyrannosaurus Arm	-	5	15
Allosaurus Brain	-	5	10
Yutyrannus Lungs	-	5	10

Tactic:
Bring a lot of support. The Dragon is the most difficult enemy. At first, it flies for some time and shoots at you with its fireballs. Use very good ranged weapons, avoid its fireballs, and command your fighting dinos to attack it as soon as it has landed. You'll definitely need to heal your fighters and yourself. It's best to bring some Daeodons with enough food in their inventory.

Reward:

- **Gamma:** 40x Element, Gamma Dragon Trophy, Dragon Flag, Behemoth Tek Gate, Behemoth Tek Gateway, Megalodon Tek Saddle, Tapejara Tek Saddle, Tek Leggings.

- **Beta:** 110x Element, Beta Dragon Trophy, Dragon Flag, Tek forcefield, Tek Transmitter, Vacuum Compartment.

- **Alpha:** 220x Element, Alpha Dragon Trophy, Dragon Flag, Tek Cloning Chamber, Tek Chestpiece, Tek Teleporter, Vacuum Compartment Moon Pool.

15.5 Scorched Earth (Manticore)

Type: Mythical Creature (Manticore)

Attack 1: Bite & Claw Attack

Attack 2: Poison Sting

Attack 3: Poison (ranged attack)

A lot of Deathworms appear in the sand below the spawning platform; later, Stone Elementals appear as well.

	Item	Easy	Medium	Hard
Portal Costs	Minimum Player Level	55	70	95
	Artifact Of The Gatekeeper	1	1	1
	Artifact Of The Crag	1	1	1
	Artifact Of The Destroyer	1	1	1
	Fire Wyvern Claw	2	10	20
	Lightning Wyvern Claw	2	10	20
	Poison Wyvern Claw	2	10	20

Tactic:
Try to avoid the floor of the arena; otherwise, you have to fight several Deathworms. One to two Wyverns should fight against the Stone Elementals should they bother you. Let some of your Wyverns attack the Manticore. Use a flying mount to keep a safe distance and to control your fighting dinos. A good assault rifle can be a useful weapon. A Griffin or Tapejara fully manned with players is possible when you're there with several other players.

Reward:

- **Gamma**: 25x Element, Gamma Manticore Trophy, Manticore Flag, Tek Gauntlets, Tek Window, Tek Window Frame.

- **Beta**: 90x Element, Beta Manticore Trophy, Manticore Flag, Tek Dinosaur Gate, Tek Dinosaur Gateway, Tek Door, Tek Doorframe, Tek Generator, Tek Rifle.

- **Alpha**: 190x Element, Alpha Manticore Trophy, Manticore Flag, Rex Tek Saddle, Tek Grenade.

15.6 The Center Boss

You must fight against the Broodmother Lysrix and Megapithecus at the same time. Both of them will conjure their support (Araneos and Gigantopithecus). Their stats are a little bit lower, however.

	Item	Easy	Medium	Hard
Portal Costs	Minimum Player Level	70	80	90
	Artifact Of The Hunter	1	1	1
	Artifact Of The Massive	1	1	1
	Artifact Of The Clever	1	1	1
	Artifact Of The Pack	1	1	1
	Artifact Of The Devourer	1	1	1
	Artifact Of The Brute	1	1	1
	Argentavis Talon	-	10	25
	Sauropod Vertebra	-	10	25
	Sarcosuchus Skin	-	10	25
	Titanoboa Venom	-	10	25
	Spinosaurus Sail	-	10	25
	Megalania Toxin	-	10	25
	Thylacoleo Hook-Claw	-	10	25
	Megalodon Tooth	-	10	25
	Tusoteuthis Tentacle	-	10	25
	Basilosaurus Blubber	-	10	25

Arena: You're fighting in an Asian style arena. Two paths lead through the village to the bosses.

Tactic:
You should focus on one opponent at first. Since Araneos can be rather annoying, we recommend killing the Broodmother first. Command two to three dinos with high health stats to attack and hold off the Megapithecus and the smaller creatures. With your main force, you should be able to kill the Broodmother quite quickly. Then, attack the giant ape. Since you can use two paths to get to the bosses, you can easily attack them in two groups from both sides.

Reward:
You receive every Tek Engram that you would normally also get from the other respective bosses.

- **Gamma**: 16x Element, Gamma Broodmother Trophy, Gamma Megapithecus Trophy, Broodmother Flag, Megapithecus Flag.
- **Beta**: 35x Element, Beta Broodmother Trophy, Beta Megapithecus Trophy, Broodmother Flag, Megapithecus Flag.
- **Alpha**: 95x Element, Alpha Broodmother Trophy, Alpha Megapithecus Trophy, Broodmother Flag, Megapithecus Flag.

15.7 Ragnarok Bosses

You have to fight against the Dragon and the Manticore at the same time. Their stats are, however, significantly lower. Stone Elementals show up as support.

	Item	Easy	Medium	Hard
Portal Costs	Minimum Player Level	70	80	90
	Artifact Of The Hunter	1	1	1
	Artifact Of The Massive	1	1	1
	Artifact Of The Clever	1	1	1
	Artifact Of The Pack	1	1	1
	Artifact Of The Devourer	1	1	1
	Artifact Of The Brute	1	1	1
	Argentavis Talon	-	10	25
	Sauropod Vertebra	-	10	25
	Sarcosuchus Skin	-	10	25
	Titanoboa Venom	-	10	25
	Spinosaurus Sail	-	10	25
	Megalania Toxin	-	10	25
	Thylacoleo Hook-Claw	-	10	25
	Megalodon Tooth	-	10	25
	Tusoteuthis Tentacle	-	10	25
	Basilosaurus Blubber	-	10	25

Arena: Nordic village with a creek and a bridge.

Tactic:
You should focus on one opponent at the first. The Dragon afflicts a lot of damage on your creatures; therefore, you should defeat it first. Meanwhile, one to three creatures with very high health stats should take care of the Manticore and the Stone Golems. Since both bosses are able to fly around a lot, we highly recommend bringing ranged weapons.

Reward:
You receive every Tek Engram that you would normally also get from the other respective bosses.

- **Gamma**: 65x Element, Gamma Manticore Trophy, Gamma Dragon Trophy, Dragon Flag, Manticore Flag, Tek Light.
- **Beta**: 200x Element, Beta Manticore Trophy, Beta Dragon Trophy, Dragon Flag, Manticore Flag, Tek sword.
- **Alpha**: 410x Element, Alpha Manticore, Alpha Dragon Trophy, Dragon Flag and Manticore Flag each, Tek Shield.

15.8 Aberration

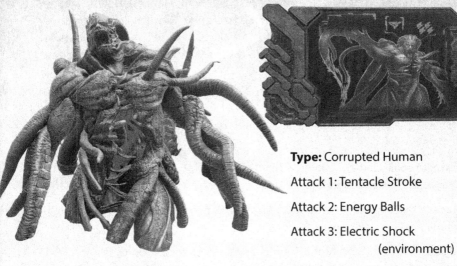

Type: Corrupted Human

Attack 1: Tentacle Stroke

Attack 2: Energy Balls

Attack 3: Electric Shock (environment)

Conjures a bunch of Nameless and Reapers (Beta and Alpha difficulty) as support.

Arena: Tek cave with a circular pool filled with liquid Element where the corrupted Edmund Rockwell appears. Tentacles appear on the edges of the pool and attack you.

	Item	Easy	Medium	Hard
Portal Costs	Minimum Player Level	60	75	100
	Artifact Of The Depths	1	1	1
	Artifact Of The Shadows	1	1	1
	Artifact Of The Stalker	1	1	1
	Basilisk Scale	0	4	8
	Nameless Venom	0	12	20
	Reaper Pheromone Gland	0	2	7
	Rock Drake Feather	0	2	7
	Alpha Basilisk Fang	0	0	1
	Alpha Karkinos Claw	0	0	1
	Alpha Reaper King Barb	0	0	1

Tactic:
First, you must destroy all of his tentacles, then you can attack the heart of the collapsed Rockwell and damage him. After a short period of time, he recovers and his tentacles appear again. Bring some good dinos that can take care of the Nameless and Reapers. You can also attack the tentacles and the heart with your dinosaurs. Stay away from the electric shocks; they paralyze you and your dinos and throw you off the mount. Wait until they've stopped or shoot at the tentacles with ranged weapons. The energy balls Rockwell throws at you, can be shot down.

Reward:

- **Gamma:** 25x Element, Gamma Rockwell Trophy, Rockwell Flag, Otter Mask, Cute Dino Helmet, Tek Sleeping Pod.
- **Beta:** 90x Element, Beta Rockwell Trophy, Rockwell Flag, Chili Helmet Skin, Rock Drake Tek Saddle.
- **Alpha:** 190x Element, Alpha Rockwell Trophy, Rockwell Flag, Scary Skull Helmet Skin, Tek Railgun.

15.9 Extinction – The Titans

Ice Titan

Type: Giant Titan that can jump very far.

Attack 1: Foot Stomp

Attack 2: Leap Attack

Attack 3: Ice Breath

Arena: Snow region in the proximity of the Blue Obelisk in the northeast.

Portal Costs	Item	Easy
	Minimum Player Level	1
	Artifact of the Void	1
	Corrput Heart	100
	Spino Sail	10
	Therezino Claw	10

Tactic:
The Ice Titan fights every creature in its proximity. We recommend letting it blow off its steam by fighting other creatures while you fight it from a distance. Bring large creatures with high health stats for support and distraction (e.g. Rex, Giga). You're best off riding a very agile, fast mount. That way, you can quickly escape from danger.

Taming:

The Ice Titan can be tamed by destroying the mutated knots on his body. First, destroy the knot on its inner right ankle, then the one on its right shoulder, and lastly, the one on its chest. After you've destroyed all three knots, the titan falls to the ground and you can tame it by clicking on the *use button*.

Make sure that you don't injure it too much since it's not able to recover. In multi-player mode, it starves after approximately one day.

Reward:

- Ice Titan Trophy, Tek Rifle Blueprint, Tek Helmet Blueprint, Tek Chestpiece Blueprint.
- Element and munition for Mek weapons.
- Advanced armor, weapons, and munition as well as their corresponding blueprints.

Forest Titan

Type: Tree Titan (giant, slow)

Attack 1: Foot Stomp

Attack 2: Vine Grab

Attack 3: Poisonous Trees (sprouts poisonous trees around the battlefield)

Though slow and having no support, the Forest titan's attacks are very intense and it can withstand a lot of damage.

Arena: Underground cave area you can access by destroying the Blue Obelisk located in the northwest of the map.

	Item	Easy
Portal Costs	Minimum Player Level	1
	Artifact of Maturation	1
	Corrupt Heart	100
	Sauropod Vertebra	10
	Tyrannosaurus Arm	10

Tactic:

This titan is very slow and stolid, but can withstand a lot of damage. Use this to your advantage and try to dodge and attack it from a distance. Fast creatures that are able to conduct ranged attacks, like the Velonasaurus, can be helpful here.

Taming:

The Forest Titan can be tamed by destroying the mutated knots on its body. First, destroy both knots on its shoulders and then, the one on its chin. After you've destroyed all three knots, the titan falls to the ground and you can tame it by pressing the *use button*. It receives a saddle automatically.

Make sure that you don't injure it too much since it will then become weaker. In multiplayer mode, it starves after approximately one day.

Reward:

- Wood Titan Trophy, Tek Replicator Blueprint, Tek Gauntlets Blueprint, Tek Leggings Blueprint, Tek Sword Blueprint.
- Element and munition for Mek weapons.
- Advanced armor, weapons, and munition as well as their corresponding blueprints.

Desert Titan

Type: Flying Titan

Attack 1: Lighting Strike

Attack 2: Swarm Attack

Attack 3: Tail Slap

This titan glides slowly above the terrain and doesn't make any fast movements.

Arena: The Desert Titan hovers nearby the red obelisk in the southeastern zone of the desert.

Portal Costs	Item	Easy
	Minimum Player Level	1
	Artifact of Chaos	1
	Corrupt Heart	100
	Fire Talon	10
	Sarcosuchus Skin	10

Tactic:

We recommend using flying mounts here. With strong flying mounts or gliders like Wyverns or Managarmrs, you can defeat the Desert Titan very easily on your own. Stay away from the swarm; it can throw you off the mount. If the lightning strike is targeting you, dodge quickly. You can even land on its back and fight it in close range; it will then, however, attack you with its tail. Always have a parachute with you unless you're wearing Tek Armor with a Jetpack.

Taming:

In the case of the Desert Titan, you also have to destroy the knots on its back. Those knots only appear when they're struck by the titan's lightning. Therefore, fly to the corrupted spot and wait until you can tell there's a new lightning strike charging up. Dodge, and the lightning strike hits the titan. As a result, the knot appears. Now, destroy it quickly. Repeat this process several times until all three knots are destroyed. A Quetzal with high health stats is very suitable for this tactic. Several players equipped with Tek Rifles mounted on a Tapejara, also work quite well here.

Then, you can land on it and tame it by simply using it. It receives a saddle automatically.

Make sure that you don't injure it too much since it will then become weaker. In multiplayer mode, it starves after approximately one day.

Reward:

- Desert Titan Trophy, Tek Replicator Blueprint, Tek Boots Blueprint, Tek Generator Blueprint, Tek Railgun Blueprint.
- Element and munition for Mek weapons.
- Advanced armor, weapons, and munition as well as their corresponding blueprints.

KING TITAN

Type: Giant Titan (similar to a Godzilla)

Attack 1: Swat & Kick

Attack 2: Meteor Strike

Attack 3: Power Fist (charges)

The largest of the titans has a Tek outfit in its Alpha version. It can't be tamed. It spawns numerous tumors that can eventually transform into the Giganotosaurus or any other kind of corrupted dino.

Arena: Platform in the upper north of the map; in the northeast of the blue obelisk in the Snow biome.

Portal Costs

Item	Gamma	Beta	Alpha
Minimum Player Level	1	1	1
Ice Titan Trophy	1	1	1
Forest Titan Trophy	1	1	1
Desert Titan Trophy	1	1	1
Corrupt Heart	150	300	300
Alpha Tyrannos. Tooth	5	10	10
Titanoboa Venom	10	20	20
Giganoto Heart	0	0	20
Spino Sail	0	0	20
Gamma King Titan Trophy	0	1	0
Beta King Titan Trophy	0	0	1

Tactic:

Against gamma and beta titans, you should be equipped with a huge amount of fire power and it's best not to come alone. Many strong Giganotos with a few Daeodons or mounted Owls as healers are a good start. Meks can inflict a lot of damage but can't handle a King Titan for very long.

If the titan's fist is charging, hit it in order to disrupt the attack.

If an Element node spawns in the proximity, the titan consequently takes less damage. If it gets destroyed, it gains health!

The best tool for fighting an alpha titan is a Mega Mek. Bring four Meks, one of them should be equipped with M.O.M.I. Enable it as soon as all four Meks are standing in the titan's territory. Then, the Mega Mek appears, which is an enormous help during the battle. It can only be enabled during the fight against an Alpha Titan. Additional support in form of Gigas is, of course, recommended.

Reward:

- King Titan Trophy
- Element and munition for Mek weapons.
- Advanced armor, weapons, and munition as wells as their corresponding blueprints.
- The credits - you've saved the world!

15.10 Valguero Bosses

This time, you have to compete with three bosses: Dragon, Manticore, and Megapithecus. Several Pteranodons accompany the Dragon, fighting you from the air, and several Mesopithecus drop to the ground.

Portal Costs

Item	Easy	Medium	Hard
Minimum Player Level	30	30	70
Artifact of the Brute	-	-	1
Artifact of the Crag	-	-	1
Artifact of the Cunning	-	1	-
Artifact of the Destroyer	-	-	1
Artifact of the Devourer	1	-	-
Artifact of the Gatekeeper	-	-	1
Artifact of the Immune	-	1	-
Artifact of the Pack	1	-	-
Artifact of the Skylord	1	-	-
Artifact of the Strong	-	1	-
Allosaurus Brain	5	10	15
Argentavis Tail	5	8	15
Giganotosaurus Heart	-	-	2
Sarcosuchus Skin	5	8	10
Sauropod Vertebra	5	8	-
Titanoboa Venom	5	5	10
Tyrannosaurus Arm	-	10	15

Arena: Quaint green valley with a ruin surrounded by high limestone cliffs.

Tactic:
A bunch of good Rexes or Deinonychus in combination with a Daeodon as a healer and a Yutyrannus as a buffer will do the job. Also bring ranged weapons in case the Manticore doesn't land that often. Remedies, good armor, and meat for our Daeodon shouldn't be missing either. First, lure the Dragon to you and fight in the spawning area; at this point, the Megapithecus shouldn't be aggro yet and remains where he is. Then, defeat the Manticore, and lastly, the Megapithecus. Should multiple creatures attack you at the same time, focus on one opponent.

Reward:
You receive every Tek Engram you would normally get from the other respective bosses as well.

- **Gamma**: 85x Element, Gamma Dragon Trophy, Manticore and Megapithecus Trophy and Flag, Manticore Armor Skin.
- **Beta**: 255x Element, Beta Dragon Trophy, Manticore and Megapithecus Trophy and Flag, Manticore Armor Skin.
- **Alpha**: 520x Element, Alpha Dragon Trophy, Manticore and Megapithecus Trophy and Flag, Manticore Armor Skin.

15.11 Genesis – Part 1

Moeder

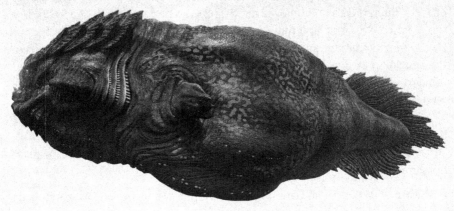

Type: Master AI of the Ocean biome in form of a giant eel

Attack 1: Bite

Attack 2: Tail Whip (local damage)

Attack 3: Electric Shock (balls of electricity all around it)

For support, it spawns a group of smaller eels that look like the Moeder but in miniature form.

Arena: Underwater cave with a whirlpool swirling around.

Habitat: The Moeder isn't a typical ARK boss since it's not absolutely necessary to defeat in order to wrap up Genesis Part 1. Moeder is a mission in the Ocean biome of Genesis. Open your inventory, select the mission tab, and choose the mission *One tough Moeder*. The mission console can be found deep in the ocean in an underwater cave system.

Tactic:
At the beginning, the Moeder is sitting in a hole at the bottom of the cave and waits until its minions have been defeated. You have to defeat each one of the creature's eel minions. Then, the Moeder leaves its cave and is vulnerable. After

severe injury, it retracts and new eel minions appear that you then have to defeat once again. This procedure repeats four times.

Pay attention to the whirlpool and stay away from it. Some good Mosasauruses should be sufficient for the battle while you can keep a safe distance from the Moeder and the whirlpool. It is, however, very annoying to lead a large group of Mosasauruses through the narrow cave system to the place where the mission starts.

> Warning: the mission currently has a lot of bugs. It can happen that the mission cuts off immediately after starting or some participants get kicked out of the mission. It can also happen that the Moeder only has 1% health and dies immediately at the beginning.

Reward:
Just like in all the other Genesis Part 1 missions, you obtain a reward containing several random items upon completion. The higher the level of difficulty, the more items you get.

Among other things, you can obtain the following: Tek Claws, Tek Sensor, Magma Saddle, Astrocetus Saddle, Ravager Saddle, Mining Drill, Hazard Suit Armor, Desert Cloth.

Corrupted Master Controller

Type: Master Controller AI of the Genesis simulation

Attack 1: Laser Stun

Attack 2: –

Attack 3: –

Corrupted Avatars and Dinotars appear repeatedly for support.

Arena: System Root - C:\ - you're at the core of the computer simulation.

Portal: You can get teleported by HLN-A to the final arena after you've successfully completed a certain number of Genesis missions:

Gamma	62 completed missions
Beta	116 completed missions
Alpha	168 completed missions

> Only the player that opens the portal has to have completed the missions. Up to nine additional players (and 20 creatures in total) can follow you without having played even one mission.

Tactic:

The Master Controller, whose head is extremely similar to Edmund Rockwell by the way, manifests in the form of a giant head on a central platform. He doesn't start an attack on his own, but instead sends in his Avatars and Dinotars. Defeated Avatars leave behind so-called Code-Keys. Collect 80 of them and bring them to the console. Then, HLN-A appears and teleports you to the next platform. You have to survive three platforms like this in total.

Enemies - Platform 1:
Avatars, Dinotars, Trikes, and Attack Drone

Additional enemies - Platform 2 and 3:
Dinotars, Raptors, Rexes, and Giganotos

Additional enemies - Platform 4:
Dinotar Reaper King

At gamma level difficulty, you have 15 minutes for each platform.

On the fourth platform, you only have to submit 40 Code-Keys, but you can only carry 20 of them at once. Then, the Master Controller becomes vulnerable for a very short period of time and after he has lost 1/4 health, he regenerates his shield and you have to collect 40 Code-Keys once again. Warning: at 50% damage, the Master Controller can't be harmed by dinos or other creatures anymore; only by weapons.

Occasionally, the Master Controller shoots purple, paralytic laser beams through his eyes.

Make sure that you're not hit by them, otherwise you'll get overwhelmed by the multitude of enemies.

Since the multitude of enemies lowers the health level of even strong dinos, we recommend controlling the Daeodons on your own and specifically healing your fighting dinos often. In groups, one of you should collect the codes and the rest should cover the collector's back. All players should fire at the Master Controller as soon as he's vulnerable. Time is short and the number of Avatars continues to increase.

Equipment:

- Many powerful dinos (Rex, Therizino, Ferox)
- Healer (Daeodon) and buffer (Yutyrannus)
- Robust armor (Tek Armor if possible)
- Heavy ranged weapons (Tek Rifle, Rocket Launcher)
- Remedies, meat for Daeodons, Element for Ferox

> The stream of Avatars and Dinotars is never-ending. There are constantly new waves of attackers. Act quickly; otherwise, you and your allies will get overwhelmed.

Reward:

You receive all the rewards from the lower levels as well.

- **Gamma:** VR Boss Flag, Master Controller Trophy, Tek Engrams: Tek Replicator, Tek Dedicated Storage, Tek Claws, Tek Hover Skiff.
- **Beta:** VR-Boss Flag, Master Controller Trophy, Tek Engrams: Tek Leggings, Tek Shoulder Cannon, Astrocetus Tek Saddle.
- **Alpha:** VR-Boss Flag, Master Controller Trophy, Tek Engrams: Tek Cruise Missile, Tek Chestpiece.

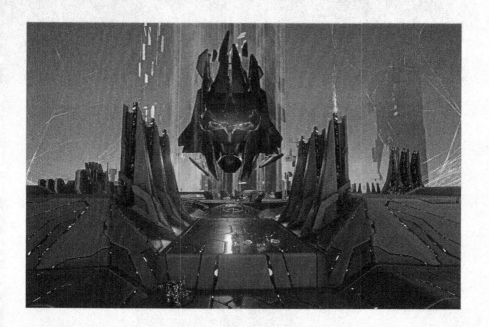

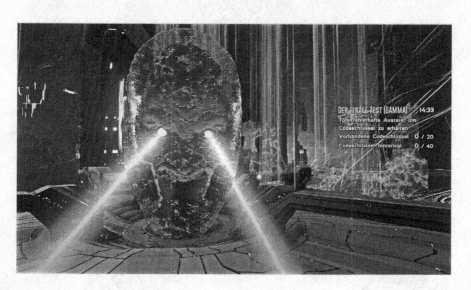

16: Ascension

16.1 Preparations

"Ascension" is the actual goal of ARK Survival Evolved. After you've defeated all three bosses on „The Island", you go to the Tek Cave in the Volcano and arrive at the platform of the Overseer. You defeat the Overseer and as a consequence, you ascend. By doing so, you have officially beat the game, and the bosses on "The Island" from ARK Survival Evolved are defeated. Additionally, you learn more about the interesting background story of the ARKs and their inhabitants and creators.

At the moment, Ascension is only available on the map „The Island". The other maps don't offer a Tek Cave or final bosses for ascension.

In order to be able to open the Tek Cave, you need some tributes first, just like with normal bosses. Here, there are the three levels of difficulty as well: Gamma, Beta, and Alpha.

Portal Costs Gamma:

Item	Qty
Minimum Player Level	60
Gamma Broodmother Trophy	1
Gamma Megapithecus Trophy	1
Gamma Dragon Trophy	1

Portal Costs Beta:

Item	Qty
Minimum Player Level	80
Beta Broodmother Trophy	1
Beta Megapithecus Trophy	1
Beta Dragon Trophy	1
Alpha Raptor Claw	1
Alpha Carnotaurus Arm	1
Alpha Tyrannosaur Tooth	1

Portal Costs Alpha:

Item	Qty
Minimum Player Level	100
Alpha Broodmother Trophy	1
Alpha Megapithecus Trophy	1
Alpha Dragon Trophy	1
Alpha Raptor Claw	1
Alpha Carnotaurus Arm	1
Alpha Tyrannosaur Tooth	1
Alpha Megalodon Fin	1
Alpha Mosasaur Tooth	1
Alpha Tusoteuthis Eye	1
Alpha Leedsichthys Blubber	1

Since you've already defeated all three bosses and killed many different Alpha creatures, you should have accumulated enough resources and very strong tames in order to be able to face the final boss. The strategy is similar to that of the other bosses:

- Bring as much armor, fire power, and support (in the form of many strong fighting dinos) as possible.
- Enter the Volcano accompanied by your team. The locked entrance to the Tek Cave is at the very bottom of the crater.
- Fight your way through the Tek Cave and teleport to the Overseer's platform.
- Go to the viewing platform and defeat the Overseer and his Drones.

16.2 Tek Cave

The entrance to the Tek Cave can be found in the Volcano's crater, northwest of the center of The Island (Lat: 42,8 Lon: 39,2):

Use the console in front of the portal, place all the tributes inside, and click on the desired difficulty level. Then, the portal opens and remains open for five minutes. A maximum of 10 players and 20 tamed dinosaurs can enter the Tek Cave.

It's very hot in the Tek Cave because a stream of lava is flowing through it. You just have to go straight ahead until you've reached the end of the cave. On your way, you have to fight a lot of high-level creatures including the Carnotaurus, Rex, and even the Giganotosaurus. These creatures can't be tamed and, when Alpha difficulty is selected, have levels up to 500.

In the second part of the cave, you don't encounter dangerous animals, instead, it's very cold. Go to the platform with a console, collect all the players and creatures, and use the console. Within 30 seconds, a portal opens up and all people being gathered there are teleported to the Overseer's platform.

ADDITIONAL USEFUL EQUIPMENT:

- Sufficient food and water (stamina decreases rapidly)
- Clothing that protects against heat (1st part of the cave)
- Clothing that protects against cold (2nd part of the cave)
- Fria Curry and Calien Soup (protection against cold & heat)

TIPS FOR CROSSING THE CAVE:

- You have one hour to cross the cave and reach the final boss.
- A fight with high-level creatures takes some time and decreases the health of many of your dinos; so you should try to avoid fights.
- Shoot enemies from a safe distance and lure them into the lava in order to kill them.
- Shoot at enemies with Pheromone Darts in order to make them attack each other.
- Try to push your opponents into the lava.
- Make sure that you're not pushed into the lava yourself.
- If you've taken a lot of dinos with you, you can simply leave some of them behind and get them to join you later. In the case of large groups of dinos, it can happen that some of them fall into the lava and are, consequently, lost forever.

- If you have several players, try to divide into smaller groups to avoid getting in each other's way.

16.3 Overseer

After passing through the lava cave and a long empty corridor containing some information concerning the ARK, you reach the Overseer Arena. Let the final battle begin:

Boss: The Overseer

Type: AI that is controlling everything

Attacks:
- Transforms into virtual versions of the three bosses (spider, monkey, or dragon) and uses their attacks.
- Conjures Defense Units that attack close-range.
- Conjures Attack Drones that can shoot.

Tactic:
- Fight the Drones; otherwise, they will overwhelm you quickly. If you're playing in teams, at least one of the players should concentrate on

the Drones. Firearms are important for fighting the Attack Drones, otherwise you won't be able to reach them. Every Drone drops Element when they're killed, which can be used as additional ammunition for Tek weapons and Tek Armor.

- You have to defeat all three forms of the Overseer in a row. When the Overseer changes into another form, he's protected by an energy shield which makes him invulnerable for a few seconds. During this time, you can fight the Drones or heal yourself as well as your creatures.

When the Overseer has been defeated, go to the platform where you've first encountered him. Don't forget that you're not allowed to ride on a dinosaur; dismount by all means. Now, enjoy the beautiful view and the last scenes of the game.

After the video sequence, you are automatically redirected to the main menu. Your character is saved in the ARK. You can now return to your former game (or a previous server). There, you can download your character again. Online, you also have the possibility to change servers (within the same server network) and download your ascended character.

If you choose to return to your former game, you can find all your dinos that survived the final battle at the entrance of the Tek Cave located in the Volcano's crater.

As a reward for ascension, your maximum level increases one time by 5 levels (Gamma), 10 levels (Beta), or 15 levels (Alpha).

17: Game Assistance

17.1 Console Commands

ARK offers numerous console commands that allow the player to interact with the game in single-player mode. When playing on a multiplayer server, only the admin can use these commands.

The cheats have to be activated first. Open the console by pressing the *TAB* button and enter the following command:

enablecheats password

The *password* is only necessary on a multiplayer server.

Here's a small selection of commands which can make the game easier. On our website, you can find commands to summon every single creature and item under the following links:

bildnerverlag.de/ark_creatures

bildnerverlag.de/ark_items

On our site, you can easily copy single commands with just a click. You can quickly put them into your ARK console by pressing *CTRL + V*.

Every cheat should start with the word *cheat* or *admincheat*, followed by the respective command and its parameters.

Example: admincheat settimeofday 18:30 (red values can be changed).

Command	Description
enablecheats *password*	Enables entering cheat commands.
admincheat addexperience 1000 0 1	The player gets 1000 experience; if you're sitting on a dino, it gains 1000 experience instead.
admincheat destroyallenemies	Destroys all creatures in the game.
admincheat DestroyMyTarget	Destroys your target.
admincheat DestroyStructures	Destroys all structures in the game.
admincheat DestroyWildDinos	Destroys all wild creatures in the game.
admincheat Kill	Kills your target.
admincheat SpawnDino *Dino path* 500 0 0 60	Summons a level 60 dino (change number). All spawn commands for copy and paste can be found under: **bildnerverlag.de/ark_creatures**
admincheat ForceTame	The targeted dino is tamed and can be mounted without any saddle.
admincheat DoTame	Tames the targeted dino as usual.

Command	Description
admincheat EnemyInvisible true	All creatures ignore you.
admincheat Fly	You can fly.
admincheat Walk	You can walk normally again (disable fly and ghost).
admincheat ghost	You can walk through walls and structures.
admincheat giveEngrams	The player learns all Engrams.
admincheat giveitem path amount 0 0	The player gets the object in the corresponding amount. All objects regarding this cheat can be found under: **bildnerverlag.de/ark_items**
admincheat giveresources	You receive 50 units of each resource.
admincheat GiveToMe	The targeted structure or tamed dino belongs to you now.
admincheat God	Turns God mode on or off. The player doesn't suffer damage anymore but can still die of starvation or thirst.
admincheat ListPlayers	Shows every player on the server.
admincheat saveworld	The world is saved immediately (warning: lag).
admincheat settimeofday 08:30	Sets the time in-game as defined (00:00 - 12:00)
admincheat slomo 5	Makes the time go by 5x faster. 1= default speed
admincheat Suicide	The player commits suicide.
admincheat teleport X Y Z	Teleports you to the coordinates X Y Z: X = (long-50)x8 Y=(lat-50)x8 Z= height (460= volcano height; -145= sea level)
admincheat TeleportPlayerIDToMe game ID	Teleports the player to you; use his test subject no. in the game.
admincheat TeleportToPlayer game ID	Teleports you to the indicated player.
admincheat ToggleInfiniteAmmo	Turns infinite ammo on or off.
admincheat ShowMyAdminManager	Shows the admin menu.
admincheat summontamed Dino path	Summons the indicated dino (already tamed).

> After activating *enablecheats* in single-player mode, you can enter commands without the prefix *cheat* or *admincheat*.

17.2 DLC / ADD-ON

ARK Survival Evolved already offers some free and purchasable DLCs (downloadable content); more to come in the future. A DLC, compared to a mod (modification), is an official game add-on. For beginners, we recommend trying the standard version without any DLCs or mods first.

Scorched Earth (purchasable)
Already described in this book. Scorched Earth offers a new ARK (a new map) in a desert scene with new creatures, items, and resources.

Aberration (purchasable)
The second, purchasable DLC, Aberration, was launched at the end of the year 2017 and offers a new map with new creatures, recipes, items, and resources. This time, the environment is a damaged ARK where you live mainly underground because everything on the surface is contaminated.

Extinction (purchasable)
In November 2018, the last part of the ARK's history (for the time being) was launched. The player fights against giant titans in order to preserve the humans' existence. Who knows whether or not the story will end happily...

Genesis: Part 1 (purchasable)
Part 1 of the Genesis saga offers a new map and thus far, mini-games for ARK. It saw a delayed release in February of 2020. You can only acquire Part 1 and 2 in combination with the Genesis Season Pass.

Genesis: Part 2 (purchasable)
According to the manufacturer's information, the second Part of the Genesis saga will be released in December of 2020. According to our experience, you should expect it in the first quarter of 2021. After six years of ARK, this could be the last official DLC, but who knows, right?

The Center (free)
A new map with numerous possibilities for discovery. Just like the other free maps, *The Center* was a mod map at first, but was then released as an official DLC.

Ragnarok (free)
Another new map with new creatures. So far, it's the largest official map with almost every creature from "The Island" and "Scorched Earth". Only here, the *Griffin* and the *Ice Wyvern* occur.

Valguero (free)
This map offers beautiful landscapes, new weather effects like rainbows, and even an underground ocean. The *Deinonychus*, the *Chalk Golem*, and the *Ice Golem* are creatures unique to the Valguero map. You can also find another variant, the *Ice Wyvern* there.

Primitive+ (free)
This free DLC extends the game with a lot of new building possibilities, numerous objects, and resources. In this gaming mode, there are no modern machines, weapons, or Tek Engrams. It's restricted to primitive weapons and buildings going back to the Iron Age, but at the same time, it adds a lot of new possibilities to the game. It's for those players who don't like ARK with Tek armor and assault rifles.

17.3 How to Install Mods

ARK also relies on a very active modding community. By now, there's a large number of mods that can expand and improve your game in a wide variety of ways.

Mods are available for the computer and for XboxOne. Unfortunately, PS4 doesn't support mods for ARK at the moment.

You can find and install mods on your computer quickly and easily via the Steam Workshop. If you're using mods on a multiplayer server, you don't have to do anything. They're downloaded automatically.

In order to install mods on your own, do as described in the following:

Open Steam and search for ARK in the game library. Click on *Workshop*:

In the Workshop, you can have a look at the available mods and read their descriptions. If you would like to try one of them out, just click on *subscribe*. The mod will be downloaded and installed automatically at the start of the next game.

But don't forget – the more mods you're using, the more unstable your game will run.

17.4 SELECTING MODS

On a monthly basis, Studio Wildcard (developers of the ARK) financially supports ten selected modding projects. For this reason, these mods are constantly upgraded and absolutely recommendable. However, there are a lot more mods and the number constantly increases. Just take a look at the Steam Workshop and search for mods you prefer. Here's a little insight into the possibilities mods offer:

Shigo Islands

Type	Description
Map Mod	A new island with a lot of possibilities.

Capitalism Series from Impulse

Type	Description
Economy Mod (e.g. "Capitalism Bank")	Numerous small mods from the Steam user Impulse, which offer an economic system with trading, banks, bounties, and a lot more.

NPC Bush People

Type	Description
AI Mod	This mod adds computer-controlled players to ARK.

Structures Plus

Type	Description
Structure Mod	Increases the possibilities you have regarding building.

Platforms Plus

Type	Description
Structure Mod	New improved tree platforms can be built.

Castles, Keeps, and Forts Series

Type	Description
Structure Mod	Nice medieval or sci-fi architecture for ARK.

Classic Flyers

Type	Description
Creature Mod	Brings back the original flying creatures with their stats. You can level up their speed stats again.

Stackable Foundations

Type	Description
Structure Mod	A small mod that makes building easier and makes it possible to stack foundations.

Upgrade Station

Type	Description
Object Mod	Provides a crafting station with which you can enhance your weapons.

INDEX

A

Aberration Arena/Boss 498
Achatina 184
Admin 28
Allosaurus 186
Ammonite 432
Anglerfish 434
Ankylosaurus 188
Anti-aliasing 21
Appearance 24
Araneo 190
Archaeopteryx 382
Arctic 143
Argentavis 384
Armor 36
Arthropluera 192
Artifacts 482
Astrocetus 380
Avatar 513
Avatars 513

B

Baryonyx 194
Basilisk 196
Basilosaurus 436
Battle Tartare 52
Beelzebufo 198
Bloodstalker 200
Brontosaurus 202
Broodmother Lysrix 486
Broth of Enlightenment 53
Bulbdog 204

C

Calien Soup 51
Carbonemys 208
Carnotaurus 210
Castoroides 212
Chalicotherium 206
Cnidaria 438
Coelacanth 440
Coloring 55
Compsognathus 214
Compy 214
Console Commands 526
Corrupted Master Controller 512
Crafting Speed 36
Crafting Stations 48

D

Daeodon 216
Dahkeya 92
Deathworm 218
Deinonychus 220
Diana Altares 93, 96
Dilophosaur 222
Dimetrodon 224
Dimorphodon 386
Dinotar 513
Dinotars 513
Diplocaulus 444
Diplodocus 226
Dire bear 228
Direwolf 230
Dodo 232
Doedicurus 234

Dragon (Boss) 490
Dragon (Wyvern) 426
Dung Beetle 236
Dunkleosteus 446

E

Edmund Rockwell 90, 498
Egg production 160
Electrophorus 448
Enduro Stew 51
Energy Brew 53
Enforcer 238
Engram points (EP) 42
Enraged 182
Equus 240
Eurypterid 450

F

Featherlight 388
Ferox 244
Ferox (small) 242
Focal Chili 51
Food 36
Fria Curry 51

G

Gacha 246
Gallimimus 248
Game, local 15
Gasbag 250
Gasbags 250
Giant Bee 392
Giganotosaurus 252
Gigantopithecus 254
Glitch 145

Glitches 145
Glowbug 394
Glowtail 256
Golem 336
Griffin 396

H

Health 35
Hesperornis 452
Hyaenodon 258
Hyperthermic insulation ... 37

I

Ichthyornis 398
Ichthyosaurus 454
Iguanodon 260
Imamu 93
Insect Swarm 400

J

Jerboa 262
John Dahkeya 92
Jug Bug 402

K

Kairuku 264
Kaprosuchus 266
Karkinos (Aberration) 268
Kentrosaurus 270
Kibble 54

L

Lamprey 456
Lamprey (Aberration) 414
Lavagolem 182
Lazarus Chowder 52
Leech 272
Leedsichthys 458
Liopleurodon 460
Local game 15
Lunar 143
Lymantria 406
Lystrosaurus 274

M

Magmasaur 276
Mammoth 278
Managarmr 280
Manta 462
Manticore 492
Mantis 282
Map 16
Master AI 510
Master Controller 512
Medical Brew 52
Megachelon 464
Megalania 284
Megaloceros 286
Megalodon 466
Megalosaurus 288
Mega Mek 507
Meganeura 404
Megapithecus 488, 489
Megatherium 292
Mei-Yin Li 91
Mek 290
Mesopithecus 294
Microbe Swarm 468

Microraptor 296
Mini Bosses 182
Mini games 144
Missions 144
Modern age 57
Modification (mod) 16
Moeder 510
M.O.M.I. 507
Morellatops 298
Mosasaurus 470
Moschops 300
Multiplayer 20

N

Nameless (Aberration) 302
Nerva 90
Nirvana Tonic 53

O

Ocean 143
Onychonycteris 408
Otter 304
Oviraptor 306
Ovis 308
Owl 422

P

Pachycephalosaurus 310
Pachyrhinosaurus 312
Paraceratherium 314
Parakeet Fish School 468
Parasaurolophus 316
Pegomastax 318
Pelagornis 410

Phiomia 320
Phoenix 412
Pin code 31
Piranha 442
Platform saddle 77
Plesiosaur 472
Prime meat jerky 54
Procoptodon 322
Pteranodon 414
Pulmonoscorpius 324
Purlovia 326

Q

Quetzalcoatlus 416

R

Ragnarok Arena/Boss 496
Raia 92
Raptor 328
Ravager 330
Reaper (Aberration) 332
Rex 370
Rock Drake 334
Rock Elemental 336
Rockwell 90
Roll Rat 340
Rusty Stufford 93

S

Sabertooth 342
Sabertooth Salmon 474
Salmon 474
Sarcosuchus 346
Scorched Earth 118
Scout 418

Seeker 420
Seeker (Aberration) 420
Shadow Steak Saute 52
Shinehorn (Aberration) 344
Shop 142
Single-player 15
Sir Edmund Rockwell 90
Snapping 65, 68
Snap point 65
Snow Owl 422
Spawn location 24
Spinosaur 348
Stamina 35
Stegosaurus 350
Supply crate 88
Supply crates 88
Sweet vegetable cake 53

T

Tapejara 424
Tek age 58
Tek Cave 519
Tek Cruise Missile 514
Tek Hover Skiff 514
Tek Shoulder Cannon 514
Terror Bird 352
The Center Arena 494
Therizinosaurus 354
Thorny Dragon 356
Thylacoleo 358
Titanoboa 360
Titanomyrma 362
Titanosaur 364
Titans 500
Torpor 36
Trent 93
Tribe log 28
Tribe member 27

Triceratops 366
Trike 366
Trilobite 476
Troodon 368
Tusoteuthis 478
Tyrannosaurus 370

U

Utahraptor 328

V

Valguero Arena/Boss 508
Velonasaur 372
Vulture 390

W

Weight 36
Window mode 22
Wolf 230
Woolly Rhino 374
Wyvern 426

Y

Yutyrannus 376

Made in the USA
Monee, IL
28 March 2021